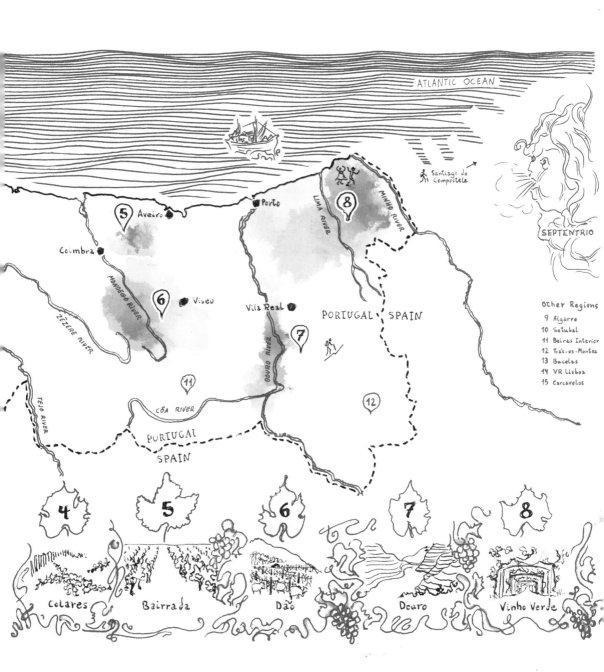

ATLANTIC OCEAN

Santiago de Compostela

SEPTENTRIO

Aveiro 5

Porto

LIMA RIVER

8

MINHO RIVER

Coimbra

MONDEGO RIVER

6 Viseu

ZÊZERE RIVER

Vila Real

PORTUGAL SPAIN

DOURO RIVER

7

TEJO RIVER

11

CÔA RIVER

12

PORTUGAL
SPAIN

Other Regions

9 Algarve
10 Setúbal
11 Beiras Interior
12 Trás-os-Montes
13 Bucelas
14 VR Lisboa
15 Carcavelos

4 Colares

5 Bairrada

6 Dão

7 Douro

8 Vinho Verde

FOOT TRODDEN
PORTUGAL AND THE WINES THAT TIME FORGOT

FOOT TRODDEN

PORTUGAL AND THE WINES THAT TIME FORGOT

SIMON J WOOLF & RYAN OPAZ

Interlink Books
An imprint of Interlink Publishing Group, Inc.
Northampton, Massachusetts

MC**P**
Morning Claret Productions
Amsterdam, Netherlands

First published in the Netherlands in 2021 by Morning Claret Productions,
an imprint of The Morning Claret, Amsterdam, Netherlands

www.themorningclaret.com

This hardback edition first published in the USA in 2021 by
INTERLINK BOOKS
An imprint of Interlink Publishing Group, Inc.
46 Crosby Street, Northampton, Massachusetts 01060

www.interlinkbooks.com

Library of Congress Cataloging-in-Publication Data available

ISBN 978-1-62371-901-2 *(hardback)*

Printed and bound in Latvia by ADverts

10 9 8 7 6 5 4 3 2

DEDICATED TO PORTUGAL'S GRAPE GROWERS

Contents

Preface 9

1 **Entrada** 18

2 **Granito**   *Vinho Verde* 46

3 **Lagar**   *Douro* 70

4 **Serra**   *Dão* 100

5 **Baga**   *Bairrada* 128

6 **Talha**   *Alentejo and Ribatejo* 152

7 **Terra**   *Colares and Madeira* 186

8 **Bom Dia!**   *Lisboa and beyond* 216

Glossary 238

Acknowledgements 243

Kickstarter supporters 244

Bibliography 248

Index 250

PREFACE

My love affair with Portugal hinged on an offhand question and a chance meeting. It very nearly never happened.

In 2003, my fiancé Gabriella and I decided on an unconventional wedding. Instead of splashing out on a big ceremony, we'd backpack around Portugal for three weeks. We had no idea what we were in for, but we had some family connections with Portugal and stories abounded of its wonders.

I was newly in love with wine and had just started working in a wine shop, while Gabriella wanted to experience Portugal and its culture on a more fundamental level. As it was our first time in mainland Europe, we decided to make the most of it by travelling from Lisbon to Porto and all points in between.

During the 1970s my aunt had lived in Portugal as an exchange student. During that time, she got to know a family who had ties to the port wine trade. The Allens had briefly owned the famous Douro property Quinta do Noval in the 19th century and still had links to several of the other estates. After my aunt's return, the Allen family's warm and welcoming nature assumed legendary status with our family – as did their house Villar d'Allen and its ancient treasures. Our interest had been piqued and we decided to visit.

On arrival in a rainy Porto, we squashed into a phone booth and tentatively called the barely legible number written on a soggy scrap of paper. A Portuguese voice answered. I mentioned my aunt and explained who I was. Before we knew it, José Allen had come to pick us up and take us to his home. We were greeted like family, despite the fact that our host had never met us before. By the time dinner was served that evening, José had already learned that I was curious about port wine.

He shared stories of the house and his family, and opened a stunning 19th-century port[1] from his cellar. We sipped history while sharing stories late into the night. Both Gabriella and I felt like we were at home. José suggested we visit the Douro valley to learn more about its history and promised to help with a contact or two. The Douro was still just a name to me at that moment, and I had no idea what to expect.

Shortly thereafter Gabriella and I booked a train ticket and, Lonely Planet guide in hand, headed to Peso de Régua. Predictably for January, it was raining as we got out of the train. We traipsed around in the damp and cold to find the most affordable hotel in town. The name sounded posh, but the Império was anything but. After a cold and miserable night, we quickly dressed and headed out in search of a warm cup of coffee and the spectacular views we'd read so much about.

The Douro in 2003 was a very different place then than it is now. There was no tourist infrastructure, no fancy brochures to guide you down the road. There were no smartphones or mapping apps. Régua felt far from welcoming, and it was not helped by the January weather. Rain and cold combined with the continual lack of heating or insulation led to a bone-shivering experience.

Thinking that my credentials as a wine shop manager might help us get into a winery or two, I set out for the only building I could find related to port wine in Régua, the Instituto dos Vinhos do Douro e do Porto (IVDP). I assumed that the IVDP would be able to direct us to a few wineries, or at least offer general recommendations that would help a budding wine lover. So, on an overcast day, I strolled up to the front door of a grand if faded granite building and rang the bell.

After explaining in my broken Brazilian Portuguese that I'd come to learn about the Douro, I received blank stares. A sacrificial official was offered up to talk to me. I laid out my idea that they would help me to know where to go and what to see. Met with slack jaws and silence, I quickly realised they weren't used to tourists asking such questions. They proceeded to explain that they couldn't help, but that they hoped I would get out and explore. I never did find out where they expected me to go. I muttered a polite thank you and left.

I felt utterly deflated. We'd travelled so far, and it felt like even the people who should have been able to help us couldn't. With a full day to kill before our scheduled visit to José's winery recommendation, we whiled away the time playing cribbage in local riverside cafes, drinking cheap Douro wine and hoping for inspiration.

. . . .

1   The wine was an 1879 Quinta do Noval.

The next morning, Gabriella and I agreed that after the morning winery visit, we'd pack up and head home a day early. We were cold, wet and tired of staring out into the rain. Little did we realise that Régua was barely the beginning of the Douro, or that we'd missed seeing any of the dramatic landscapes we'd hoped to see because we simply hadn't ventured far enough up the valley.

We strung out breakfast for as long as possible to kill time and fill up on free food (backpacker survival rules), before jumping into a taxi to go to the address written down by José in our worn travel journal. After a five-minute taxi drive up one hill and around the next, we arrived at a winery named Quinta do Vallado. Perched on a steep hillside and surrounded by vines, it looked like it had seen better days. We got out of the car and were greeted by the deep resonant voice of Cristiano Van Zeller.[2] Cristiano is a big character in every way. Standing approximately six and a half feet tall, he cuts an imposing figure. But when that smile breaks across his broad face, you know you are with a new friend.

We were welcomed into the winery and introduced to his friend and business partner, Francisco Olazábal.[3] I don't remember much of the tour. It was well before the existence of the designer hotel and modern winery, and the building was utilitarian rather than impressive. We finished in a scenic tasting room where blending took place. We tasted and talked and heard all there was to know about the region, its wines and history. Finally, we felt we'd had a glimpse of something authentic.

As we were about to leave, Cristiano asked a throwaway question that arguably changed my life forever: "So, both of you, what do you think of the Douro?"

I've never been one to skirt around the truth, so I hit him with it. Out poured all my disappointment with Régua, the lack of things to do, the lack of information, the endless wet and cold and the inability of the IVDP or anyone else to help us. "Honestly, I think we're just going to head back to Porto and continue our journey," I blurted out. When the jaw drops on a man as large as Cristiano, the ground shudders. He made it absolutely clear that we could not leave the Douro without giving it a second chance.

· · · · · · · · · · · · ·

2   Van Zeller is based at Quinta do Vale D. Maria but was instrumental in helping set up the winery at Quinta do Vallado in the early 2000s.

3   Quinta do Vallado is owned and managed by cousins João Ferreira Álvares Ribeiro and Francisco Ferreira; Francisco 'Xito' Olazábal is also involved as consultant winemaker.

Gabriella and I stared in disbelief as Francisco and Cristiano hatched a plan. Within minutes, Cristiano had phoned a hotel further up the valley. I remember the feeling of anxiety as we reluctantly agreed to 100 euros a night on our backpacker's budget. When he asked if we'd like dinner at the hotel, we nervously suggested that we would head out and eat locally. He laughed, "You can't, there isn't anything for miles! Don't worry, my treat."

Cristiano drove us back to Régua to grab our belongings. Apologising as he left us for a lunch appointment, he assured us a short train ride and taxi would get us to our new accommodation. We resigned ourselves to spending more money we didn't have, but clearly this was going to be an adventure.

Leaving Régua and heading inland, our eyes opened wider and wider as the landscape unfolded. The hills rose higher, the terraces became more precarious, and we began to understand why people were so in love with the Douro. We drove up one of the sheerest hillsides to a stunning 18th-century manor house named Casa do Visconde de Chanceleiros. To say it was in the middle of nowhere would be an understatement.

We were met by a very tall German woman who greeted us with a warm smile and ushered us into our 'cottage', which boasted proper heating and big fluffy duvets. It was the first time in days that we'd felt dry or warm. It was pure heaven.

That evening we headed up to the main house for dinner, where we sat alone in a grand and formal dining room. Though our backpacker clothes weren't quite in sync with the setting, we savoured a traditional meal of soup, roasted meat, the obligatory rice and potatoes and plenty of wine. Satiated and happy, we joined the owner by the fire with a glass of port and two large dogs lounging at our feet. Chatting about the history of the house and my experience in wine, she namedropped a recent guest, the American wine critic Matt Kramer. I felt like I was on the right track.

That night, we slept better than any other on the trip.

Casa do Visconde de Chanceleiros is not on the Douro river, but nestled in the heart of the valley. When we woke up the next morning, we were treated to a magical scene. At night the temperature had dropped, and the frost left a blanket of what looked like fairy dust over the vines. They sparkled like diamonds in the morning sun. Something clicked at that moment. I knew I would be back.

After breakfast and a reluctant departure, we headed over to Cristiano's winery at Quinta do Vale D. Maria, near Pinhão. The taxi driver just needed his name and we were on our way. As we wound around the hills, we looked at them in awe rather than with the contempt we'd felt a day ago. Pulling up at the Quinta, we shook hands with Cristiano and another man, who transpired to be a local mayor. Excusing himself for his meeting, Cristiano left us in the hands of his winemaker Sandra Tavares da Silva.

Sandra is almost as tall as Cristiano but rather more statuesque. We later learned that she'd had an earlier career as a basketball player and an international model, neither of which came as a surprise. Sandra took us around the winery sharing stories and let us taste some wines direct from the barrel – a first for me at the time. Her kind smile and evident love of the valley made us feel blessed that we'd given in to Cristiano's insistence.

When we later moved to Europe, we would get the chance to know both Cristiano and Sandra much better. But for the time being, our adventure was over. We headed back to Pinhão, and after a simple lunch at a local tavern caught the train back to Porto.

In 2005, we moved to Spain. Then in 2013, we decided to move to Portugal permanently. Our son was on the way and Portugal, its people and simple way of life had won us over. Our wine communication business Catavino gradually morphed into a tourism agency, and I now introduce guests to Portugal on a regular basis. Every time I bring someone to the Douro, I get to relive that moment when I woke up in the valley, through their eyes. I can't think of a better job.

Portugal is beautiful. I've tried to capture the moments and people which make it so special, and I hope my photos do it justice. But this book can only show a small slice of the many amazing stories and landscapes. Had I included every discovery that moved me, it would stretch to 50 volumes. As I continue on my journey to learn what it means to be Portuguese, that number of volumes is sure to keep on growing.

And all this might never have happened without Cristiano's surprise intervention on that cold January day in 2003.

RYAN OPAZ, *Porto, June 2021*

There was a moment in autumn 2016 when Ryan and I first started talking about a book. It was late one night in the Douro, after a few good bottles had been dispatched. My focus at the time was on my first book, *Amber Revolution*, so my head and heart were in Italy, Slovenia and Georgia even if I was physically elsewhere.

But since 2013, Ryan had engineered regular invitations and temptations to get me to come to Portugal and learn more about its wines. He knew there was treasure that I'd appreciate. It worked, and I was becoming smitten with the wines and the country. But as we both tried to deepen our understanding of Portugal, we were floored by a huge and seemingly impenetrable question:

Why does the wine-loving world have so little appreciation of Portuguese wines?

This book is, in many ways, our long-form answer. By setting down the stories we collected, the experiences we shared and the tasty bottles that sustained us during four years of research, we hope to show you the inner workings that helped us unravel this conundrum.

Perhaps the question seems surprising or even presumptuous, but it is borne out of my own experience as much as I observed it in others. As someone who was always wine-curious, I started out with a crush on France, before broadening my outlook to Italy and all points east. Spain was well and truly on the menu too. But Portugal remained a closed book. I absorbed all the technical stuff about port and madeira – both of which I loved – and had a rough idea about Vinho Verde, mainly gleaned from drinking industrial quantities of a Spanish lookalike (Pescador) during visits to Barcelona.

Beyond these predictable choices, I couldn't figure out where to look. Attending a major London tasting organised by Wines of Portugal in 2012 ('50 Great Portuguese Wines', selected that year by Julia Harding MW), I was struck by the predominance of heavily oaked wines and the worrying number of cripplingly heavy bottles.[4] It felt as though Portugal was still stuck in the Robert Parker groove, producing over-ripe, overbearing wines shouting, "me, me, me!" in some kind of wine-Esperanto. It was a language that didn't communicate anything I could identify as authentically Portuguese.

. . . .

4   A bad habit of producers who want their wine to be positioned as super-premium or high-status. The heaviest 75cl bottles can be as much as 500g heavier than the lightest – a significant difference when the cost and carbon emissions of shipping around the globe are factored in.

Harding had more than done her homework. She ferreted out a clutch of leftfield gems such as Quinta da Palmirinha, Aphros and Casal Figueira, and arguably produced the most varied iteration of this tasting to date. Richard Mayson, a well-known British writer on Portuguese wine, selected only red wines when he curated the same tasting in 2005, as he didn't feel that there were any Portuguese whites that would pass muster. Times have certainly changed.

Revisiting Harding's list, and those of her colleagues who curated the selection in other years, a few truisms about the Portuguese wine industry rose to the surface. The same consulting winemakers cropped up again and again, as did a clutch of big-name producers. Douro red wines dominated the proceedings. Was this really an accurate representation of everything great in Portuguese wine?

It took a few more years for me to answer that question, and the truth turned out to be more complex than a simple yes or no. Yes, it was what the Portuguese thought they should be showing the world, but no, there was certainly a lack of diversity. And that in turn was due to the scarcity of small, family-run grower producers.

During successive visits to Portugal, I got to grips with its many liquid treasures, some fabulously obscure and others shockingly uncelebrated. Old ideas such as *palhete*, *clarete* or *curtimenta* were clearly embedded into Portuguese wine culture, but until very recently, no winemaker dreamed that these styles had any commercial potential.

Then there were the forgotten jewels such as the regions of Colares or Carcavelos, the much-maligned wines of Lisboa and the barely footnoted activity on the islands of the Azores. Most shocking of all was the discovery that the Alentejo's clay pot, or *talha*, winemaking culture was alive and well, and not the museum piece it is made out to be in so many magazine articles.

I began to uncover wines that bucked the trends I'd seen back in 2012. There *are* Douro wines which are deliciously fresh and light, both red and white, not to mention orange or rosé. When you know where to look, new winemaking talent, fresh ideas and increased focus on authenticity are proliferating everywhere. In many cases, the newer, younger faces are also the ones driving the adoption of organic or biodynamic farming – both methodologies that I feel are crucial for the wellbeing and sustainability of people and planet.

While natural wine and conventional wine have tended to become somewhat ghettoised in some European countries, in Portugal this polarisation has hitherto been much less evident. Nonetheless, there is a noticeable move to less intervention in the vineyard and the cellar. It's a development that I welcome because it allows Portugal's most exciting characters to speak louder. Native grapes, diverse climates and ancient wine styles don't need to be dumbed down or have their rough edges smoothed out. There is a growing international audience of liquid adventurers ready to appreciate them as they are.

The more Ryan and I talked, the more we saw the place for a book that focused on the unsung heroes and obscure corners of Portuguese wine. But to answer our overarching question, a deep dive into the culture was also needed. What makes people tick, and what indents has the weight of history left on the wine industry? Why are things the way they are, and why are the Portuguese sometimes their own worst enemies when it comes to promotion?

In our opinion, the answers to these questions shed far more light on Portuguese wine than a barrage of technical information. Much as we are both card-carrying wine geeks, we wanted to write a book that gets beyond the minutiae of tasting notes, geological analyses or the intricacies of winemaking.

What makes Portugal special, as Ryan and his photos constantly remind me, are its people and their stories.

So, *Foot Trodden* is first and foremost a collection of those stories. It is not a complete guide to Portugal or its wines. Instead, we've selected a small sample of growers and producers whose personal narratives clamour to be heard, and whose work fascinates and satiates our palates. The following eight chapters are grouped loosely by region, with the exception of chapter one which sets the scene and intro-duces key cultural and historical themes. We've traversed roughly north to south, with a few omissions. Regions such as Trás-os-Montes, Setúbal and the islands of the Azores all hold interest for wine lovers, but our narratives have not yet lead us down those paths.

We're confident that the real Portugal and its authentic wines speak loud and clear through the tales we've told. We hope that they inspire you to seek out the bottles and contemplate your own travel to Portugal.

SIMON J WOOLF, *Amsterdam, June 2021*

For those who want an exhaustive guide to every grape variety grown in Portugal, every soil type or every producer worth knowing across the country, we have listed additional resources in the bibliography. Please also check the *Foot Trodden* website (foot-trodden.com) where we provide short profiles of all the growers featured in this book and much more besides.

CHAPTER 1

ENTRADA

• • • • • • • • • • • • • •

On 8 February 2013, a group of 16 Portuguese winemakers gathered together in a dank cellar in downtown Porto, within staggering distance of the Douro river. Over the next two afternoons and evenings, a few hundred of their friends, customers and colleagues crammed themselves into the space to taste wine, hang out and party.

The event had been organised by João Roseira (owner of Quinta do Infantado, Douro) and Mateus Nicolau de Almeida (Muxagat/Trans Douro Express), who christened it Simplesmente Vinho. Pressing the design skills of João's son Gustavo into service, they advertised it as an off-salon next to the huge Essência do Vinho, Porto's highest profile wine fair, which was celebrating its tenth birthday just a few streets away.

It might not have seemed like it at the time, but this hastily thrown together happening defined a key moment for Portugal and its wine. Like a movie trailer, it tantalised with the promise of things to come. And it heralded the start of a new age for Portuguese wine: one that would be more uncompromising, more diverse and more exciting than anything that went before.

What made Simplesmente so significant? It gave the platform to independent winemakers, a species long recognised and celebrated in other European wine countries – for example, by France's Vigneron Indépendant syndicate, created in 1976 – but almost unheard of in Portugal until the 1990s.

Simplesmente wasn't the first such salon to take place in Portugal. Roseira, together with João Tavares de Pina (Quinta da Boavista/Rufia), had organised an event called Dão e Douro that took place annually between 1999 and 2008. And since 2010, pioneering natural wine importer Os Goliardos has organised the Vinho ao Vivo (Live wine) tasting in Lisbon, a relaxed, outdoor event featuring independent winemakers from all over Europe.

But Simplesmente was audacious enough to stage itself right in the lap of Portugal's biggest and most corporate wine fair, deliberately inviting comparison and posing the rhetorical question, "Why do the small guys never get any attention?"

Roseira and Nicolau de Almeida drew inspiration from similar salons outside Portugal and from their shared renegade spirit. Specifically, they had both attended a peripatetic tasting called Haut les Vins in January 2013. That year it took place as a fringe event to Vini Sud – a giant trade fair held every year in Montpellier.

"Why don't we do something like this during Essência?" was the question on their lips as they travelled back to Porto. Nicolau de Almeida had the perfect idea for a venue. He gave Roseira an address on Largo do Terreiro and suggested he go and take a look. The subterranean location comprised three cramped and dark stone arches, owned by an architect's firm named Skrei. It had just been used for another event where straw bales were used as audience seating. Debris and loose bits of straw were all over the floor. "There were mice running around, and as soon as I saw that I said right, we're gonna do it!" says Roseira. "I mean, how much more natural could you get?" Then, he recalls, "I called my friends, Mateus called his friends, and we had 16 winemakers."

Their event was conceived as the polar opposite of Essência do Vinho. Essência takes place at the stunning Palácio da Bolsa, Porto's old stock exchange building and effectively the centre of the port trade in the past. It's a venue that reeks of grandeur, establishment and high finance. Wineries pay a substantial four figure sum to exhibit. Those that can afford it construct elaborate marketing displays, and inevitably have 'pretty young things' on hand to staff their stands. For the exhibitors it's about being seen and having their brand register with the great and the good of the Portuguese wine industry. For many of the visitors who aren't wine professionals, the attraction – once the entrance fee has been factored in – is the more or less unlimited and free wine. This means that Essência do Vinho can feel more like a bacchanalian endurance test than a wine fair. Sharp elbows are required.

WINEMAKERS WHO EXHIBITED AT SIMPLESMENTE VINHO IN 2013

Vinho Verde: Aphros, Quinta da Palmirinha, Anselmo Mendes

Douro: Mateus Nicolau de Almeida, Conceito, Quinta do Infantado, Quinta da Covada, Quinta de Vale de Pios

Dão: João Tavares de Pina, Lagar de Darei, Quinta da Pellada

Bairrada: Quinta das Bágeiras, Luís Pato

Lisboa: Casal Figueira

Alentejo: Quinta do Mouro, Vitor Claro

Simplesmente charges its producers a tiny fraction in comparison to Essência. And every winemaker has the same amount of space and the same setup – a single wine barrel, around which they and their customers can congregate. There are no roller banners or elaborately designed booths, and there's a very good chance that the person who pours you a taste will be the winemaker themselves. It's a gritty, grassroots event that reflects Roseira's edgy, hellraising character.

As Roseira and Nicolau de Almeida witnessed in France, Spain and other parts of Europe, there was nothing conceptually new about Simplesmente Vinho. But in Porto that year it felt like a revolution. It marked a fundamental change of direction from the previous 300 years of wine business in Portugal.

REGULATION AND RESTRICTION

There's a commonly held view that France is where wine classifications and appellations first emerged, but France has nothing on Portugal. In France, the first wine regions to be demarcated and regulated under the Appellation d'Origine Contrôlée system included Arbois, Cassis, Cognac, Châteauneuf-du-Pape, Monbazillac and Tavel in 1936. But Portugal's first comparable demarcation and regulation of a wine region happened way back in 1756, for port production in the Douro valley.

That demarcation, theoretically a royal decree but in practice entirely the work of King Joseph I's prime minister Sebastião José de Carvalho e Melo, set the precedent for a long tradition of oppressing and controlling Portuguese farmers and grape growers to facilitate trade and commerce that took place far away from the vineyards. Arguably, it also set Portuguese wine on a trajectory where it would be driven by major brands and corporate interests, not by notions of viticulture, terroir or the equivalent of France's *vignerons indépendants*.

Sebastião José de Carvalho e Melo later became the first Marquês de Pombal, and it's this latter name by which he's better known. Historian David Birmingham describes him as "one of the most innovative rulers that Portugal ever had", but also makes clear that his methods were highly dictatorial. Following his appointment as prime minister in 1755, Pombal quickly won praise due to his handling of the huge earthquake that hit Lisbon in the same year. His innovative rebuilding of the city to withstand future quakes was just the start of many planned modernisations.

Pombal also had wine, and specifically the port wine trade, in his sights. He wanted to regain control of what had by the mid 18th century become a kind of British cartel and one that was desperately unpopular with the Portuguese. The mainly British-owned port shippers of the time had created a market where they could dictate almost any price they wanted to the Douro growers and winemakers. They were raking in profits that Pombal wanted to have in the government's coffers instead. A lot of the trade was facilitated by secretive negotiations held at the Factory House, a kind of private members' club for British shippers in Porto.

Pombal's audacious plan for regulation, described by Birmingham as "a mixture of shrewd economics tempered with venal corruption", involved the creation of the Companhia Geral da Agricultura dos Vinhos do Alto Douro (otherwise known as the Douro Wine Company), a government body that would oversee and regulate port production, and wrest control away from the shippers. The shippers were thus forced to buy their stock of port wine from the Douro Wine Company, at prices effectively set by the government, in place of the price fixing that they had profited from for years. Furthermore, Pombal generously gave the Douro Wine Company exclusive export rights for Brazil (a key market at the time) and exclusive distribution rights to sell to the restaurants and cafes of Porto.

What Pombal got away with was quite extraordinary. His demarcation of the area allowed for the production of port wine encapsulated the Douro, but he conveniently allowed the grapes from his personal vineyards to be used for port wine too, despite the fact that they were located in Carcavelos, some 400 kilometres further south! The area for port wine was physically demarcated by granite posts known as *marcos da feitoria* or sometimes called *pombalinos*, and further reinforced by mandatory grubbing up of vineyards that lay outside the area. Pombal ordered the destruction of vineyards in Bairrada and Minho, both of which border the Douro, and in Ribatejo, with the justification that wine from these regions was commonly used to adulterate port blends.

He introduced further reforms to improve the quality of port wine, which had plummeted as exports ballooned in the early 18th century. Elderberry juice had become a popular additive, as it could cover up deficits in grape quality or ripeness by adding a deep colour to the ferment. Pombal not only banned the practice, but additionally ordered every elderberry tree within five leagues[5] of the Douro river to be uprooted and destroyed. He also banned the use of manure as a fertiliser, in an attempt to curb excessive vineyard yields.

. . . .

5 Portugal used several different units all called leagues during this period. The distance would in any case have been approximately 25 kilometres or 15 miles.

By now, Pombal was on a roll and implemented further reform via the Douro Wine Company in 1761. He granted the company a monopoly for the supply of *aguardente* (brandy) for the fortification of port, although his attempt to restrict the fortification of port exclusively to Portuguese *aguardente* was unsuccessful.

LAND OF WINE BRANDS

Port wine is effectively a value-added product. A British wine merchant supposedly discovered a Cistercian monastery in Lamego in 1678 where brandy was added to wine that was still fermenting. The result was a beverage that was not only pleasingly sweet and alcoholic, but also stable and able to resist the ardour of a long sea voyage. Although the practice of arresting fermentation did not become commonplace until over a century later, by the early 19th century port wine had evolved into a style that would be recognisable today.

The business of port shipping began with companies such as Kopke, Warre and Croft (three of the earliest established shippers), who would buy the wine in barrel, and have it transported down the Douro river to Vila Nova de Gaia where it would age and then be shipped to its final destination. Until Pombal's regulation of the industry in 1756, the shippers took virtually all the profit. After 1756, it was shared out between the government and the shippers, but the farmers who actually grew the grapes and made the wine still only received a pittance.

The port wine model works by having a large number of mainly small growers, or grower/winemakers, none of whom sell direct to the market, and a small number of bottlers/exporters (the shippers or port wine houses). This model has been enshrined in law since 1756. The commercial restrictions were tightened in 1908, when the prime minister João Franco ruled that port wine could only be exported from Vila Nova de Gaia, effectively limiting its commercialisation to the port shipping companies. This ruling was strengthened later by prime minister António de Oliveira Salazar in 1933. It wasn't until Portugal joined the EU in 1986 that the restriction was lifted.

At the height of the port trade in the early 20th century, there was a total of 81 port shippers in Vila Nova de Gaia. Today's picture is more complex, with a shrinking global market for fortified wines, yet an overall increase in the number of companies producing, bottling and selling port. The historic shippers of Vila Nova de Gaia have seen massive consolidation and a reduction in numbers to barely a quarter of the peak. But there are still 21,000 growers in the Douro valley, of whom no more than 500 also vinify or bottle wine.

What becomes clear from these figures is that port wine is, by and large, a blended, branded product, divorced from the land or from individual vineyards. Quinta do Infantado became the first independent producer in the valley to bottle its own ports in 1979, and an increasing handful of small grower producers followed suit in the 1990s. But most port is still overwhelmingly sold under major brand names such as Sandeman, Porto Cruz or Taylor's.

The evolution of madeira wine followed a similar path. In some ways, madeira has remained even more rooted in the tradition of blend and brand than port wine. The deliciously salty, high-acid fortified wine, with production delimited to the island of the same name, or its off-island Porto Santo, has long since fallen out of fashion worldwide. But even if the scale is different today, the structure of the wine industry on the island has barely altered.

Two centuries ago, there were approximately 70 companies bottling and selling madeira wine. Today, there are just eight. Vine growing was decimated in the 19th century due to *Oidium* (powdery mildew) and *Phylloxera* (a vine-eating louse which nearly wiped out vine cultivation in Europe and which wreaked havoc in northern Portugal from 1868), while consolidation and reduced markets have taken care of the rest. Currently, the island still has around 2,000 registered growers, most of whom farm minute parcels, with an average size of just 0.3 hectares.[6]

The madeira wine market is also restricted, partly because the regulating Instituto do Vinho, do Bordado e do Artesanato da Madeira (IVBAM, which also promotes the island's traditional embroidery and other artisanal products) requires that any new madeira producer must have stocks of 120,000 litres of madeira wine before they are granted their licence. This has effectively prevented any of the growers from creating boutique madeira wineries, as they would have to first acquire stocks of old madeira.[7]

As with port, madeira is a blended and branded product, with close to zero connection between the consumer and the farmer. Whether your favoured brand happens to be Henriques & Henriques, Barbeito or Blandy's, this has nothing to do with where on the island the grapes were grown, or who grew them. Grape growers are

. . . .

6   According to 2020 figures from the Instituto do Vinho, do Bordado
    e do Artesanato da Madeira (IVBAM).

7   There is one exception to this rule, which we profile in chapter seven.

often elderly and content to surrender their grapes to whichever agent or producer first steps forward to buy them. Although many produce their own simple wine (*vinho seco*) for home consumption, it is strictly forbidden to be sold.

Both the Douro and Madeira were hit hard by the twin scourges of *Oidium* and *Phylloxera* during the 19th century. The availability of port wine became so scarce that its best customers, notably the British, had to look for alternatives. One small wine region escaped destruction by *Phylloxera*, due to its sandy soils which are inhospitable to the pest. A little way up the west coast from Lisbon, Colares produces a lean, briny red wine that used to require a decade of ageing, but nonetheless it shot to popularity during the first two decades of the 20th century, when there were few other alternatives. This in turn exposed it to over-production and fraud.

To combat this problem, the regional government of Lisbon intervened with a ruling that the wines of Colares could only be produced from vines grown on the sandy soils next to the cliffs. They then established the Adega Regional de Colares in 1931, the first of Portugal's state-managed cooperative wineries. A ruling was passed a few years later requiring all growers in the region to become members, meaning that their grapes must be delivered to the cooperative, which became the only winery approved to vinify the wine.

The introduction of these restrictions was understandable and logical, but yet again they ruled out any possibility of the small-scale grower-producer getting a foothold in the business. Instead, Colares became a region with 690 growers, one winery and a single-digit number of négociants who would buy the wine in barrel, age it further and then sell it. If this sounds familiar, that's because it is a very similar model to the one established in the Douro and Madeira.

Co-operative wineries were established across the entire country over the next few decades. Production in Dão was particularly restricted, forbidding the sale of grapes to private wineries and in effect forcing all the wine to be vinified at the government's facilities.

New state, old rules

There are few periods in modern history that have shaped Portugal as much as the Estado Novo, or new state, founded by Salazar in 1933. Even today, more than 50 years after his death in 1970, no-one in Portugal lacks an opinion about this single-minded ruler.

Born in 1889 near Viseu, Salazar would come to rival the Marquês de Pombal in terms of his absolute and dictatorial rule. In all other respects, he was very different to the flamboyant Pombal. Salazar is often described as a dictator, although some historians maintain that he is better described merely as authoritarian. The Estado Novo enforced its iron will discreetly via the PIDE, its secret police, but did not utilise fascist or totalitarian rhetoric. This differentiated it from overtly fascist regimes such as Nazi Germany or Franco's Spain.

Salazar shunned public appearances and became increasingly reclusive over the course of his 36-year term. He was not a powerful orator, nor was he given to displays of pomp or grandeur. His living quarters were humble, and he never married. As Tom Gallagher writes in his biography of Salazar, he would often place a blanket over his knees while he worked, rather than heat his offices. He maintained a deep connection to his homeland in Dão and would retreat to his country house and vineyards at key points during the agricultural year.

Salazar's main goal was to restore stability to Portugal's turbulent economy and to ensure that he remained in power. He was successful on both counts. His economic policy had two main thrusts. He was keen to stimulate the growth of major corporations and exports, as a way of ensuring that the government's coffers remained full. He was also anti-liberalism, anti-modernisation and anti-development. Salazar effectively froze Portugal in time while turning it into a closed society. He famously denied Coca-Cola an import licence, seeing the brand as a symbol of the modern world that could only pollute the Portuguese soul.

Salazar did not want the proletariat to have boundless opportunities, better education or wealth. He aimed to create a docile electorate who would allow him to govern without question. As David Birmingham notes in *A Concise History of Portugal*, the government preached a gospel of "patriotism, paternalism and prudence". Salazar saw virtue in the country remaining, as he put it when explaining his rejection of Coca-Cola, "backward, a term that I consider more flattering than pejorative".

There was supposedly honour and pride to be taken in being a farmer or a grape grower, but such glory certainly wasn't rewarded financially. The Estado Novo significantly omitted to introduce any form of pension or welfare payments for agricultural labourers. The rural areas of Portugal remained undeveloped and poor, with many parts of the north still off-grid and without running water until the 1970s. Wine trade visitors who visited the Douro valley in the 1980s were often amazed at the lack of infrastructure.

Salazar's regime was also strictly protectionist. For instance, a 1937 ruling required cigarette lighter owners to purchase an annual licence in an attempt to safeguard the profits of the state-owned matchstick monopoly. The *New York Times* reported on the relaxation of the ruling in 1970, citing it as a sign that Portugal might finally be opening up to the modern world.

The Estado Novo had a huge influence on Portugal's wine industry, and its hand can still be felt today. Salazar was pro-corporatism and did not stand in the way of proven and profitable enterprise. In that respect, existing companies such as the major port and madeira wine shippers had a free hand to continue doing business much as they always had.

When it came to wine regions that were seen to be inefficient or inconsistent in terms of their production quality, government intervention was swift. This was the justification for the creation of state-owned co-operatives across the country. Again, there was clear separation between the farming or labouring classes (vine growers) and the captains of industry who bottled and commercialised the wine.

Salazar was very clear on the importance of the wine trade for the country's economy, famously saying, "Drinking wine provides food for one million Portuguese". But like Pombal before him, he attempted to restrict production to particular regions. He'd written about what he termed a "crisis of subsistence" in 1916, and during the late 1920s and early 1930s (just before his ascent from finance minister to prime minister) he enforced campaigns to plant wheat in the Alentejo, instead of vines. As grower and winemaker 'Professor' Arlindo Ruivo explains, the Alentejanos often flouted the rules and planted new vines underneath olive trees, to keep them away from prying eyes.

A number of major Portuguese wine businesses did well during the Salazar years, such as Vinho Verde giant Aveleda, who launched their entry-level brand Casal Garcia in 1939, and their sister company Sogrape (then known as Sociedade Comercial dos Vinhos de Mesa de Portugal), who created an off-dry and slightly fizzy rosé wine brand in 1942. Mateus Rosé, sold in a flask-shaped bottle that was meant to resemble a world war one water canister, took time to find its markets but became a runaway success during the 1960s. A decade later, it had reached 120 countries. A wine with no geographical designation at all beyond "Portugal", Mateus Rosé is made with a major percentage of Baga in the blend – a fact that will amuse anyone who knows how unloved this tannic, high-acid grape variety used to be. Whilst Mateus Rosé has been an untold success for Sogrape, it's open to question whether its ubiquity has tarnished Portugal's wine reputation, in the same way that Liebfraumilch turned a generation off German white wines.

José Maria da Fonseca, another major winery group based in Setúbal, got in on the mass-produced rosé act in 1944 with Lancers Rosé, targeted more specifically at the US market. Just as with Mateus, Lancers came in a specially shaped bottle and had no geographical indication. It remains hugely popular.

While the entire western world was getting buzzed on cheap Portuguese rosé (there are photos of everyone from Jimi Hendrix to Steve Jobs enjoying bottles of Mateus), Salazar's power was waning. The strain of a decade of ill-advised colonial war in Portuguese Africa started to show, and he suffered an undiagnosed stroke in 1968. Reports at the time suggested that he fell while trying to unfold a deckchair, but the truth may have been even less dignified as, according to correspondence which surfaced in 2009, he fell into a bathtub.

Salazar was admitted to hospital 16 days later and fell into a coma. When he re-gained consciousness, those around him shielded the ruler from the reality that he was no longer in power. His successor Marcello Caetano could not match Salazar's determination and drive, and the Estado Novo collapsed in 1974 with the largely bloodless Carnation Revolution. But even if the revolution was peaceful, it still spelled trouble for the wine industry.

First came two years of chaos, and a period when a revolutionary, communist-leaning faction tried to implement a people's popular republic. Banks, the press and much of the farming industry in the south were all nationalised. Many indus-trialists and company owners fled the country, others were arrested and corporate assets were seized.

Major wine producers were hit hard, especially those, such as the big port pro-ducers, who relied on huge short-term bank loans during the harvest to pay their growers. Following the forced nationalisation of banks, the government refused to make any credit available to private businesses. Paul Symington, who was chairman of his family's well-known port wine company until 2018, recalls that his father had no choice but to go to their many hundreds of growers with a tough proposition: he couldn't give any guarantee of payment, but if the growers agreed to deliver grapes to the Symington's cellars then he guaranteed them payment in wine if the money didn't come through. Symington recalls walking through the cellars and seeing long lists of farmer's names written on each tank as a simple form of credit note.

Symington has described this brief revolutionary period as a near-disaster for the entire port wine industry as the government of 1974–75 wanted to nationalise the entire sector. One major port shipper, Royal Oporto, had already been seized by the government with zero compensation given to the owners. He acknowledges Mário Soares, who was the leader of the Socialist Party in 1974, as "the man who effectively saved port". Soares, who had been in exile during the Salazar years, successfully pressed for democratic elections in 1975, prompting Portugal's first free election since 1932. He won the election and helped bring the country back on to a stable footing, avoiding the eventuality that the entire port industry was nationalised.

CHALLENGING TIMES

Another iconic Portuguese wine business was nearly quashed by the aftermath of the Carnation Revolution. In 1972, a wine-loving entrepreneur named Joaquim Bandeira made an appointment to visit the chief financial officer of his local bank. The CFO's name was José Roquette, and he'd been recommended to Bandeira by a friend of a friend. Bandeira needed financing to buy an historic property in the Alentejo named Herdade do Esporão (herdade is a ranch or farm). Bandeira had seen an opportunity to plant vineyards and make high-quality wine at scale. He felt that the Alentejo had untapped potential, which was quite a radical view at a time when the region was known only for knocking out bulk quantities of low-quality wine.

Bandeira won over Roquette with an elaborate and impassioned presentation, but Roquette was unable to convince the bank's board. They reportedly responded, "You must be crazy, there's no way we're going to lend money for a project like this." After talking it over with his wife, Roquette decided to invest in the project privately, so he and Bandeira each put up 50% of the money and bought the ranch.

Disaster struck almost immediately. The first vineyards were planted in 1973, but after the revolution in 1974 the pair lost everything. As the employee of a private bank, Roquette was in the firing line as a dangerous capitalist and was arrested by the revolutionary government in 1975 and thrown into prison. Herdade do Esporão was immediately nationalised and Roquette and Bandeira effectively lost their entire investment.

Roquette was released from prison later in 1975 as the government had no valid charges on which to hold him. He was seriously disillusioned and decided to move to Brazil and build a new life for his family there. Bandeira continued to work at Esporão, making a deal with the government and managing to secure a Soviet-style worker's commission to help tend the vines.

By 1980, Portugal had pulled back from its flirtation with communism, and the government started to redistribute seized property back to its original owners. Roquette returned from Brazil, and together with Bandeira negotiated the return of the entire Herdade. The property was only relinquished on condition that all of its grapes were delivered to the local co-operative for the first five years. José Roquette likes to joke that the co-op's wine between 1980 and 1985 was of decidedly superior quality.

The pair invested heavily in the winery and by 1985 were ready to release their first commercial vintage. Esporão was extremely forward looking. José's youngest son João, who is Esporão's current CEO, says it represented "total disruption" in the Portuguese wine industry at the time. The winery was gravity-fed and boasted stainless steel tanks with built-in temperature control. There were even oak barrels for ageing the wines, the inspiration for which had come from the Australian and Californian wineries visited by Bandeira and his winemaking team.

By the late 1980s, Esporão had 350 staff and was burning money. Bandeira didn't prove to be quite as good at business as he was passionate about wine. Following a disastrous harvest in 1988, the results of which were quietly sold in bulk to an undisclosed buyer, the pair had to face a grim reality: Esporão needed refinancing, and it also needed a more professional management team.

Roquette and Bandeira tried unsuccessfully to sell the company, first to Sogrape and then to the Rothschild family (who at the time were poking around the Alentejo with interest). Things didn't work out and in the end Roquette bought out Bandeira and started to rebuild the operation. Today, Esporão is one of Portugal's largest wineries and biggest success stories. And it hasn't lost the drive to innovate.

In 2019, Esporão completed the conversion of almost 700 hectares of vines to certified organic farming, a forward-looking move that remains unprecedented in Portugal, a country that has been slow to embrace less polluting alternatives for farming and viticulture. Esporão joins a small number of certified organic wineries in Portugal and is by far and away the largest.

Esporão changed the conversation around the wines of the Alentejo, and João Roquette believes it prompted a fundamental change in Portuguese wine in general. "People started looking at wine as a branded product instead of a commodity product," he suggests.

Projects like Esporão were only feasible in 1980s Portugal when there was a good supply of private finance. Martim Guedes, part of the fifth generation of the family who own and manage Aveleda, explains that "capital was very scarce in Portugal in the 1980s, not like it is now". This wasn't the only challenge in a country that had yet to join the EU. Getting modern winery equipment into Portugal from Italy or Germany was a logistical and bureaucratic challenge in the immediate aftermath of the revolution.

Established companies like Esporão, Aveleda or Sogrape thrived during the 1980s and 1990s. But opportunities for those lower down the economic scale to get into the wine business were still close to non-existent. Aspiring independent wine-makers or growers without deep pockets would need to wait for Portugal to join the EU before there was any chance of realising their dreams.

THE PORTUGUESE LOVE OF MELANCHOLY

Making generalisations about national characteristics can be dangerous, but there does seem to be a very Portuguese way of coping with hardship, and the ordinary working Portuguese who lived through the years of the Estado Novo certainly endured plenty of it.

Saudade is one of those untranslatable words which describes a very Portuguese condition. It encompasses longing, melancholy and mournfulness. It is a kind of Portuguese equivalent of the British stiff upper lip: a coping mechanism, a fallback when life seems bleak and nothing goes the right way. And just as the British are proud of that stiff upper lip, there is also pride in saudade.

Writing for the *Huffington Post*, Laurie Burrows Grad describes saudade as, "the presence of absence... a longing for someone or something that you remember fondly but know you can never experience again." The Portuguese journalist and writer Sonia Nolasco, who lived much of her adult life in New York, says that it can be a feeling of longing for something in the past or the future, and that it can be so intense that it is like physical pain. She suggests that the origins of saudade are from the 15th century when the Portuguese first started going on long sea voyages. Saudade would be felt by the voyagers for their homeland, and by those they had left behind for their loved ones. No-one could be sure if they'd ever return.

The work of the celebrated Portuguese writer and poet Fernando Pessoa provides a window onto saudade for many. His short poem from 1930 tackles another facet of saudade, a kind of existential nostalgia:

> *Recalling who I was, I see somebody else.*
> *In memory the past becomes the present.*
> > *Who I was is somebody I love,*
> > *Yet only in a dream.*
> *The longing that torments me now*
> *Is not from me nor by the past invoked,*
> > *But his who lives in me*
> > *Behind blind eyes.*
> *Nothing knows me but the moment.*
> *My own memory is nothing, and I feel*
> > *That who I am and who I was*
> > *Are two contrasting dreams.*

Fado (meaning 'fate' in Portuguese) is a kind of musical embodiment of saudade. It's a folk tradition that was popularised in 1820s Lisbon, although its roots may well be much older. *Fadista* and fado authority Rodrigo Costa Felix says of its origin that, "It was originally the music of prostitutes and pimps, drunks and thieves". Fado songs are often sad and mournful, with lyrics that express resignation, longing or melancholy in general. The vocal wail at the end of a phrase – the *rubato* – is a key characteristic and is sometimes likened to the blues.

Comparing fado with southern Spain's best known folk tradition, flamenco, gives an interesting perspective on the Portuguese character. Flamenco is flamboyant and extroverted with a highly ornamented style of singing or playing. It can encompass a wide variety of emotions and goes hand in hand with an elaborate dance tradition and colourful dress.

Fado, by comparison, is often much more introverted. Listening to an intense fado performance can be a harrowing experience, like overhearing something desperately personal that seems as though it wasn't meant to be shared. The song lyrics often concern loss, death or other subjects worthy of saudade. Wine is another popular topic, as in the classic 'Oiça lá ó Senhor Vinho' ('Listen, O Mister Wine') written by fado legend Amália Rodrigues. Fado lyrics are virtually never political.

Fado became discredited after the fall of the Estado Novo, who had used it as a kind of propaganda, much in the same way that Franco appropriated flamenco. According to Felix, Amália Rodrigues was cast out by the nation and moved to

Brazil. The political climate had changed by the time she died in 1999, and in a demonstration of how important fado had become, her death was marked by three days of public holidays during which time the Portuguese flag flew at half-mast.

Felix notes that fado and wine are inextricably linked. "For the Portuguese, a good fado evening needs to include baked chorizo, caldo verde and cheap red wine," he says. The experience of fado singing and dinner is offered at many specialist fado restaurants in Lisbon, which are now a major tourist draw. The more ad-hoc *fado vadio*, or 'vagrant's fado', can still occasionally be observed in backstreet cafes or late at night after scheduled performances have finished.

The Portuguese penchant for melancholy and longing is bound up with a sense of inevitability, and a character which is often humble. The relevance to wine is not purely cultural. Hesitance when it comes to promotion is virtually a national sport, and this has arguably held back the effectiveness with which the Portuguese market their own wine.

There are plenty of winemakers in Mediterranean[8] or south-east European countries who excel at self-promotion, often delivered with a healthy dose of machismo. Sentiments such as "my wine is the best wine", "I'm different/better than all my neighbours" or "I was the first and I'm still the best" are frequently implied, if not overtly stated. In the four years during which we undertook the bulk of our research for this book, we never heard any Portuguese winemaker utter such a comment. In fact, the reverse was true – it was often hard to get people we saw as innovators or pioneers to accept their seat at the historical table. João Roseira muses on this aspect of the Portuguese: "In our soul, we think we're not that great. We don't believe so much in ourselves." There's a real reticence to shout it loud or to sing one's own praises.

Perhaps it seems contradictory to write about the successes of major companies such as Esporão or Aveleda, whilst implying that the Portuguese are useless at promoting what they do. But there is a very real dichotomy here: the Portuguese can be extremely adept at building major businesses, but historically have been less than ready to market any authentic notion of themselves or of Portuguese-ness. Instead, the Portuguese became masterful at taking external narratives and utilising them to sell their wine. The port industry is a case in point. João Roseira explains that, "We all say that port wine is the best wine in the world, but we never drink it. The special bottle only comes out when the next American tourist arrives".

. . . .

8   Portugal is, for the avoidance of any doubt, not a Mediterranean country.

Bearing this in mind, perhaps it's not a surprise that large swathes of the wine-drinking world still believe that Portugal has little more to offer than the major port, Vinho Verde or rosé brands. The notion that Portuguese wine is excessively driven by brands is not without basis. For all the reasons explained in this chapter, it has been close to impossible for 'the little guy' to get in on the act over the past few centuries.

KEEPING IT IN THE FAMILY

In terms of the wine establishment, it's not just brand that matters, but also family. As Portugal shook itself free from the straitjacket of the Estado Novo, it revealed a wine business that had become consolidated into the hands of a few powerful and interrelated dynasties. While many of these families are Portuguese, a significant proportion have their origins elsewhere.

The port and madeira wine industries in particular have always been driven by families from abroad. Many of these families have integrated over the centuries. When John Blandy arrived on the island of Madeira in 1808, he was very much a Brit. But seven generations later, Chris Blandy (who is now at the helm of the Madeira Wine Company) is bilingual and dual-national, born to one English and one Portuguese parent. Typically for the family, Chris was educated in the UK. When he speaks English, he's every bit the classic British gent. The Blandys are part of a phenomenon which is sometimes dubbed the 'British Portuguese'.

The Symington family, now the largest landowners in the Douro, have a similar story to tell. After five generations of living and working in Portugal, the youngest two generations have effectively become Portuguese. That said, Paul Symington, born in 1953 to British and British/Portuguese parents admits that he was the first family member to formally apply for Portuguese nationality, which he did in 2018 in response to the UK's exit from the European Union.

Other significant families in the wine business include Niepoort (originally Dutch, but as with Blandy's and Symingtons, now very much naturalised), Van Zeller (past owners of Quinta do Noval), Guedes (of whom one arm owns Sogrape, currently Portugal's largest wine group, and another arm owns Aveleda), Ferreira/Olazabal (although Ferreira port is now owned by Sogrape, direct descendents of Dona Antónia Ferreira own two significant Douro properties, Quinta do Vale Meão and Quinta da Vallado) and Soares Franco (owners of the JM Fonseca group, which includes the Lancers brand).

Some of Portugal's major wine groups and brands have more corporate ownership or management. The Taylor Fladgate partnership (which owns Taylor's and many other port wine brands), Sogevinus and AXA Millésimes (the current owner of the prestigious Quinta do Noval) are examples. But wholly family-owned businesses, with no external investors or shareholders, are still a prominent feature of the Portuguese wine landscape.

All of these major companies and consolidated winery groups are good at efficiency and consistency, and they've undoubtedly powered much of the expansion of Portugal's wine production and exports. But wineries and winemakers who produce large volumes tend to steer well away from risk-taking or too much diversity when it comes to the wine itself. This has inevitably had an effect on Portugal's wine industry, or at least its perception outside the country.

Seminal US wine distributor and writer Kermit Lynch pre-empted a modern wine movement when he published *Adventures on the Wine Route: A Wine Buyer's Tour of France* in 1988. Covering his travels throughout France in the 1970s and 1980s, the book rails against the increasing homogenisation and the use of technology or manipulation in place of craftsman-like skills. During this period, interventionist winemaking and the rise of international wine critics threatened to transform a mystical beverage into a mere set of numbers on the page, not just in France but worldwide.

Lynch's manifesto contained the germ of the modern natural wine movement: a philosophy of minimal intervention in the cellar and the vineyard which aims to produce more honest, additive-free wines that better express the grape and its regional characteristics. A new generation of wine lovers and winemakers embraced these ideals in the late 20th and early 21st centuries, and the touchstones of less intervention, more natural or additive-free winemaking and more environmentally conscious practices in the vineyards became a significant and ever-expanding niche in wine-making. Meanwhile, oblivious to these changes, the Portuguese wine industry remained frozen at an earlier point in time and style of production.

Ironically, Portugal has all the raw material and rich tradition anyone could possibly desire when it comes to crafting authentic, low intervention wines. So why has it not made better use of these assets until now?

Blending in the vineyard

Diversity could be Portugal's watchword, at least in terms of grapes. Its vineyards teem with native varieties that are rarely seen outside the country. The fashion for ripping them out in favour of Cabernet Sauvignon or Chardonnay never took hold in Portugal as much as it did in other parts of Europe.

This is partly due to the fragmented nature of Portugal's vineyards. Grape growing in regions such as the Douro, Vinho Verde and Dão is often still an amateur or week-end pursuit. With many tens of thousands of individual growers, the average plot size is minute and the incentive to replant or modernise is non-existent. A grower who owns a third of a hectare (an area a bit less than half a football pitch in size) and sells 100% of their grapes to the local co-operative has no interest in replacing their vines with a more fashionable variety or a better vine-training system.

A document published by the Portuguese government in 2017, the *Catálogo Nacional de Variedades de Videira* (National Catalogue of Vine Varieties or NCVV), lists no less than 230 varieties indigenous to Portugal. But it also notes that there are likely to be many more varieties as yet unidentified and many that survive only in very old vineyard plots which are at risk of being abandoned or even destroyed.

One of the challenges of identifying such varieties is that they are typically inter-mixed in old vineyards. This planting technique – the field blend – is an important concept in Portugal. Vineyards were historically always interplanted, sometimes even with a mix of white and red varieties, with the intention that all varieties were harvested and fermented together. Field blends have remained particularly important in the Douro, and for port wine, but are also still common in Dão, and in the older vineyards of the Alentejo and the Lisboa wine region. The idea can seem random to outsiders. As Richard Mayson has written, asking a small-scale grower in the Douro, "What's growing in your vineyards?" is very often met with a shrug and the words "*não sei*" (I don't know). Yet the field blend has a sound basis.

Vineyards were historically planted with a view to hedging bets. Some varieties would be planted for their ability to ripen reliably, others because they contributed colour, body or acidity to a blend. Having a mix of early and late ripening grape varieties was always wise. The field blend is best seen as a kind of natural insurance policy. Depending on the vintage conditions, if one variety succumbed to disease or didn't ripen properly, another would fill the gap and ensure that the harvest was not lost.

Field blends are by no means unique to Portugal. They have historical importance in the Austrian wine growing region of Vienna, where their use is enshrined in law for the production of Gemischter Satz. In Bordeaux, a region that used to be considered as having marginal climate for ripening grapes, the intermixing of Cabernet Sauvignon, Cabernet Franc, Petite Verdot, Malbec and many other ancient varieties was common throughout history.

That said, field blends in Portugal tend to be far more complex than elsewhere. It is not uncommon to find centenarian plots in the Douro containing 40 or more interplanted varieties. Quinta do Crasto's Maria Teresa vineyard, with vines over 100 years old and more than 50 known varieties, is one example. Another is the Pintas vineyard owned by Sandra Tavares da Silva and Jorge Serôdio Borges, which is approximately 88 years old with 40 varieties identified so far.

Winemakers and growers in Portugal fell out of love for co-planted vineyards in the late 20th century. Perhaps the association with the long-distant past and with smaller farmers and growers contributed to a feeling that the idea was old fashioned. Field blends do present challenges, and in some ways fly in the face of everything that modern winemakers and vine growers are taught.

For a producer who wants to harvest each variety at its supposedly optimal physiological ripeness, a co-planted vineyard is a nightmare. Either the pickers need to harvest in multiple tranches on different days, a labour intensive and thus expensive business involving picking off those varieties that have ripened and leaving those that haven't, or the winemaker accepts that they will have a blend of variable ripeness levels in their ferments, something that no modern winemaking school would countenance.

Really old vineyards with mixes of red and white grapes present still greater challenges. It is rare these days to ferment red and white grapes together, not to mention commercial suicide as the resulting wine can then only be bottled as a lowly table wine under EU rules.[9] Furthermore, the global wine industry has become obsessed with the concept of the single varietal wine, since New World countries such as Australia and New Zealand first popularised the idea in the 1970s and 80s.

· · · · · · · · · · · · ·

9   Small amounts of white grapes can often be seen in the lagares of the Douro's port producers. This is never mentioned officially, and usually would be a very low percentage (5–10%).

Foot treading at Quinta da Gricha

Mass-produced wines now inevitably state their grape variety on the label, and most customers buying wine in large supermarkets or chain retailers look for their favourite variety as if it were a brand. Wine is bought as a Chardonnay or a Cabernet Merlot, and not necessarily because of who made it or where it comes from.

This shift in fashion to varietal labelling hit Portuguese wine hard. So many of Portugal's traditional styles are and have always been blends, and that makes them a hard sell beyond niche markets and customers who already know and love them. This in turn has led to Portugal's most forward-looking wine region, the Alentejo, forging a love affair with the single varietal. Syrah is now on the list of Portugal's top ten most planted grape varieties, and most of it is bottled in the Alentejo with the grape variety featured prominently on the label.

Even the Douro valley started to forsake the idea of the field blend. Research done by João Nicolau de Almeida and José António Rosa in the late 1970s narrowed down Douro grape varieties to five that were recommended for their superior quality. Their work had a huge influence on new planting decisions from the 1980s on. Touriga Nacional has become the absolute favourite, giving its name to hundreds of new varietal wines ranging from humble co-operative bottlings to Quinta do Noval.

Conversely, there is now increased interest in older field blend vineyards and their ability to lend complexity and an indefinable sense of authenticity to the wines. Luis Seabra, who makes wine in the Douro and further afield, feels that the older the vineyard is, the less important the individual varieties become. Winemaker Rita Marques has conducted comparative trials between field blended vineyards and single varietal plantings in the Douro Superior, and found that the field blends created more harmonious results in the cellar.

Seabra admits that old vineyards and field blends can be extremely labour inten-sive when it comes to pruning or harvesting, yet he acknowledges that they are part of a tradition that is worth preserving. Whilst it is rare for new vineyards to be co-planted with a field blend, it's not unheard of. Field blends have become marketable and even – dare we say it – fashionable.

These feet are made for treading

If field blends are Portugal's vineyard signature, the equivalent in the cellar is surely the practice of foot treading grapes. In antiquity, virtually all wine would have been made this way, but mechanical crushers, or crusher-destemmers, have long since replaced this manual process in most winemaking parts of the world.

Foot treading of grapes usually takes place in a *lagar*, a shallow-sided, square or rectangular stone basin that can be made of granite or whatever material is available. Modern lagares are also made from concrete or even stainless steel. They vary in size, but at their largest can accommodate 20 or more workers, who methodically walk backwards and forwards, shoulder to shoulder in a line.

Its survival in Portugal is due in large part to the port industry, but also reflects the glacial rate at which Portugal modernised under the Estado Novo. As previously mentioned, much of the Douro valley remained off-grid until the 1980s, which is one reason why mechanisation of any sort was uncommon.

Foot treading isn't a cheap solution for port, as it requires a large team of people who need to work continuously for a whole evening to thoroughly crush grapes and stimulate the start of fermentation. However, despite a great deal of research and development into motorised alternatives in the form of the robotic lagares pioneered by Symington and others in the 1990s, there is still a lot of love for the human foot's gentle but persistent extraction.

In comparison, foot treading a small lagar for table wine can often be accomplished with just two people working for an hour or two. For table wines, compared to port, far less extraction of colour and tannins from the grape skins is needed, and a slower fermentation may be desirable. Luis Seabra says he often foot-treads his Douro wines, for the simple reason that he lacks the equipment to do it any other way.

Just as the idea of the field blend is enjoying renewed popularity, foot treading and lagares are experiencing a resurgence in Portugal's boutique wineries. Anyone who cynically believes this is done purely for marketing reasons should try treading grapes themselves. The process is monotonous and tiring, but it can unquestion-ably produce thrilling and very elegant wines. Furthermore, it creates a primal bond between human and wine. The atmosphere at a winery when a large group of people spend the night treading is palpable, beginning with the concentrated intensity of the *corte* and progressing to the wilder and more raucous *liberdade* which is accompanied by live music and libations galore.

At the same time, manually crushing grapes in a granite trough, or working with a vineyard that was planted by your great-grandfather might seem primitive. For the many Portuguese who spent their careers working in the wine industry as it slowly modernised during the 20th century, there has occasionally been a feeling of shame that these old ideas are still so prevalent. Surely it's time to move on and upgrade to more modern, hygienic and scientifically proven methodologies?

But the survival of old lagares or co-planted vineyards is part of what makes Portugal special; it's just that it took the Portuguese a long time to realise it. As Bento Amaral, technical director of the Port and Douro Wines Institute (IVDP), says, "The Portuguese are quite humble. In the beginning we were trying to follow what people were doing elsewhere in the world, to come up with an international style of wine." But he's seen a change over the past decade. "The world has discovered Portugal now. We're a little bit more at ease, a little bit prouder of what we produce."

The 16 winemakers gathered together at Simplesmente Vinho in 2013 were front-runners when it came to this realisation. They were a diverse bunch, culled from all corners of the country. Some were boutique in size, others like Anselmo Mendes had already developed major businesses. What united them was their goal to make wines that were authentically Portuguese and that truly expressed their various regions, grape varieties and traditions.

João Roseira adopted a phrase coined by Filipa Pato (whose story is told in chapter four), who says that she makes "wines without make-up". It concisely sums up the qualities that Kermit Lynch sought during his travels, and what was missing from the Portuguese wine landscape at the time: wines with soul, made by people with dirt under their fingernails and grape pulp between their toes. And wines that make a virtue of being Portuguese, with all the idiosyncrasy, diversity and difference which that entails.

The growers showing their wines at Simplesmente Vinho enjoyed a weekend of banter, laughter and togetherness. Those who walked outside for a breath of fresh air could see the river Douro flowing past and, on the opposite bank, Vila Nova de Gaia and its port lodges. For lovers of symbolism, it was perfect: the epitome of the Portuguese wine establishment on one bank, and a tiny fringe event ranged against it on the other.

The process of building a whole new wine paradigm, almost in defiance of the establishment, was just beginning.

CHAPTER 2

GRANITO

• • • • • • • • • • • • • • • •

A grainy Super 8 film shows a slice of rural life from the Minho valley. Friends, family and children go to church, celebrate at a local fair and tend their land. The fields are ploughed with a pair of oxen. A man guides the plough, while women follow behind with rakes to break up the soil.

Vines grow everywhere, by the church, on the edges of the maize fields and around an imposing granite house. They're trained over two metres high on pergolas. During the harvest, the grape pickers perch high on ladders to pluck the fruit. Large wicker baskets are carefully handed down to receiving hands on terra firma. It takes two or three people to heave a full basket up onto a co-worker's head, from where it's transported to a waiting trailer. The baskets are inscribed in white paint with the text "C Paço".

At the winery, everything is human powered. A man balanced precariously on a wooden plank enthusiastically crushes the grapes in the lagar below. He's using an implement that looks like a giant three-pronged hoe. His son joins in with gusto. Later, the crushed mass goes into a massive steampunkesque basket press constructed from cast iron and wood. The farmer strains with his full force to push round a long horizontal beam, slowly applying pressure to the pulp and releasing the juice.

An eight-year-old boy walks purposefully across the field carrying a hay bale. His name is Vasco Croft, and although he was born and lives in Lisbon, he's a regular visitor. His family has owned the house and vineyards, Quinta Casal do Paço, since the 17th century.

Only the children's clothes and a small beat-up tractor provide a clue that this film was shot in 1970 and not 100 years earlier. Life in the Minho region barely changed during that time, retaining its focus on the land and the bare necessities of subsidence. It was a way of life that Vasco describes – perhaps rather sentimentally – as medieval and beautiful. "People lived without money, but in an ecological way," he explains. "Everyone was self-sufficient, people had cows for milk and manure, and pigs for meat. They'd kill one pig for the year and use the meat to season their beans and vegetables."

This medieval way of life, with each family having their own arable crops, vines and animals, still survives today. In far-flung parts of the Minho, houses with animals on the ground floor and the family living above can occasionally be seen. The warmth generated by the livestock provides valuable extra comfort and economic benefit. These days, the family's TV screens and internet routers add to the heat.

The idea of the closed-loop farm, or self-sufficiency operation, lies at the core of a more modern philosophy: biodynamics. Rudolf Steiner's farming methodology was conceived in the 1920s as a response to concerns about decreasing soil fertility. Whilst its more esoteric concepts might puzzle the average Minho resident, the eight-year-old boy with the hay bale would later embrace it as a way to reconnect with his ancestor's land.

GREEN WINE
· · · · · · · · · · · ·

The Minho valley is much better known globally as Vinho Verde – a name that, contrary to the belief of most wine drinkers, does not primarily describe its lightly effervescent, off-dry wine, but rather the wet and verdant landscape. With over 16,000 hectares of vines[10] and the highest annual rainfall in Portugal (at 1,500mm per year comparable to Wales), it's an accurate description.

Minho, or Vinho Verde if you prefer, forms Portugal's sister region to Galicia. The national border runs roughly perpendicular to the Atlantic coastline, claiming the most northerly quarter of the peninsula for Spain. Heading south, Vinho Verde country runs right up to Porto's city limits. It's defined as much by its stony ground as it is by vines. Everything here is made from the local granite – buildings, troughs, lagares, stairways and gate posts.

Vinho Verde was one of several Portuguese wine regions first demarcated in 1908 and it remains the largest. But what might surprise today's fans of Vinho Verde wine is that in 1908 it was most often red, albeit an extremely lean, tart and spiky red. As noted by John Delaforce, author and family member of port shipper

· · · · · · · · · · · ·

10 Comissão de Viticultura da Região dos Vinhos Verdes (CVRVV) figure, 2020.

Delaforce Sons & Co, red Vinho Verde was probably the first Portuguese wine to be exported to Britain in the early 17th century. It did not compare positively with the French wines of the day and it's not surprising that the British went looking for something a bit more full bodied, leading them to the Douro valley.

The combination of Vinho Verde's cool climate, high-acid granite soil and typical grape varieties is bound to produce light, low-alcohol wines. Grapes such as Vinhão (red) or Loureiro (white) will ripen at levels of just 10% or 11% potential alcohol.[11] The regional tradition of making and consuming mildly effervescent, young or 'green' wines evolved from the habit of early bottling or drinking while the wine still had some natural spritz left over from fermentation.

Aveleda created an innovative mass-market example in 1939. Casal Garcia wine was a stroke of genius. Aveleda fashioned a budget-priced, non-vintage white Vinho Verde which simulated the traditional style by artificially adding the bubbles at bottling time (in much the same way as with canned fizzy drinks). Casal Garcia is also bottled with a healthy slug of residual sugar, offsetting the wine's naturally high acidity. It retails for under three euros a bottle in Portugal, and not a whole lot more elsewhere.

The company has remained entirely family owned through five generations and began with just nine barrels of wine in 1870. Now, 15 million bottles of Casal Garcia are produced every year. As Vinho Verde's most voluminous producer, Aveleda sheds interesting light on how viticulture has developed in the region. Despite owning a massive 200 hectares of vines at the original Quinta da Aveleda, they also purchase grapes from 2,000 growers in the region, making them a more significant economic force in the region than even the largest co-operatives.

Martim Guedes, one of the current generation who manage the company, says that the main challenge is productivity. Most growers work with older vineyards that were planted at a much lower density than modern viticulturists would recommend.[12] Vines work themselves harder when given a bit of competition, hence at low planting densities the yields can be disproportionately small. Most growers, after all, are not professionals and their vines are just a weekend hobby that brings in some pocket change come harvest time. Some even elect to be paid in wine rather than cash.

· · · · · · · · · · · ·

11 It is common to chaptalise, ie add a source of sugar such as rectified concentrated grape must to increase the alcohol level of the final wine.

12 1,500 vines per hectare is quite normal for these older vineyards, whereas a modern planting regime would typically have at least 4,000 plants per hectare.

Quinta da Covela

Despite many vineyards being sub-optimal, there have been improvements. A few decades ago, it wasn't uncommon for growers to struggle to achieve even the minimum permitted ripeness level: a measly 7% potential alcohol. Now, as Guedes explains, 10% is the norm due to increased knowledge amongst the growers, better vineyard plantings and a helping hand from global warming.

Despite the oceans of Casal Garcia that are produced (not to mention Aveleda's many other labels) there's plenty of competition in the budget Vinho Verde sector. British wine writer and Portuguese expert Sarah Ahmed dubs them "swimming-pool wines", referring to the likely location of their consumption.

Even Vinho Verde's most prestigious sub-region competes on price. The denominated area of Monção and Melgaço sits right up next to Spain. Here, the modern-day focus is on Alvarinho, a perfumed, grapefruit and peach-filled beauty of a white grape that's also popular in Galicia under its ever-so-different Spanish guise Albariño.

At a T-junction on the main road through Monção is a nondescript looking entrance and car park. Behind it, the drab buildings look like they might house a funeral parlour. There's a small reception area with a typed price list taped to the wall. This is the Adega de Monção, Vinho Verde's largest and most important cooperative cellar. For three euros and some change it's possible to buy a bottle of their Muralhas de Monção. The label looks like it hasn't been redesigned since the Marquês de Pombal walked the earth, but the liquid inside doesn't disappoint – it's textbook Vinho Verde: fresh, spritzy and thirst-quenching, with zesty fruit and lunchtime-friendly low alcohol.

Perhaps this sounds like paradise: tasty wine, typical of its region and at a knock-down price. But there's trouble in paradise. These honest-enough wines are far from the bottom of the barrel. Vinho Verde is frequently sold in Portuguese super-markets for under two euros, with unclassified bottles dipping down to half that amount. At these price points, don't expect more than a near-tasteless, character-less and colourless liquid, with only the artificially added CO_2 and hit of sweetness on the finish to make it recognisable.

Due to the predominance of ultra-budget Vinho Verde, a kind of two-tier system evolved in Portugal's restaurants. The question, "Would you like wine or Vinho Verde?" is a bit like asking if you want grand cru champagne or cheap prosecco.

The Minho valley's ability to produce vast lakes of cheap Vinho Verde has shot it in the foot. Not only does it create huge challenges for the few serious wine-makers who want to elevate the region, it's also kept grape prices at starvation levels. A kilo of grapes goes for a mere 45 eurocents, according to Aveleda. That's an average price, not the lowest. And that in turn has hastened a massive population drain to the cities or abroad. For the younger generation growing up in the post-Salazar age of increased education and mobility, there has been no stimulus to remain in the Minho's rural backwater.

Back in the 1940s, when Casal Garcia first transformed poolside drinking, there were an astounding 116,000 or more grape growers in Vinho Verde. Even in 1981, there were still around 70,000 faithfully tending their vines and trucking their grapes to the cooperative wineries, or to Aveleda's doors every harvest. But that number has plummeted in the last few decades, and now hovers around 16,000. Given the scant rewards on offer for a whole years' work in the vineyard, it is hardly a surprise.

Vinho Verde still feels like it has one foot in the past, when feudal systems and serfdom predominated. In contrast to the large number of growers, there are only 600 wineries in the region that produce and bottle commercially. Many of these producer-bottlers do not sell directly to the public, but only to other larger wineries who inevitably take most of the profit.

Plenty has changed since the region was demarcated in 1908. The high pergolas, called *vinha de enforcado*, are now seldom seen. Back in the day, their purpose was to allow a row of beans or tomatoes to be grown underneath, but it wasn't a recipe for high-quality grapes. The ratio of red to white grapes has altered out of all recognition, with reds now making up a scant 20%, much of which is destined for the newly fashionable category of rosé Vinho Verde. What hasn't changed is the measly price paid for grapes or wines. The two-euro Vinho Verde is alive and well, and the region's tarnished image still needs a polish.

High quality

· · · · · · · · · · · · ·

A minute proportion of Vinho Verde's winemakers dare to set their sights higher and produce wines that are more than just simple quaffers for the beach or the pool. Their wines are bone dry and certainly don't have artificially added CO_2. They rely instead on the region's natural climate to provide the pure fruited, zesty acid signature. First amongst equals in this elite group is surely Quinta de Soalheiro in Monção and Melgaço, where the Cerdeira family pioneered the idea of planting Alvarinho and making upmarket Vinho Verde in the 1980s.

Brother and sister Luís and Maria Cerdeira took over from their father in 1994 and Soalheiro has since gone from strength to strength. Luís has a point to prove that Vinho Verde is a wine for serious ageing. When we visited in 2016, he proudly opened a 1996 Soalheiro, one of the earliest vintages that the winery still has in its cellars. He pulled the cork, took a sniff and then said dolefully, "Sorry, it's gone… no good anymore". Then with perfect comic timing, he pulled back and enjoyed our reaction. He had us hook, line and sinker. The wine was fighting fit, still of freshness and vitality but with the added depth and nuance of maturity.

Maria began the conversion of the quinta's original 10 hectares of vineyards to organic viticulture in 2004. It was quite an achievement in this wettest of wet regions where seasoned growers and winemakers insist that working without synthetic products would be suicide. These vines now form the core of a premium cuvée named Primeiras Vinhas. Maria also masterminded the creation of Quinta da Folga, a neighbouring property where the family keeps rare-breed Bísaro pigs and produces a range of cured meats. Added to that is a range of herbal teas (*infusões*), harvested or foraged from their own organically farmed land. It's a typical throwback to the Minho valley's farming traditions. This is a land where vines have never been a monoculture.

Although Luís likes to joke about the natural wine world and its supposedly weird, funky or faulty wines, his winemaking is pretty hands off. He's proved that Vinho Verde can be incredibly exciting when it's made in a back-to-the-roots fashion. Terramatter (a wild fermented Alvarinho which spends some time in chestnut wood barrels) and Nature (an unfiltered, zero-added sulphites version) are his more experimental examples. They provide an apt demonstration that if the grapes are up to scratch, no winemaking tricks are needed to create beautifully characterful Vinho Verde.

Anselmo Mendes was later off the starting block than the Cerdeira family, but swiftly gained recognition for Vinho Verde outside the region. A native of Monção, he became obsessed with Alvarinho and how it would respond to various fermentation and ageing techniques. After a decade of research from 1987, he rented vineyards in 1997 and made the first vintage of his Muros de Melgaço (a 100% Alvarinho wine) a year later.

Mendes achieved considerable success with a modern and precise winemaking style. His wines have mainstream appeal and have found a broad audience. The fascination with Alvarinho has continued, earning him the affectionate name 'Senhor Alvarinho'. Mendes expanded both his own production and his winemaking consultancy business rapidly, and in terms of quantity has now far eclipsed Soalheiro or anyone else in the boutique Vinho Verde sector: his output approaches a million bottles a year.

One of Mendes' protégés has forged his own reputation. Márcio Lopes not only has one of the most impressive beards in the whole of the Minho valley, but he's also responsible for some of its most exciting wines. Following experience with Mendes in Monção, and additionally in Rutherglen and Tasmania, Australia, Lopes created his Pequenos Rebentos ('small shoots') label in 2010. He makes a large range of wines, mainly from rented vineyards (including some with very old vines), and with minimal intervention in the cellar. Many are quirky and made in tiny quantities.

Lopes' À Moda Antiga is an absolute stunner of an Alvarinho, made with skin fermentation – an orange wine, in short. He's also made a virtue of an old pergola-trained Vinho Verde vineyard, planted with the traditional and rather rare red varieties Cainho, Alvarelhão and Pedral. This field blend creates Atlântico, a super-lightweight but characterful vin de soif. Lopes is a busy chap – he also makes wine in the Douro and Ribeira Sacra (Galicia).

While Soalheiro and Mendes are the standard bearers for Monção and Melgaço, their equivalent in the Lima valley could be Quinta do Ameal, an estate that started producing high-quality wines in the late 1990s. Here, the focus is not on Alvarinho but rather on the limey, floral Loureiro grape variety.

Pedro Araújo, who is related to the port shipping family Ramos Pinto, took over management of the quinta from his father in 1998 and developed it into one of Vinho Verde's most prestigious estates. Although he is not alone, Araújo has been one of the more vocal disparagers of brand Vinho Verde, pointing out that its associations with cheap wine make it almost worthless as a label marketing term. Araújo often declassified his wines to the theoretically more lowly Vinho Regional Minho denomination to make the point. Other quality producers such as Soalheiro have got around this problem by just listing their sub-region, with the wording "Vinho Verde" seldom appearing on the front label at all. Approaching retirement age, Araújo sold the winery to Esporão in 2019.

Further east, sitting almost on the dividing line between Vinho Verde and the Douro valley, Quinta de Covela has always been a beacon for quality (despite the fact that during the 1990s and 2000s its then owner Nuno Araújo focused on red wines made from international grape varieties including Cabernet Sauvignon and Merlot). After being abandoned for several years, the estate was acquired in

2011 by Lima Smith Associates[13] – a partnership between Brazilian entrepreneur Marcelo Lima and British journalist Tony Smith, who previously worked for Condé Nast International and now lives on the property. Smith's colourful and cosmopolitan past spans young adulthood living in Austria, where he originally fell in love with wine, and working as a foreign correspondent in Brazil..

The pair have breathed new life into the beautiful estate, transitioning it to a focus on two white grape varieties which are considered to be more typical in this part of the region: Avesso and Arinto. Winemaker Rui Cunha has a long history at Covela as well as with his own project Lacrau in the Douro valley. Working with Lima & Smith, he creates wines that stay true to the Vinho Verde imprint of freshness and purity, whilst injecting welcome diversity in terms of the grape varieties and styles. Rui was reportedly delighted that he could finally produce wines that were more typical of the region, something that the previous owner had little interest in.

From Steiner to Buddhism to wine

While Vasco Croft spent childhood holidays at Quinta Casal do Paço, and helped with the harvest on several occasions, it never occurred to him for a minute that his future might involve making wine.

Grappling with the eternal questions of existence and the meaning of life, Vasco discovered the works of Rudolf Steiner when he was 18. Steiner was an Austrian philosopher and esotericist who famously developed both the Waldorf school system (also known as the Steiner school system) and the biodynamic farming methodology in the early 20th century.

Steiner conceived an underlying philosophy, which he termed anthroposophy, as a way of connecting the human experience with a spiritual dimension. Vasco would go on to study philosophy and developed a powerful connection to Steiner's ideas. By the time he was 22, Vasco was married and had already become a parent. The discovery that there was a Steiner kindergarten in Lisbon proved pivotal.

. . . .

13 In 2013, Lima & Smith also purchased two properties in the Douro valley. They continue to manage Quinta das Tecedeiras, but have now sold the more prestigious Quinta da Boavista to Sogevinus.

"It was marvellous to meet the teachers, to see how the children played, to see their joy," says Vasco. His first experience of taking his son to kindergarten had been very negative, but as soon as they arrived at the Steiner school his son was relaxed and welcomed. Two years later, in 1987, Vasco and his first wife Paola decided to move to the UK, to better immerse themselves in the anthroposophy community and to study at a Steiner teacher training faculty.

The couple rented a cottage in the Ashdown Forest in East Sussex and enrolled at both Emerson College and the Steiner teacher training facility Michael Hall. Both colleges are located in Forest Row, a small and charming village. It was here that Vasco had his first head-on encounter with biodynamics. Emerson College had a biodynamic farm on its campus and its produce was used to create meals for the students.

Vasco remembers buying delicious vegetables, meat and yoghurt from another nearby biodynamic farm which had an honesty box outside the house. It was an idyllic and slightly otherworldly life, seemingly untroubled by the desolation and hardship that characterised 1980s Britain during the last gasp of the Margaret Thatcher regime.

During this period, Vasco had no interest in wine. He consciously abstained, taking on board Steiner's misgivings about wine and alcohol in general as potentially disruptive to a meditative way of life. That said, he couldn't help noticing that the most inspiring and creative of his teacher colleagues enjoyed it. They had a tendency to hang out at each other's houses, like a hip community of artists. And inevitably, when they got together, there would be wine.

Paola's father fell ill in 1989, drawing the family back to Portugal. They moved into a house in Carcavelos, a seaside location not too far from Lisbon, that had once been famous for its wine. Vasco's enthusiasm for Steiner education continued unabated. Wanting to start a Waldorf school in Lisbon, he realised that he would first have to create a teacher training programme. Vasco went further and became president of the Portuguese Waldorf School Association (Associação Portuguesa de Escolas com Pedagogia Waldorf) and started a furniture design business.

Life sometimes throws a spanner in the works and that's what happened in 1995. Some years previously, Vasco had got to know a Buddhist monk, the Brazilian Dr Gustavo Pinto who follows the Japanese school of Buddhism. By the 1990s he was already renowned as the west's leading expert on the I-Ching, the ancient Chinese 'book of changes' from which Buddhism and many other beliefs draw guidance and inspiration.

Pinto didn't get to Portugal that often, so when Vasco and the monk met for lunch at Hotel Praia Mar (in Carcavelos), the day was already shaping up to be auspicious. As they sat in the plush restaurant surroundings enjoying its magnificent view out over the Atlantic, Pinto revealed the reason for his choice of venue.

"It's great to meet you here – what a surprise!" said the smiling, bald-headed monk. "But since we have the unique possibility of this meeting, I want to share a new discovery with you that has completely changed my life."

He asked, "What year did we first meet?" and Vasco answered, "1985". Pinto summoned the waiter and said, "Please bring us a bottle of Buçaco 1985". Lovers of Portugal's more arcane treasures will know what a rare treat this was. The wine stood a good chance of being transcendental even for those not accustomed to meditation.

Pinto and Vascao enjoyed a red Buçaco[14] that day. The wine is produced by the famed Buçaco Palace hotel near Coimbra. Both Buçaco whites and reds are wines that can age beautifully for many decades. However, in the 1990s they were nearly impossible to find without visiting the hotel itself. Pinto had not selected the restaurant at random: the Praia Mar is part of the same hotel group as Buçaco Palace, so they stocked its wines. Pinto and his guest were in for a treat.

The wine was brought to the table, and Pinto continued, "Remember the year when we met and how we were, what we were living through, what were our aims, expectations, troubles, joys? They were unique to that year and unrepeatable. Like those events, this wine was only possible due to the conditions of that year, the actions of the people who cared for the vines, the rains from that year. The winds are never the same, the rains are never the same and the wine is never the same."

Pinto intoned slowly, almost meditatively. He kept going with his vinous sermon: "The wine is kept inside this vessel with this cork. I'm going to remove the cork now, and the air in the bottle – which is the air that we were breathing in that year – will be released. The wine inside is going to be released too, and it's going to suffer a transformation. Oxygen will enter, and the wine has to wake up and grow, to show us what it is. It will have an ascending curve and then after some time it will start to slow down and decay, just like human life."

Finally, he got to the nub of his riff on the joys of fine wine: "And this period will give us time for human conversation. Nobody who loves wine will open his best

. . . .

14 The spelling is frequently anglicised to Bussaco.

The view from Quinta Casal do Paço

bottle of wine unless he's with a friend or a lover. This is not just something to taste, our whole human nature is revealed through sharing with others."

The Buddhist sermon continued throughout the meal, and the wine more than lived up to its expectations. For Vasco it was a revelation, and one that he would later describe as a personal meeting with Dionysus. The lure of wine was irresistible after Pinto's inspired introduction. From then on, every time he and the monk met, they would share a special bottle, working their way through many of Portugal's finest appellations.

Vasco continued with his furniture design business and the work in the Waldorf community, but wine was about to seep into his life on a much more fundamental level.

Vasco's family had long employed a farmer (Vasco likes to use the word 'peasant', a word which for him does not have negative connotations) to keep things at Quinta Casal do Paço ticking over since none of the family lived in Vinho Verde. But by 2002, the farmer Senhor António was in his early 80s and well overdue for retirement. The quinta was falling into disrepair and something had to change.

Conjuring up a vision of his childhood, and the simple lifestyle that had once prevailed in Vinho Verde, Vasco dreamt of recreating it at the quinta. He started to spend time at the property and looked into the possibility of revitalising the wine cellar.

It was no surprise that Vasco was given Anselmo Mendes' name as the best source of advice. Anselmo came to look at the estate in 2002. He confirmed that the vineyards and the location were great, and that Vasco was lucky to have plenty of Loureiro vines, which Anselmo advised had the brightest future. But what about the red varieties, namely Vinhão? "Take it out!" said Anselmo. "It's rustic and very tough, no-one will understand it outside this region."[15]

Vasco had no idea how to make wine. Anselmo gave him a shopping list of the basic equipment that he'd need: "You need this-and-that machine, stainless steel tanks, a pump, start like this". Vasco talked it through with Senhor António, who was horrified. "If all that equipment comes in one door, I leave through the other" he said.

· · · · · · · · · · · · ·

15 His advice notwithstanding, Anselmo Mendes does still produce one solitary Vinhão.

But Vasco forged ahead, aided by one of Anselmo's assistants. He came up with a brand name and a label: Aphros wines.[16] Initially, he'd thought about making wine as a kind of hobby. It could be sold locally to restaurants, recouping enough to cover the costs of running the estate. But selling the wine didn't prove to be quite so straightforward.

Going door to door with cases of his first bottled 2004 vintage under his arm, the challenge was evident. He was a nobody, with no track record, and he was trying to sell wine in a saturated market. No-one locally wanted to pay more than two euros a bottle. It's hard to imagine Vasco doorstepping for clients. His quiet, laid-back demeanour is more art school professor than smooth-talking salesman.

What also hit home was that Vinho Verde was considered to be a second division wine. Vasco laughs, "And if Vinho Verde is second division, red Vinho Verde is fourth division!" Anselmo had been right on that count, even though Vasco had ignored his advice to rip out the Vinhão vines. Clearly, he was now in for the long game.

BIODYNAMICS

From 2005, Vasco threw himself into converting the estate to biodynamic farming and restoring the beautiful 16th-century house and chapel. Whether or not to farm biodynamically was never a question, given his long devotion to Steiner's philosophies. He sees biodynamic farming as a complex and holistic practice which needs to be understood and implemented on a deep level, and he bemoans the fact that many modern biodynamic wineries implement the methodologies with scant understanding of what they really mean.

Biodynamics, with its absolute rejection of any synthetic inputs to the field or vineyard, and its focus on manure, silica and quartz-based preparations to help build the vines' strength, is a challenging farming methodology to implement in a wet region like Vinho Verde. European vine cultivars[17] are susceptible to mildew. Conventional viticulturalists insist that it is madness to work without systemic fungicides unless one is prepared to wave goodbye to a significant proportion of the harvest.

. . . .

16 Originally the brand name was Afros, but Vasco later changed it on advice that it could cause confusion in the US market.

17 The *Vitis vinifera* subgenus.

Yet those like Vasco who are willing to invest the time and keep faith in the philosophy often manage to triumph against the odds. In many ways, the value of biodynamics is that it provides a way for the grower to connect on a deep level with plants and the soil. Biodynamic growers spend a significant amount of time in their vineyards, observing and responding to the needs of their vines.

Visiting Quinta Casal do Paço today, it's hard not to be seduced by its calm and beauty. A grand and almost baroque granite staircase transports you from the gate to the house. Vasco has retained some of the old pergola-trained vines on the terrace and it doesn't look so different to the 1970 video. The surrounding vineyards exude vitality and health. Depending on the time of year, you might catch sight of a flock of sheep as they come for a munch of the grass between the rows. Their presence in the vineyard is vital, according to Vasco, not least because they leave behind valuable manure.

Behind the house, a set of stone water-dynamising bowls are built into the hill. Water cascades down, forming into large and beautifully clear droplets as it reaches the bottom. A walk-through shed houses all of the biodynamic preparations and herbal tisanes that are used to enrich the soil and strengthen the plants. Vasco makes everything himself, unlike many other biodynamic growers.[18] He does admit that it was challenging to find a local source of cow manure – the solution involves a long drive – which is a reminder of how much of the local population have abandoned the land and farming.

RECOGNITION

· · · · · · · · · · · · · · ·

While Vasco had scant success trying to sell locally, or in Portugal, his wines started to get the attention of wine critics and importers outside Portugal. In a cyclical twist of fate, British wine writers were some of the first to appreciate the unpopular Vinhão. Vasco recalls International Wine Challenge founder Charles Metcalfe telling him, "This is the first truly delicious Vinhão I've had!", whilst Portuguese wine specialist Richard Mayson was also impressed with the 2005 vintage.

· · · · · · · · · · · ·

18 The biodynamic certification body Demeter often advises certified biodynamic
     farmers or winemakers to buy in the mandatory preparations 500 and 501,
     if they feel the practitioner has insufficient skill or experience in producing
     them in-house.

Before too long, he'd been signed up by importers in the UK, Germany and Japan, the last being one of the world's largest and most important markets for natural wines. A chance meeting with film director Jonathan Nossiter helped secure a deal with a US importer. Nossiter famously directed *Mondovino* in 2004, a film that takes up the Kermit Lynch riff and rails against homogenisation in wine. Vasco describes it as a game changer.

Vasco's story is typical of many artisan Portuguese winemakers who started in the early-to-mid 2000s. Once Aphros wines started to be sold outside Portugal, invitations to wine fairs followed. "We started to have a social life as a winery thanks to Vinho ao Vivo and Simplesmente Vinho," he says. But it was when Vasco attended events such as the 2012 Real Wine Fair[19] in London that he was suddenly exposed to "all the freaks from other countries".

Georgian wines, made in the traditional *qvevri* (a large, buried clay pot with a pointed bottom) left the strongest impression on Vasco, leading to a number of new developments for Aphros. Having outgrown the small cellar at the quinta, Vasco built a larger, modern winery a few kilometres away.[20] This in turn freed up space in the original cellar for a more daring experiment. Vasco decided to return the Quinta's cellar to its traditional state as a winery without electricity. But there was a twist. In homage to the Georgian qvevri wines that had so impressed him, he also installed six antique *talhas*, the Portuguese clay pot equivalent of the qvevri.

A new line of wines were created in this zero-electricity cellar, with grapes hand-destemmed using a *mesa de ripar*[21] and then fermented in talha. The wines are also bottled by hand and labelled under the name Phaunus, a disciple of Dionysus, the first winemaker according to Greek mythology. Stylistically, they are some of the most adventurous in the Aphros range.

Vasco's wine Phaunus Loureiro subjects the indigenous white grape to a few months of skin contact in the talha before it emerges with an enticing savoury complexity and refined texture. The range also includes a Vinhão, a palhete – a traditional Portuguese style where red and white grapes are co-fermented to produce some-

. . . .

19 An artisan/natural wine fair organised by his importer Les Caves de Pyrène.

20 As with so many Portuguese winery projects of the 2000s, this was partly financed with EU funding.

21 An old-fashioned wooden framed device which traps stems and allows grape clusters to be pushed through.

thing not dissimilar to a rosé but with more colour and texture – and two pét-nats (sparkling wines made with a single fermentation that finishes in the bottle).

Vasco has long since accepted his destiny. He's now the owner of a successful winery with a worldwide profile. He works in collaboration with two local wine-makers, Miguel Viseu and Tiago Sampaio[22], who both share his commitment to biodynamic farming and natural winemaking. Every aspect of his life has changed. His first marriage didn't survive, and he closed the furniture business in 2014, the year when he also moved from Lisbon to become a full-time Minho valley resident.

In many ways, Vasco's vision of life as it used to be at the quinta has been recreated. Senhor António's son Alberto Araújo, a childhood friend of Vasco's who grew up at Casal do Paço, played a key role[23] in revitalising the vineyards and installing beehives at the estate. Beekeeping forms a vital part of a holistic, biodynamic farm. Vasco delights in filming scenes from the harvest, much as his mother did half a century ago. Fashions have changed again and, amusingly, while the swinging sixties had yet to reach Portugal in 1970, a half century later the atmosphere was noticeably bohemian. New-age hippies trod grapes in the lagar to the accompaniment of gongs and Buddhist chanting.

Vasco's 2019 video was shot in his modern winery, with shiny new lagares and stainless-steel accessories. It's a far cry from the more primitive cellar at the original quinta, or the simpler lifestyle of the 1970s, but what prevails is the joyful atmosphere and obvious enjoyment of all concerned.

· · · · · · · · · · · · ·

22   Tiago is profiled in full in chapter three.

23   He left in 2018 to run a nearby hotel.

Quinta da Palmirinha

When Vasco Croft converted his estate to biodynamic farming and achieved Demeter certification in 2007, he was certainly a pioneer, but he wasn't the first. About an hour's drive south from Quinta Casal do Paço, near the town of Amarante, there's another pioneering estate which started down the same path a few years earlier.

The 3.5 hectares of vines at Quinta da Palmirinha were inherited by Fernando Paiva in 2000. He was 56 years old at the time and decided to retire from his position as a professor of history and Portuguese and take on the vineyard. A course in biodynamic agriculture with the late Pierre Masson, a legendary French exponent of Steiner's philosophy, provided inspiration for how he would work.

*Fernando Paiva with a bag
of dried chestnut flowers*

White-haired and with the lean, weathered look of someone who spends a lot of time outdoors, Paiva isn't a big talker. When he's asked how biodynamics can work in the wet and challenging climate of Vinho Verde he just smiles doggedly and says one word: "Faith". He counts himself as an agnostic, however when it comes to biodynamics he's now very much a believer. Paiva and Croft met around 2004, although they did not collaborate directly.

The vines at Quinta da Palmirinha are still interplanted with vegetables in traditional Vinho Verde style and Paiva has chickens on grass-cutting duty among the vines. Taking the Steiner idea of closed-loop farming to its extremes, Paiva even uses the fronds of his palm trees to attach the vines to their trellises. He's fashioned a contraption with a wooden board and two nails which allows him to strip the fronds into thin ties.

Wanting his winemaking to be as minimalistic and additive free as his viticulture, Paiva started experimenting with making wine without any added sulphites in 2016. Simultaneously, he discovered that the Polytechnic Institute of Bragança were trialling powdered chestnut flowers as an alternative antioxidant to sulphur dioxide for the production of cheese. Paiva felt that if it could work for cheese, there was no reason why it wouldn't work in wine.[24] He has worked closely with the institute ever since, and now uses this naturally occurring substance made from chestnut trees that grow on his land in all his wines.

He's convinced that it's the perfect substitute for sulphur dioxide, an additive that many natural winemakers want to minimise or avoid altogether as there are rare cases where wine drinkers can show allergic reactions or mild intolerance. That said, it is possible with perfect grapes and winery hygiene to work without any additives whatsoever, so not everyone is convinced about the replacement of sulphur with another additive, even if it is a naturally occurring one.

· · · · · · · · · · · · ·

24 One of the most useful properties of sulphur dioxide is as an antioxidant. It's used by winemakers to stabilise wine at multiple stages of the winemaking process.

CHAPTER 3

LAGAR

· · · · · · · · · · ·

As cities go, Peso da Régua is at best unremarkable and at worst just plain ugly. But location is everything, and Régua, as it's usually abbreviated, is the gateway to the Douro valley. It plays host to three of the Douro river's scarce bridges, notably the IP3/A24 motorway bridge which towers above even the highest of the high-rises. And Régua is also the administrative headquarters of the port industry.

The Casa do Douro and the Instituto dos Vinhos do Douro e do Porto form two historic pillars of port production, both located on Rua do Camilo. Sandwiched in between them is a café, a no-frills place much like the others on the street. Its clientele visit to grab the morning's caffeine shot or to refuel over a simple lunch and a beer. The awning advertises the brand of the coffee, while a couple of wooden tables and chairs sit optimistically on the pavement.

But the café also plays host to a less than official activity. On a September morning, two men sit at the back, coffees drained and business underway. After a few minutes of discussion, they reach an agreement and a piece of paper is passed under the table from one to the other.

The transaction that just took place does not involve any land, grapes or wine, yet it has just made one man richer by a sum of €30,000. It is also completely illegal. The piece of paper[25] is a *benefício*, the annual licence issued by the Instituto dos Vinho do Douro e do Porto (IVDP) which allows for a certain volume of grapes to be used for the production of port wine. So, why would anyone want to buy the licence without the grapes that it is supposed to accompany? And why do port grapes need a licence anyway?

Welcome to the Douro valley, Portugal's most famous wine region. Welcome to one of the most tightly regulated wine industries in the world, and one of the most dysfunctional.

. . . .

25 It is more likely to be digital these days.

Casa do Douro and IVDP offices in Régua

Port wine and the not necessarily beneficial *benefício*

· ·

The Douro valley is sizeable. While neighbouring Vinho Verde covers more ground, the Douro feels more monumental. At more than 100km long, it snakes its way through increasingly remote and climatically diverse zones. Closer to Porto, the lower lying, temperate Baixo Corgo receives around 900mm of rainfall per year. Further east is the hotter, higher Cima Corgo, gouged with its dramatic slate and schist terraces and scattered with most of the historic quintas. The Portuguese side of the valley ends in the arid savannah of the Douro Superior, a flatter and more desolate landscape that survives on a scant 300mm of rainfall per year, with granitic soils in addition to the slate and schist of the Cima Corgo.

Modern-day visitors to the Douro may complain that the roads twist and turn or that there are insufficient bridges crossing the river, but they have it easy. Travelling to or from the region in the past was a formidable undertaking that could even result in death. Before the river was dammed in 1971, the Douro often swelled to a raging torrent as it rushed past the steeply terraced cliffs on either side. When it reached Porto, it could cause serious flooding, as it did in 1909, when a number of port lodges in Vila Nova de Gaia were destroyed. Many of the older cellars in Gaia have giant metal grids in their doorways, to prevent barrels from rolling too far and getting mixed up in the event of a flood.

Two centuries ago, the plucky souls who navigated the *barcos rabelos* downriver from the vineyards to Vila Nova de Gaia were lucky if they completed the journey with cargo and crew intact. Still, the effort was worth it financially, at least for the port shippers. The Douro's robust, deeply coloured wines have had an appreciative overseas audience since 1689, when the war between Britain and France sent British merchants scrambling to find a replacement for the copious amounts of claret drunk on the sceptred isle.

The story of how Douro red wine evolved into the port styles known and loved today warrants its own book. But in short, it developed from the merchants' habit of adding a slug of *aguardente* to the barrels before they were shipped, to protect the wine from oxidation during its long sea voyage. Over the course of a century, this evolved into the modern technique of fortification where the grape spirit is added directly at the winery, and before fermentation has completed. This process not only stabilises, but also locks in unfermented sugars to create the toothsome style that is known and loved today.

While the Brits and their fellow shippers focused entirely on the sweet, fiery port wines, this wasn't the style that the Douro locals were accustomed to drinking. Growers in the valley have always made their own simple table wine, known locally as *consumo*. As winemaker Tiago Sampaio notes from conversations with his father, it would often have been made from a mix of red and white grapes, producing a light and refreshing beverage. Writing his travelogue about living in the Douro Superior in 1939, John Gibbons wrote, "I never saw water as a regular drink. It was always that *consumo*, the local red wine. The stuff was in the people's blood, and the infant seemed to go on to sips of *consumo* as soon as it left its mother's breast."

The regulation of the port industry, which began so dramatically in 1756 with Pombal's demarcation of the Douro, really gathered speed in the 20th century. As described by Portuguese author and Douro wine expert Gaspar Martins Pereira, one of Salazar's first acts as prime minister in 1933 was to create the Instituto do Vinho do Porto (IVP) to oversee port production, the Casa do Douro which managed the vineyard holdings, and the Grémio dos Exportadores de Vinho do Porto (Exporter's Guild) to which all the shippers had to belong.

This bureaucratic trinity laid the groundwork for many additional restrictions. All Douro vineyards were catalogued and registered with the Casa do Douro, which also acted as a market regulator, buying up surplus stocks of port wine each year. Membership of the Grémio was only granted to companies holding a rolling stock of at least 150,000 litres of port and possessing a sizeable lodge in Vila Nova de Gaia, something which sealed the fate of the many thousands of small growers.

Over-production continued to be an issue during the 1930s, leading to the introduction of the *benefício* in 1947. The system was devised by an agronomist working for the Salazar government. Álvaro Moreira da Fonseca came up with an exhaustive method to classify every vineyard in the Douro for its potential to produce port wine. The classifications, which are still in use today, range from A for the top vineyards to I for the lowest quality. Vineyards graded below F are not permitted for port production at all. Moreira da Fonseca based the grades on a fabulously complex points system, with plus and minus points awarded for location, altitude, productivity, soil type and texture, vine training methods, grape varieties, the steepness of the vineyard slope, aspect, exposure, and shelter, plus the age of the vines and the planting density.

Each vineyard is granted a licence for a certain volume of port production. The licence is renewed each year by the IVDP (the successor to the IVP), based on market factors, with the aim of avoiding over-production and over-supply and thus also guarding against price drops.

The system has its heart in the right place and is supposed to protect growers and shippers alike. But like many bureaucratic constructs that have remained in place for decades, it is not just showing its age but is in serious danger of self-combusting.

Paul Symington is one of the system's most vocal detractors, describing it publicly as scandalous. As he explains, none of the major port-wine houses receive anything like a sufficient *benefício* to utilise all the grapes that they either grow or purchase. What to do with the leftovers?

Most producers use the surplus grapes to produce Douro table wine, which is not restricted by the *benefício*. The challenge is that the grapes in question tend to be those of lower quality. This in turn has created a flood of bargain-basement Douro wines made from grapes that are frequently sold at below the cost of production.

Symington notes that the true cost of growing grapes in the Douro is around 90 euro cents or more per kilo per year. This is high compared to many other parts of Portugal because the Douro's steep slopes and terraces make mechanisation close to impossible, and also because yields in the Douro's drier climate zones tend to be low.

It has created a situation where canny négociants swoop into the valley to buy grapes at rock-bottom prices, and then sell the wines at a price-point that com-pares with mass-produced bottlings from Chile. Mechanisation is easy in Chile's huge valleys and plains, allowing grapes to be grown and wine to be made at prices that would bankrupt most European producers. Symington shakes his head in frustration at the thought that wines from the Douro's heroic viticulture must compete in this bottom tier.

There is another solution, as observed in the cafe in Régua. Purchasing an additional *benefício* without purchasing the grapes from a grower who has no intention of making port or selling their grapes for port production has become serious business. Symington insists that his family doesn't participate in this trade, but he's reliably informed that, "one of the largest port houses spends over a million euros a year on buying additional *benefícios* without grapes".

How do producers cover their tracks when they use bought-in *benefícios* and then reassign other parts of their harvest? Permitted yields in the Douro are generous in the extreme, allowing up to 55 hectolitres of wine to be produced per hectare of vines. As Symington confirms, this theoretical maximum yield is close to impossible to achieve in the Cima Corgo or the Douro Superior, where growers are lucky if they harvest half that amount. So, a port producer who might suddenly have a mismatch between *benefício* and yield will claim they had an exceptionally good year with yields at the maximum level. The IVDP has a mere four inspectors to cover the entire Douro, making it more or less impossible to police such dubious claims.

The illegal activity of purchasing *benefícios* without grapes is no secret. Every Douro grower and winemaker acknowledges that it is common practice. Even the IVDP are aware of the illicit trade. Their technical director Bento Amaral admits that the *benefício* system needs overhauling, yet stasis prevails. Symington says that this is because there are far too many vested interests. He's talking about landowners in the Douro who make a good income just from 'selling the paper'. Paul Symington is personally a vineyard owner, with 35 hectares of vines in the Douro Superior. He mentions a neighbour (he declines to name them) who doesn't make any attempt to look after their vines, letting mildew run rampant and leaving the grapes to rot. Selling the *benefício* is much easier work than nurturing a vineyard or finding pickers for the harvest.

With the huge rise in production of Douro still wines, the entire valley's economy has become skewed by the *benefício*. Growers are keen to get the considerable price premium paid for port wine grapes – €1.20–€1.40 per kilo, versus as low as €0.25 for Douro wine – yet the production of Douro wine in volume terms is now more or less on a par with port. Prices are kept artificially high for a static or shrinking port market and pitifully low for Douro wine. It's hardly a sustainable scenario.

Just a century ago, port was the only game in town. Unfortified Douro wine didn't exist as a commercial category. How has it come to dominate the valley's production today?

The reversal of fortunes

Inevitably, as Portuguese winemakers and growers started travelling abroad, and as sail gave way to steam and then to combustion, thoughts turned to whether the Douro valley could also produce high-quality table wine for export. Fernando Nicolau de Almeida, technical director of port house Ferreira, dared to dream a little bigger. Inspired by a visit to Bordeaux, he envisaged a super-premium Douro wine that could be compared to France's grand crus. After much experimentation, he made the first vintage of what would become a Portuguese wine icon, in 1952.

Barca Velha was a wine born out of a port sensibility. Nicolau de Almeida envisaged it as a robust, complex wine that would be aged for a lengthy period in both barrel and bottle. He surmounted many technical challenges to make it, not least that the winery at Quinta do Vale Meão[26] had no electricity. To keep the grapes and the cellar cool enough to produce an elegant red wine[27], ice blocks wrapped in straw were trucked up from Porto. Nicolau de Almeida's son João (born 1949) still remembers the excitement as a child when he and his twin brother were allowed to ride up to the remote winery on the same truck carrying the ice. The wine was then transported to Vila Nova de Gaia immediately after fermentation, where it could age safely at a cool temperature and avoid taking on the undesirable 'Douro bake' character.

João recalls that his father would often bring wine samples home. An important part of his quality check for Barca Velha was serving the wine from an unmarked bottle at lunch, to gauge the reaction of his wife. Legend has it that if she shook her head, that particular vintage would not be bottled as Barca Velha. She was clearly rather choosy, as during the first four decades of its production only 13 vintages saw the light of day. The most recent vintage, 2011, was released in 2020 and is coincidentally the 20th release since 1952.

Perhaps because the project was owned by a port house, Barca Velha was treated with slight scepticism for years, although it now enjoys considerable prestige. Critics award high scores and the wine sells for hundreds of euros a bottle. It remained one of a kind in its price bracket and at its quality level for decades.

. . . .

26 Production of Barca Velha was later transferred to Quinta da Leda.

27 The typically fast, high-temperature fermentation that is common in port wine would likely produce a still wine that tasted unpleasantly cooked and jammy.

The many other attempts at making table wines in the 1970s and 1980s were often afterthoughts, where producers utilised leftover grapes not used for making port. Furthermore, few took heed of what Fernando Nicolau de Almeida had learned.

Key to the success of Barca Velha was a much gentler extraction process than the prolonged foot treading used for port wines, ensuring that its tannins were not aggressive or mouth-drying. Nicolau de Almeida also settled on Quinta do Vale Meão because of its relatively high altitude. He knew the grapes would have more natural freshness and acidity, which was important to make an elegant and balanced Douro wine. Again, these parameters are quite different to those required for port.

João Nicolau de Almeida would take his father's experience and successfully apply it to his own Douro wine, almost half a century after the birth of Barca Velha. João hadn't particularly chosen wine as a career path, but when his father suggested in 1970 that he went to France to study oenology he recalls, "I had no idea what oenology was, but I just heard 'you will go to France' and I said 'I'm ready!'"

After his return to Portugal he started working for Ramos Pinto, the port house owned by his mother's family, in 1976. His first major task was to undertake a systematic study of the grape varieties that were best suited for the Douro. Working together with his uncle, José António Rosas, he studied a dozen different varieties by planting and vinifying them in each of the valley's three sub-zones. The five-year study resulted in five preferred varieties. They were Touriga Franca, Touriga Nacional, Tinta Cão, Tinta Roriz and Tinta Barroca. Even though the findings were poo-pooed at the time – João recalls, "It was a disaster, everyone said you just came back from Bordeaux, what do you know?" – they had a huge influence thereafter. Even today, these five varieties are still seen as the cornerstones for quality port wine or new vineyard plantings.

In 1990, Ramos Pinto was absorbed into the Champagne Louis Roederer group of wineries. On the day the deal was signed, João came to meet his new boss Jean-Claude Rouzaud, the then CEO of Roederer. He had something he wanted Jean-Claude to taste – samples of a Douro red wine which he hoped to introduce to the range. Having tasted the samples, Rouzaud was enthusiastic and said, "What are you waiting for?" So, the first vintage of Duas Quintas was born.

From an initially slow start, the concept of high-quality Douro wines began to gain traction in the 1990s, but it needed some of the valley's younger winemakers, a rather raucous party and an Austrian marketeer to really get the wheels turning.

THE DOURO BOYS

Dirk Niepoort is the larger-than-life head of his family business, which he has led since 1997. Born of German and Portuguese-Dutch parents and partly educated in Switzerland, he has the stature and curly hair that one would expect from a Dutchman. The softly spoken manner with disarming directness is entirely his, however. Niepoort brought a cosmopolitan view of wine to what was then a very traditional port négociant. In particular, he was enthusiastic about table wines.

It was an enthusiasm borne out of his own extraordinary cellar, which ranges from grand cru Burgundies to classic Portuguese wines half a century old. Niepoort loves to open these jewels at the legendary dinners and lunches that he regularly hosts. Dressed invariably as if he has come straight from the vineyard, in shorts and a fishing vest, his manner is always convivial and informal. "Wouldn't you like to try something good?" he'll ask with a conspiratorial look, before wondering over to what looks like a discarded cardboard box, only to return with a 19th-century Madeira or a 1966 Frei João.

Niepoort was quick to see the potential for Douro wines and despite his father's reticence he produced his first attempt in 1990. Robusta lived up to its name and was a big bruiser of a wine. It was never released, but Niepoort wasn't about to give up. In 1991 he made the first vintage of Redoma, a more elegant style that has since become a staple of the Niepoort range. With the Douro's warm climate and its many old vineyards, achieving concentration and complexity in the wines is straightforward. What requires much more skill is to rein in the Douro's power in order to show refinement.

His contemporaries and friends were at it too. Cristiano van Zeller had experimented with making still wines at Quinta do Noval in the late 1980s. His family sold the property to the French AXA Millésimes group in 1993. It was a watershed moment, the first time that one of the Douro's old family properties had been sold to foreign interests. It also left Cristiano with a void in his winemaking activities. He phoned his friend Miguel Roquette, co-owner of Quinta do Crasto, and asked if he'd be interested in a joint venture to make some Douro wines.

The pair produced the first Quinta do Crasto Douro wine in 1994 and showed it at a trade fair in London the following year. But the UK trade was not ready for the idea of premium wine from the Douro; "They all said £4.99 is the maximum price for a Portuguese red wine," laughs Cristiano. By the end of the 1990s, he had also developed his wife's estate Quinta do Vale D. Maria into a boutique winery for both ports and Douro wines, and had a hand in restoring an important historical property in the Baixo Corgo.

Quinta do Vallado was originally owned by Dona Antónia Adelaide Ferreira, the legendary grand dame of the Douro, famed for her philanthropic work in the valley. Today it's run by cousins Francisco Ferreira and João Ferreira Álvares Ribeiro, with the help of Francisco 'Xito' Olazábal, who is now owner and winemaker at Quinta do Vale Meão. All three are great-great-great grandsons of Dona Antónia.

Niepoort, Van Zeller, the Ferreiras and Xito, plus their friends Tomás and Miguel Roquette (Quinta do Crasto), met often to chat and taste. They had a shared goal to create Douro wines that would really put the region on the map for more than just port. The wines they made were a perfect mirror of the Douro's hot, dry climate, with power, ripeness and structure that were perfectly in tune with the moment. The motor was running, but it needed someone to put it into gear and press on the accelerator.

When Niepoort attended the huge trade fair ProWein in Düsseldorf in 1999, there was one visitor to his stand that he wouldn't forget in a hurry: a spectacled, strawberry-blonde Austrian who was upfront, smart and in no sense unnerved by Niepoort's directness. Her name was Dorli Muhr and she was the director of a wine PR agency in Vienna. Muhr is a force to be reckoned with – she founded Wine+Partners in 1991, and after 30 years it occupies an enviable top spot in the industry. When the pair met at ProWein, Niepoort quickly invited her to dinner. She declined, but he reissued his invitation on multiple occasions throughout the year.

Muhr wasn't initially sure what to make of the maverick Portuguese winemaker, but later that year he convinced her to come to Portugal and drove her up to the Douro valley on his motorbike. Badly needing to decompress due to a punishing work schedule, she spent three hours alone in the vineyards in contemplation. She likes to joke that it was the Douro valley, rather than Dirk, which eventually won her over.

In 2002, Muhr and Niepoort decided to marry. Meanwhile, Niepoort and his colleagues had coalesced into an informal group, calling themselves the 'Douro Boys'. They became one of Muhr's clients by default; as she says, at that time there was no PR agency in Portugal with a comparable international network to Wine+Partners.

Drumming up interest for Douro wines turned out to be a serious challenge outside Portugal. Muhr remembers two rather desperate events she organised in Germany in 2003. "In Munich, we had ten guests, and in Hamburg eight people. My friends would come just to be polite, but it was tough to get people to taste wines from Portugal. No-one had heard of the Douro!"

Realising she needed to think a bit more outside the box, Muhr tried a different approach the following year. Their next opportunity was another major wine trade fair, VinExpo in Bordeaux. The Douro Boys teamed up with some Spanish colleagues from Ribera del Duero and Muhr had a plan. "We realised that most people were coming for the big, black-tie events at the top châteaux," she says, "so we decided to do something different that was more in the Iberian way."

Muhr's idea was a pool party, and she hired a house with a big garden and swimming pool. The invitation was a small beach towel with a printed message. Below their logo 'Douro Duero', the text invited guests to forget about donning their black tie after a long hot day at the fair, but instead to don their swimsuit and jump in the water.

The winemakers expected around 50 guests, but over 150 people showed up in the first 15 minutes alone. "It was beautiful," Muhr recalls. "There were all these winemakers and guests in the pool with a glass of wine, chatting and having fun." The challenge was that the catering was woefully inadequate for the unexpectedly large crowd. Muhr had booked a DJ and urged him to start playing immediately. She figured that if everyone started dancing, they might forget how little food they had eaten. The snacks and charcuterie were eked out while the good times rolled.

The party was an extraordinary success and continued until around 3am. As Muhr recalls, it only stopped when the police arrived to shut it down. The event was also a turning point for the Douro Boys. Suddenly, they had exposure and an image that was unconventional, modern, yet totally serious when it came to the wines.

More than 15 years later, at a time when Douro wines are now a common sight on wine merchant's shelves around the globe, it is hard to imagine the impact this event had. But at the time the Douro Boys[28] were a massive force for spreading the word. Importantly, their wines were confidently priced at a premium level. They were not as rarefied or unobtainable as Barca Velha, but neither were they the £4.99 bargain basement wines that the UK trade had previously insisted on.

. . . .

28 Muhr and Niepoort's marriage did not last, and they decided to separate in 2007. Muhr moved back to Austria, and in addition to running Wine+Partners, now also makes wine at her family's estate in the Carnumtum region.

During that decade and a half, winemaking skills blossomed in the valley. Wine-makers learnt to harness the Douro's best qualities – the haunting violet perfume that Touriga Nacional brings to the blend, or the velvety texture of Touriga Franca. Curbing excess ripeness or oak ageing reveals the Douro's thirst-quenching fruit acids, and a similar textural refinement to the wines of Saint-Chinian or Priorat. Old vines – and there are many in the valley – lend a gnarly complexity to the flavours, bringing a panoply of dried herbs, mint and woodsmoke to the party.

THE AGE OF INDIES

Even though it would theoretically have been possible for small Douro estates to bottle and sell their own table wine before Portugal's accession to the EU, few considered the idea. Port's dominance was ingrained into the minds of growers and shippers alike. Just one grower, Quinta do Infantado, managed to break the monopoly of the major port houses in Vila Nova de Gaia when they gained permission to bottle their own estate ports in 1979. But otherwise the idea of boutique port producers remained purely theoretical.

Five generations ago, the Quevedo family started out in the grape-growing and port-wine business. Based in the small town of São João da Pesqueira, in the heart of Cima Corgo, they had just one option when it came to selling their produce.

Once a year, a well-dressed, polite Englishman would come to the Quevedo's door, doing his best to speak some Portuguese. There was no such thing as a contract or guarantee. How much wine he chose to buy, and for what price, was not under the control of the Quevedos or any other Portuguese family living in the region.

By the time Oscar Quevedo (born 1946) took charge, he'd amassed a considerable number of vineyards. His 60 hectares, pooled from inheritance on both sides of the family, required him to have several employees to manage the vineyard work. Nonetheless, it wasn't an especially profitable business, so Oscar also worked a day job as a lawyer and notary while his wife worked as a doctor.

Meanwhile, the family had weathered two serious financial setbacks. The worst occurred in 1954. Oscar's uncle Jorge Teixeira Costa was all set for his sister's wedding day and decided to drive himself and the family to the church in Lamego. Swerving to avoid a taxi that had stalled on the road bridge crossing the Varosa river, he piled into a truck coming in the opposite direction. The truck driver narrowly avoided going to a watery grave, but his cargo of full port-wine barrels rolled one

Cláudia and Oscar Quevedo

by one into the river below. The traumatic nature of the event was far from being the only problem. Jorge had no driving licence, so the insurance company refused to pay any compensation for the lost wine. Neither did he have any money. The family had to foot the bill of 175,000 escudos[29], a ruinous sum which set them back for years.

The following decade didn't smile on the family either. The port shipper that the family had dealt with throughout the 1950s and early 1960s went bankrupt and did not pay for two consecutive harvests. Oscar's grandfather Raul died aged 69 from a heart attack which many suggested was caused by the massive financial pressures on the family.

Needless to say, entrepreneurship and risk taking were hardly valued qualities in the Quevedo family by the end of the 20th century. But Oscar's youngest child, Oscar Junior, would change all that.

Born 1983, Oscar junior remembers that growing up in São João da Pesqueira, almost every family lunch or dinner would end up in a discussion about the wine business. The Quevedos continued to struggle to keep their sales steady enough to cover all the costs. Oscar junior hated the way the topic dominated the conversation.

From a young age, his shrewd business sense and affinity with financial matters was clear to see. By the time he was 12, he had tried setting up a booth on the street outside the family's home, attempting to sell a few bottles of port to passers-by. His father gave him 10% of the sales. It wasn't exactly a booming business, so Oscar junior began looking for alternative ways to make a better return.

Eyeing up a patch of unused ground at the back of the family home, he made a deal with his parents to convert the land into a vegetable garden. It wasn't so straightforward, as the space had to be cleared and then pumped to remove excess ground water. Still, Oscar persevered for two years, at first selling vegetables to local establishments and then to his parents themselves. He didn't get all the initial investment back and ultimately had to admit that while it was fun, it didn't make financial sense.

Reading about the stock market in a magazine, Oscar got fired up. It sounded like the holy grail: a quick way to make money. From the age of 13 he started buying and selling stocks and shares. As he was underage, his older sister Cláudia would sign the forms and go to the stockbroking office to make the deals that he'd carefully researched. Oscar started out just investing his own funds, but when Cláudia noticed that her brother was an astute trader, she put in some of her own money too.

. . . .

29 About €100,000 today.

Wine and farming clearly weren't the way forward, that much was clear to the youthful Oscar. A few years later, he went to study economics in Porto, and then developed a career in finance. His first big break came when he landed an asset management role for an investment bank in Geneva, where he moved to in 2005.

Cláudia was the polar opposite of Oscar in many ways. From a young age, she fell in love with wine, and insisted on studying to be a winemaker, despite the protestations of her grandparents. After she completed her studies in Vila Real, she joined Oscar senior in 1999 as winemaker. It was a significant moment for the Quevedo wine business – the first time her father felt he didn't have to go it alone.

Oscar junior doesn't look especially like a banker or a bigshot businessman. Slighter and more wiry than his dad, his smile is boyish and infectious. If he carries any baggage from the family's history on his shoulders, it never shows. But however hard he tried, he couldn't detach himself from his home town or the family's wine business.

Living in Geneva, he would fly home to Portugal and the Douro more than once a month. After he met his Spanish wife-to-be, Nadia Adria, Geneva's allure started to wane. In 2007, he managed to land a new job working in mergers and acquisitions in Madrid. In retrospect, he admits "the way I left my job in Geneva was a bit brutal. Perhaps I was too emotional". Oscar junior did not give his employer the opportunity to negotiate or to find a solution to his geographical conundrums. He just tendered his resignation as a fait accompli.

After moving to Madrid, Oscar's homeland was only a five-hour drive away and he'd regularly leave Madrid after work on a Friday, and drive back from the Douro again on the Sunday night. "I'm so close to the Douro and my little village that it was hard for me to stay away for too long," he explains. The saudade is strong in his voice when he talks about São João da Pesqueira. "If you ask me where I'm from, I still say I'm from there," he says. "Somehow in my mind, I still believe I live there, I'm still the little boy that knows every backstreet and everyone."

Despite his hatred of the family wine business dominating mealtime conversations, Oscar junior was still drawn to it. He started working in his spare time with his sister Cláudia, attempting to build an export market for the family's wines.

In 2007, Cláudia contacted her brother with what sounded like a great opportunity. An American couple who had just moved to Barcelona were organising a Douro wine tasting event. Cláudia asked Oscar privately if they should send samples of their wines for the tasting, guessing that her father wouldn't see it as a good investment. They did, and Oscar soon met the pair, whose names were Ryan and Gabriella Opaz.[30]

Calling themselves Catavino, their mission was to shake up the wine communications landscape. In a move that was groundbreaking at the time, they suggested that it was essential for wineries to have an online presence and an effective website. They spoke a whole new language of blogging, Twitter feeds and search engine optimisation. For many of Portugal's and Spain's family wineries it might have sounded like gibberish, but some could see that it spelled the future.

Oscar established a bond with Ryan, realising that digital expertise might be key to breathing new life into Quevedo's lacklustre export sales. Again, fearing that his dad would veto the investment, Oscar paid Catavino in cash for some consultancy. Quevedo gained a website and a blog, and both started to show results.

The death of Oscar junior's grandfather in early 2009, a person he describes as "my best friend", was the turning point when he realised he wanted to move back to Portugal. He remembers telling his parents one weekend in the Douro. They were in the kitchen preparing lunch when Oscar mentioned that he wanted to quit his job in Madrid and move back home to work at the winery.

"My dad barely reacted. He just said 'OK, fine'." Oscar interpreted that in several ways. His dad didn't want to pressure him, but pride was also at stake. Oscar shouldn't feel that he was somehow the saviour, the prodigal son who would return to save the family business. He would have to earn his place at the table.

In part due to the groundwork that Oscar and Cláudia had laid, things started to move quickly. Inspired by the possibilities of social media and export sales, Oscar opened a Twitter account and quickly began to build a network. In 2009, Quevedo signed a deal with Naked Wines, a new wine club that had launched a year earlier in the UK. Simultaneously, they created a range of Douro table wines in part so they could utilise excess grapes that were not covered by their *benefício*. Oscar's Wine and Cláudia's Wine featured quirky, hand-drawn label designs[31] and were attractively priced. They were a world away from the super-premium

· · · · · · · · · · · ·

30 Simon writes: readers may find it strange that we mention Ryan here. He and Gabriella were unquestionably part of this story, and their work was a source of inspiration for Oscar Quevedo junior. I felt it would be disingenuous to write them out of the story.

31 The hand-drawn designs were abandoned in 2015 for a new label which, while it looks slicker and more commercial, lacks the personality of the original drawings.

styles created by the Douro Boys or Casa Ferreirinha (Barca Velha), yet they still had the Douro imprint of bold, ripe fruit and firm texture, and were good honest wines for drinking any day of the week.

By 2013, export sales were booming and the Quevedos decided to stop selling wine in bulk to the big port houses. The era of the well-dressed Englishman was over, and Oscar junior was vindicated. "We don't have to go and knock on the door of the merchants in Vila Nova de Gaia," he said. "There's another way."

Oscar still doesn't come across as a traditional CEO or businessman. Visiting the winery in São João da Pesqueira, we noticed a worker on a small digger enlarging a water drainage ditch in the car park. But then the cab opened and out jumped Oscar, who had been taking a break from the paperwork and demonstrating some additional skills that one suspects he did not learn in Geneva.

The company has transformed itself into a very serious enterprise today. Quevedo now owns an impressive 104 hectares of vineyards and produces approximately one million bottles of wine a year. It's a serious achievement for a business that didn't and couldn't exist in the Douro before the late 1980s.

Small is beautiful

While Quevedo has grown to quite a significant size, the 21st century has also seen the emergence of a truly boutique winemaking scene in the valley, much of it powered by millennial Portuguese driven not primarily by commerce but more by the wish to fulfil a dream or to create something authentic.

Rita Ferreira Marques has been in the Douro wine game for long enough that she's seen massive change, from the tiny handful of serious Douro wine producers in 2000 when she started out, to some 400 or more now. Not that wine was her first love. Growing up in Coimbra, wine and the family's vineyards in the Douro Superior didn't hold much allure. The grapes were sold to port producers just like they had been for decades. It was a useful cash cow for her mother, but that was it.

Things changed when Rita went to study engineering, which seems to be the lot for all future Portuguese winemakers. She decided it wasn't for her and switched to a winemaking degree at Vila Real instead. By the time she graduated in 2001, the siren call of the Douro was strong.

Although she comes across as a quiet and reserved character, this slender-framed winemaker is clearly a driven soul if not an outright workaholic. Following experience at Niepoort between 2002 and 2003, she went travelling. As she says, "It's super important to get out of your comfort zone and see something different." Initially, that meant more studying in Bordeaux, then further afield to University of California, Davis, New Zealand and South Africa.

When she returned home, her mother Carla Ferreira made an offer she couldn't refuse – she could take some of the family's vineyards and make wine instead of just selling the grapes. Rita did that and more. With a keen eye for marketing, she engaged a graphic designer and created a brand, a winery and quite literally a concept: Conceito. Her first wines hit the market in 2005.

Rita had taken inspiration from her time at Niepoort, and her goal was to turn the notion of Douro wines on its head. Instead of the big, burly reds that were the stock-in-trade of many early pioneers in the region, she wanted to make a lighter and more delicate style. This was not just personal preference, but also a decision that was perfectly in tune with the family's vineyards.

Although the Douro Superior is generally the hottest and driest part of the region, Rita works with vineyards in the Teja valley which are far from the river and at a relatively high altitude. It's a landscape of more gently rolling hills here, with none of the drama of the Cima Corgo's vertigo-inducing terraces. The temperature difference when compared to nearby estates such as Quinta do Vale Meão is significant, allowing Rita to produce the cool climate style that she prefers.

Ironically, the high altitude and cooler site of the family's vineyards means that they're not graded very high on the scale for port production, which tends to favour ripeness and alcohol above all else. This is a lesson that the Douro wine industry has gradually learnt, that the best grapes for table wine are often quite different to the best grapes for port. When a wine is fortified with almost one fifth of grape spirit, it needs to be robust to go the distance. Port producers look for as much ripeness, colour and tannin as they can reasonably get. But these exaggerated qualities are far less attractive in a bottle of red table wine.

Rita hasn't stopped travelling just because she now has her own winery. "The Douro is super cold and boring in the winter," she says. She prefers to spend her winter squeezing in a second round of winemaking in South Africa, rather than sit at home doing nothing. Every year, she travels to the Boekenhoutskloof winery in Swartland, to make a Bordeaux blend that is also sold under the Conceito brand. Two vintages of a Marlborough Sauvignon Blanc were made in 2010 and 2011, but even the energetic Rita has decided not to make that trip an annual fixture.

One wine in particular has become her calling card. Simply named Bastardo, it has its own story to tell. The grape variety after which it's named is native to Jura, where it's known as Trousseau. Thus far, there is no confirmed theory of how it migrated to Portugal or specifically to the Douro. Carla Ferreira's family always had a plot of it, unusually not in a field blend but just planted on its own, apparently because it was prized for its ability to ripen and produce high sugar levels, even if it struggles in the colour department.

Rita's Bastardo is light on its feet, vivacious and pleasantly peppery. It's a typically individual reading which in some vintages is barely darker than a rosé. It's also the only one of Rita's wines that is foot-trodden in lagares. Despite all the nods to authenticity by using old vines, old techniques and very little intervention in the winemaking, her Bastardo is routinely refused the Douro DOC classification, because the IVDP tasting panel struggles to reconcile it with the typical character of the region's red wines. Still, being bottled as an 'illegitimate' and lowly table wine hasn't stood in its way as it sells out every year.

• • •

Descend from the Teja valley and cross the Douro, then climb back up the other side and you reach the village of Sanfins do Douro. It's a sleepy place that often feels like it has more dogs than people. The streets are cobbled, the buildings hewn from weathered slate and shale. Of course, there is wine, although Sanfins enjoys none of the prestige of its Cima Corgo neighbours, because its vineyards are high in the hills up to an altitude of 700 metres. And that means minus points on the Moreira da Fonseca scale.

The village got its own co-operative cellar, the Adega Cooperativa de Sanfins do Douro, in 1958. And that was roughly when Tiago Sampaio's grandfather stopped making wine. After all, it was a whole lot easier just to truck the grapes around the corner to the Adega and collect some cash.

The family cellar and grandma's old house form three sides of an open courtyard. The house no longer has grandma in it, but feels like a snapshot in time with its old flock wallpaper and dark interior. In the courtyard, a few twisted, high-trained vines mingle with a washing line and some laundry. An expansive view opens out over the church and the hills below the village.

Although compact, the cellar is a well-designed space with a row of traditional granite lagares running along most of its length. They look a little like a set of giant hot tubs, each one a raised-up square basin that could probably accommodate half a dozen people to foot-tread the grapes. But when Tiago was growing up in the 1980s, there was no love for the building any more. The roof fell in and a tree started growing out of one of the lagares.

Tiago was fascinated with winemaking and farming in general, and started studying at agricultural college when he was just 13, much to the disdain of his grandmother who thought he should aim higher, get a good education and work in the city. He persuaded his father to let him make his first wine in 1999. The old cellar was pressed into service, despite the fact that the tree was now reaching for the stars and pushing its way up through what was left of the roof. He also took his education seriously. Following the obligatory winemaking degree from Vila Real, Tiago headed to Oregon in the early 2000s and completed a PhD in viticulture and oenology.

By the time Tiago returned to the Douro, his head was full of modern winemaking know-how. He'd absorbed all the prevailing fashions in Oregon, such as leaving the grapes to ripen as long as possible ('long hang-time'), fetishising higher alcohol and serious extraction. And he'd also fallen hard for one of Oregon's specialities, Pinot Noir.

Working with his family's old vineyards, high up in the hills, one of the first things Tiago did was to plant a few rows of Pinot Noir. He had a feeling it just might work at such lofty altitude. The first harvest was 2007, and Tiago did his best to emulate everything he'd learned in the US. The Pinot was harvested with more than 14% of potential alcohol and aged in oak barrels.

Looking back over his first years of winemaking back in the Douro, Tiago admits that he was playing a tug-of-war with his vineyards. The high-altitude plots were perfect for producing fresh, lively wines that didn't deliver a sucker-punch after the second glass, but Tiago still had the Oregon style in his mind. Eventually the penny dropped and he realised he couldn't impose his will on nature.

The apparently anomalous corners of the Douro, such as Sanfins and its surrounding area, point to its Achilles' heel. It is talked about as one wine region, with one set of regulations, one idea about the typicity of the wines. But a drive up to Tiago's vineyards is enough to ram home the point that there is not one Douro, but many. Even the three sub-regional divisions provide insufficient recognition of the valley's true diversity.

Little of the received wisdom about the Douro really works for Tiago, and for him the recommendations that came from João Nicolau de Almeida's lauded study make little sense. Strolling through a plot of his favoured Tinta Francisca, he says, "The last thing I'd plant here would be Touriga Nacional. It's a myth that it does well everywhere." His winemaking has moved in the opposite direction to his teachers, and now sits firmly within the minimal intervention oeuvre. Sampaio now works with his hands off as far as possible, not trying to control his ferments by adding yeasts, nor airbrushing out any of their personality with filtration or fining when he bottles.

Tasting his wines, it is abundantly clear that Tiago knows exactly what he's doing, even though his cellar sometimes seems like utter chaos. Visiting in 2017, the lagares were filled with a jumble of variously sized barrels, as the available floor space was already piled high with yet more barrels and tanks. There were many experimental cuvées, including a Moscatel ageing under flor yeast and a late harvested white which had failed to reach more than 5.5% alcohol after two years of fermentation.

Tiago took a tortuous route with his branding. His first few vintages were bottled with punkish labels and branded as Olho no Pé, meaning literally 'eye on the foot' or 'watch your step'. Realising it wasn't such a catchy name for English-speaking markets, he changed the brand to Folias de Baco. Yet most of his wines are now bottled as a range which he calls Uivo, except in Portugal where he still uses the Olho no Pé branding.

Whatever might be written on the label, Tiago's style is now quite recognisable. The wines have a feeling of energy and a lightness of touch yet are never simplistic. Whites and reds alike tend to have fascinating textures. Pét-nats have become a small obsession, and are very good, as is the Moscatel Gallego, with pin-sharp, minty aromatics. Moscatel is a specialty of the area around Favaios, where Tiago has some of his vineyards.

Tiago has also made a port wine, albeit a bone-dry style with less than half the amount of residual sugar than is common. It's quite delicious, but quite impossible for him to sell as a port, which would require costly investment to build up stock and to adhere to the prevailing law which requires one third of port production to be held back each year.

One experiment that has become a regular fixture is 'Renegado' (no translation needed). This is Tiago's homage to *consumo*. Produced from an old field blend vineyard that has a significant proportion of white grapes, everything is harvested and fermented together, with very delicate handling and zero oak to ensure a result that is playful and featherlight. Think of it as a rosé with attitude, or a spicy vin de soif. It is apparently the only one of Tiago's wines that his dad deigns to drink.

By Portuguese standards, Tiago is a giant, towering over most of his peers. Skinny as a rake, with a shock of jet-black hair and a schoolboy grin, he projects a laid back, easy-going persona. Yet there is fire in his belly and nothing incites that more than talking about every Douro winemaker's favourite organisation: the IVDP.

Tiago's wines are regularly penalised by the IVDP's blind-tasting panels, with many of the wines refused for the Douro DOC classification and thus bottled without any indication of the region. He's clearly frustrated by what he sees as the panel's preference for discernible oak influence, especially for wines in the reserva category. Sampaio is not alone in his feeling of rejection from the IVDP. Bento Amaral acknowledges that the institute needs to move with the times and has invited Sampaio to present all of his wines to the panel tasters in a more informal setting. For the moment though, the institute and the renegade winemaker haven't quite figured out how they can talk or how they can best help each other.

Even if Tiago's winemaking skills don't appear to impress the IVDP, his work has increasingly caught the attention of his colleagues. Vasco Croft invited him to become a consulting winemaker for Aphros, in Vinho Verde, a role which Tiago took on in 2017 with great enthusiasm. With typical Portuguese modesty, he refused any offer of payment insisting that it was a great learning opportunity. Croft resolved the situation by gifting him two antique talhas, which Tiago now uses to make his own Uivo Anfora wine.

Luckily, Tiago upgraded from the cramped conditions at his family's old cellar just before he took delivery of the massive clay pots. As the Adega Cooperativa de Sanfins do Douro had long since lapsed into bankruptcy, its grim but sizable head-quarters was finally put up for sale. Tiago jumped at the chance and moved Folias de Baco to its new location in early 2019. It makes for beautiful if ironic symmetry. The very same building that killed off winemaking in Tiago's family – and countless others – has now been reborn as the host of Sanfins' most unconventional yet successful wine artisan.

• • •

João Nicolau de Almeida once lamented "the schizophrenic situation in which there was almost no connection between viticulture and wine." As he put it, historically the blenders were in Vila Nova de Gaia and the growers were in the Douro. Times changed, and Nicolau de Almeida's own sons opened his eyes to a better way to connect with the land.

Mateus and João junior transitioned Quinta do Monte Xisto, the family's property in Douro Superior, to biodynamic viticulture. They produce table wines under the labels Trans Douro Express and Muxugat. Sceptical at first, Nicolau de Almeida was quickly won over. "There is something natural and human about this new way of looking at the earth," he said in an interview with the Portuguese newspaper *Publico*. "Nobody wants to die on polluted ground".

The focus has shifted in the Douro. Winemakers such as the Nicolau de Almeida brothers, Tiago Sampaio or Rita Marques want to let the valley express itself through their wines. Not the other way round.

Port no longer dominates the conversation, even if the *benefício* continues to distort the Douro wine market. Instead, what's on everyone's minds is when climate change will really start to bite, as 45°c summer temperatures and July harvest dates are already a reality. The endangered species that is the seasonal vineyard worker is also a significant issue.

The only constant is the Douro river, which continues its placid flow past the ancient terraces and historic quintas. And the fact that Régua remains as plain as ever.

Oscar Quevedo and his grandfather João Batista Quevedo

Terraces in the Cima Corgo, Douro

CHAPTER 4

SERRA

● ● ● ● ● ● ● ● ● ● ●

It's possible to drive right through the middle of Dão without ever realising it's a wine region. Its vineyards are so parcellated and broken up by hills, mountains and granite outcrops that most are invisible from the main roads – not that there was anything resembling a highway until 1989, when EU funds dramatically improved access to this rural and increasingly depopulated part of the country.

Boasting mainland Portugal's highest mountain range Serra da Estrela, which tops out at 1,993 metres above sea level, Dão is wilder and more rugged than the neighbouring Douro or Bairrada regions. It remains well off the beaten track, and close to impossible to visit without a car. Even its main urban centre, Viseu, lacks a train station.

Serra da Estrela itself couldn't be more Portuguese. It's the ultimate low-key mountain, despite its superior elevation. Rather than a single notable peak, the highest point of Serra da Estrela, Torre, is on a plateau. A cheese with the same name arguably enjoys more worldwide fame. It's soft and made with sheep's milk, and unusually is made without rennet.[32] It's not uncommon for international cheese fans to be completely ignorant of the fact that their favourite dairy product also happens to be a mountain.

Apart from hikers, tourists tend to give Dão a miss. Even wine-loving visitors are likely to head straight to the Douro valley or Vinho Verde. No-one gives Dão a second thought. It shouldn't be this way. Not only is Dão a beautiful and largely unspoilt region, it's also the home of what many consider to be Portugal's most important red grape variety, Touriga Nacional. At least, this is the opinion of experts such as José Vouillamoz, who notes that Touriga's clonal diversity is higher in Dão than anywhere else in Portugal, which is a key pointer to its likely origins.

· · · · · · · · · · · · ·

32 *Silybum marianum*, commonly known as milk thistle, is used instead.

Pruning at Quinta da Pellada

Named after the river that diagonally bisects the region from northeast to south-west, Dão once had a reputation for producing some of Portugal's most elegant and classical red wines. Its climate and soils are perfect for the production of structured, dark-fruited reds with crunchy tannins and fresh acidity. It has been demarcated as a fine wine region since 1908.[33] But its reputation was destroyed by 30 years of government intervention which sent the quality of the wines tumbling down as steeply as the Serra da Estrela's escarpments. There is more than a little irony in the fact that António de Oliveira Salazar was himself from Dão, and owned vineyards in the region throughout the time he held office.

Dão's Achilles' heel, as Richard Mayson outlined in the 1992 edition of his book *Portugal's Wines and Winemakers*, was that most of its 100,000 or more growers owned tiny vineyard plots that were more akin to a back garden than a serious vineyard. Subsistence farming, with wine as one of the staples produced for home consumption, had always been the norm, but such fragmented production could neither provide the consistency nor the scale of production expected from a modern wine region.

The Salazar government was keen to consolidate wine production and make it as efficient as possible. From 1954, they built ten large co-operative wineries in Dão, simultaneously introducing a ruling that forbade privately owned wineries from buying in grapes. This granted the co-ops an effective monopoly when it came to winemaking. The co-operative winery model was rolled out across the entire country, but the restriction on buying in grapes was specific to Dão.

Even though the co-operatives were brand new, they were not particularly well equipped and the winemaking and hygiene practices were perfunctory. Worse still, they tended not to make much if any selection between the best and worst grapes delivered to their weighbridges. Not only did the standard of the wines plummet, but the motivation of growers also fundamentally altered. The co-operatives paid solely on the basis of weight, not quality. Higher yields rewarded the grower with more money, never mind whether it would produce a better wine.

It wasn't until 1989 that this restrictive and anti-competitive model was repealed, due to pressure from the European Union. By then, the damage had been done and Dão was in the doldrums. Look no further than the pronouncements of wine writers at the time. Jancis Robinson recalls that prior to the 1990s, Dão was pro-ducing "some of the toughest, hollowest, most uncharming wines in the world". Michael Broadbent reputedly described the special taste of Dão wines as "goaty".

. . . .

33 Originally Região Demarcada, now Denominação de Origem Controlada or DOC.

Writing in the *New York Times* in 1984, Frank J. Prial cautioned, "Critics are divided on the quality of Dão reds. Some say they are too dry and papery, even when well made." He adds his own editorial: "In fact, the Dão reds seem to come in various styles, ranging from soft and drinkable to unbalanced and rough."

By 1989, growers had become used to a guaranteed sales route and relatively easy money. The co-operatives continued to dominate. Winemaker António Madeira explains that the traffic queues to deliver grapes during harvest were often so long that growers would sleep in their trucks overnight. The alternative was losing their place in the queue to drive onto the weighbridge and calculate their payment.

Tending vines in Dão had started to become the preserve of the elderly by the 1990s. When Portugal joined the European Union in 1986, it brought opportunity to the younger generation, who were encouraged by their parents to get city jobs and who moved to Lisbon or Porto, or left Portugal altogether.

João Tavares de Pina

There are always exceptions to the rule, and winemaker João Eduardo Tavares de Pina is one of those. Having grown up in Porto, at the age of 30 he chose to move to his family's isolated Dão estate in 1991.

João is an engaging narrator, in Portuguese or his heavily accented English. He mentions that he's much more fluent in French, which was the most common second language in Portuguese schools up until the 1980s. His rough sandpaper drawl of a voice feels like it's forming his face into a permanent grin. He's also a master of surprise – he'll typically sneak in the most unlikely detail almost as a throwaway and wait for you to stop and do a double-take.

We chatted one February evening as he prepared dinner at home, near the small town of Penalva do Castelo. He's a keen and very skilled cook. "This is my routine," he explained. "I come home, light the fire and start cooking. And then I'm happy." We were happy too, with our appetites building as we watched him slice a fresh sea bass into carpaccio-like slivers and marinate them in lemon juice and olive oil.

João talked about his family roots, which are embedded in Penalva do Castelo, as evidenced by the profusion of street and village names in the nearby area which contain the family surname: Travanca de Tavares, Chãs Tavares and Várzea de Tavares for example.. The family's farm, Quinta da Boavista (not to be confused with the prestigious Douro property of the same name), was established as a commercial winery in 1894. João's grandfather was what he describes as a "serious winemaker", although the estate sold in bulk and did not bottle its own wines until the fall of the Estado Novo.

His father, João António, had a career working for what is now the major winery group Sogrape. Like most fathers at the time, João António hoped that João junior or one of his three brothers would follow the same career path and also become a consultant winemaker for a major company. Consequently, João junior was sent to Bordeaux to study winemaking between 1980 and 1983.

He learned from a number of up-and-coming luminaries, including the now legendary late Denis Dubourdieu. João recalls that he neither liked nor disliked the wines of Bordeaux, but just accepted that they had the highest status in the wine world of the 1980s. He formed a stronger opinion about the city. It was incredibly dirty and racisim appeared to be widespread.

Returning to Portugal in 1983, João continued his studies at the University of Trás-os-Montes and Alto Douro (UTAD) in Vila Real. It's here that he teases in a surprising biographical detail: "You know I discovered one of the world's most popular selected yeasts?" he says as we walk around his simple winery where such products have not been used since the 1990s. It's a mildly shocking and provocative statement, given that he is now famed for making natural wines which ferment spontaneously using just the wild or ambient yeasts that occur naturally on the grape skins or in the atmosphere.

He's not joking though. After studying for his degree in agronomy, João embarked on a three-year research project, working his way through 700 samples from the Vinho Verde region, which resulted in the isolation of a yeast now named QA23. It might not sound catchy, but QA23 has since become one of the world's most popular selected yeasts, sold in plastic blister-packs to millions of winemakers around the globe via its Canadian licensee Lallemand. Amongst other qualities, it is recommended by the manufacturer for "developing passion fruit character in Sauvignon Blanc".

João laughs at the apparent contradiction – "I came from the dark side to the green side" – but he also acknowledges that having sound technical knowledge is essential for a winemaker who then wants to work without the interventions or additions used by mainstream producers.

Back to Boavista

Although it would become the source of a great deal of tension between João and his father, he passionately wanted to make wine at the family's estate that had lain dormant for decades. The opportunity came shortly after João married in 1990. His wife Luisa Lopes is from Lisbon. As João puts it, "Luisa was from the south, I was from the north, and we needed to find somewhere in the middle." Quinta da Boavista was perfectly located, even though it meant swapping city life for an intensely rural existence.

João and Luisa moved to the property in 1991, supporting themselves with a combination of Luisa's job teaching biology and geology at a local school and João's part-time work in technical drawing. Meanwhile he'd reached a slightly uneasy agreement with his father, who still owns the entire estate. João would make wine, his father would cover all the costs but also exclusively handle the sales.

As João explains, an estate like Quinta da Boavista in the unfashionable Dão is more of a liability than a serious business proposition. "Who would want to spend money on a property like this?" he asks rhetorically. Explaining why none of his three brothers seem to mind that he has sole use of the estate, he says, "We never had profits from this place, we just had expenses. So, my brothers said do what you want, just don't ask us for money."

João did just that. He made his first vintages from 1996, and his father sold some of the wine to Portugal's largest wine club, Enoteca. The wines were classic Dão, linear, fresh and firmly structured. João's 1997 Terras de Tavares still tastes wonderful today (he kindly opened a bottle during one of our visits), but back in the late 1990s and early 2000s fashion was moving in a different direction.

The era of super-ripe, overtly oak-influenced wines had arrived in Portugal. Producers were ripping out Portuguese grape varieties and planting Cabernet Sauvignon or Syrah. Parker Points – the currency of the celebrated American wine critic Robert Parker – were highly desirable. Understated, classical wines from Dão were, as João puts it, "not trendy".

João continued working part-time, this time selling winery equipment to other winemakers. It enabled him to befriend many of the country's leading winemakers, such as Dirk Niepoort and Jorge Serôdio Borges. Finally in 2004 his father was sick of "losing money and losing time", and their collaboration ended, along with the financing.

Some very lean years loomed and João decided it was time for a change. Looking back, he describes 2005–07 jokingly as "my commercial period". He figured that, as things weren't going well, something had to change. His solution, much to the disgust of the more traditionalist Tavares de Pina senior, was to follow fashion with a riper, more late-harvested style and the use of French oak barriques for ageing.

The stylistic change paid off to a degree, perhaps in part since João was now selling his own wines and he could deal with customers that his father had rejected out of hand. In 2007 he started exporting outside Portugal, yet the sales volumes remained less than exciting. "No-one wanted my wines back then," he says, noting that he still even has stock of his 1997 Jaen.

PUNK'S NOT DEAD

João had started hearing about the concept of natural wine, and it resonated. "This was exactly what my grandfather did," he says. "He just tried to harvest the grapes at the right time and do nothing in the cellar." As an experiment, he made the first batches of what would become Rufia, an irreverent label, meaning 'punk' in Portuguese. He released the 2012 vintage in 2014, and it sold out immediately. The provocative labels, designed by Australian-born, Brazilian-raised cartoonist Marguerita Bornstein[34], were a key part of the package.

"The idea was just to go back to tradition," he explains, "with lower alcohol, lighter wines. But they are meant to be serious wines, too". And although the Rufia project started as a kind of side label, it now represents João's main production and has opened doors for him worldwide. He smiles as we taste the latest vintage of his *curtimenta* or orange wine. "I started making an orange wine because it was trendy," he says with a grin.

For all the lack of artifice, that *curtimenta* has gone from strength to strength and, as with all the Rufia wines, João says it now sells out to his distributors on pre-allocation. In many ways, the style and the winemaking are simply a return to the traditional methods that João started out with. It's just that now fashion has come full circle and the world has caught up.

. . . .

34 Her work has frequently appeared in the *New Yorker* and *Time* magazine.

Despite the success, João's relationship with his father continues to be complex, to say the least. Although his father has no day-to-day involvement in the wine production, he still co-owns the land on which the house and the vineyards are sited.

It's not the only problem with the land. By 2010, a pernicious invader had infested almost all his vineyards. Esca is a potentially devastating disease, borne by fungi, which kills off the trunk of a mature vine. It's nigh on impossible to treat once it takes hold in a vineyard. His drastic solution was to pull out the entire 13 hectares of vines, including some plants up to 60 years old, and to start again from scratch.

João now works increasingly with a 'no till' methodology, a form of permaculture that was originally popularised by Japanese farmer Masunoba Fukuoka in his seminal 1975 work *The One-Straw Revolution*. By creating a naturally balanced and healthy ecosystem, João aims to prevent esca from taking hold in the future. To mitigate the more familial problem, he's also planting new vineyards on adjacent sites that he's purchased himself. Walking over to the new plots, we passed an impressive granite corner-post. "That's the Romanée-Conti of Dão," he laughs.

For all the complications, it is not hard to see the appeal of Quinta da Boavista. It's a typical Dão landscape, with rolling hills and forests surrounding the cultivated areas. João and Luisa live in a simple and compact house, while the historic granite building and courtyard, which were formerly rented out as holiday apartments, currently sit empty due to a disagreement between father and son about its use.

On a sunny morning, the hill that tumbles down outside their front door glistens as if it is covered in frost. But, although it's decidedly chilly during our February visit, the bejewelled appearance is actually due to the quartz deposits in the soil catching the light. João looks at the sky and pronounces that sunset that evening will be a sensational deep red – and he's not wrong. It's a *boa vista* indeed.

Although he clearly loves living in this isolated spot, there is nothing inward looking about Tavares de Pina. He's an enthusiastic promoter of his region and his colleagues. From 1999 he started organising tastings together with long-time friend João Roseira. It was a collaboration that would eventually lead to the creation of the pivotal wine fair Simplesmente Vinho. He also befriended a young Frenchman who moved permanently to Dão in 2017 and needed all the help he could get.

THE OLD-VINE WHISPERER

If you met António Madeira at a wine fair in 2014, as we did, you'd have been forgiven for thinking that he was a moody character. Madeira would stand by his tasting table, unsmiling and seemingly dour, but with two bottles of his first and only wine, an impressive and rather elegant 2011 Dão red.

Madeira admits that he'd been very close to a nervous breakdown at the time.

Despite being born and raised in Paris, his name easily gives away the family's Portuguese heritage. Madeira's parents were originally from the Serra da Estrela area – at the very heart of Dão. Like so many families, they left Portugal during the Salazar era, and like so many they chose France, which now has the largest Portuguese diaspora in Europe – a total of around 1.7 million people according to France's 1999 census. Poverty in Portugal and the almost total lack of development or opportunity during the Estado Novo were the main factors that drove people elsewhere. Portugal and France have had strong links throughout the 20th century, as evidenced by French becoming the default second language taught in many Portuguese schools.

Madeira and his parents would visit every summer for holidays, and he loved the rural contrast with Paris. In 2004, he met Marina Almeida (his wife-to-be) in his grandparent's village of São Martinho.

Wine wasn't part of Madeira's life at that point. He remembers that his father always had a glass of wine with dinner, but it was invariably a cheap Côtes du Rhône from the supermarket, which Madeira found quite disgusting. The lightbulb wine moment came later, after he'd graduated with an engineering degree and started working in the logistics sector.

"My colleagues had plenty of money and some of them started a wine club," recalls Madeira. "I started to taste wonderful things and I fell in love." And this being Paris, he discovered natural wines from the Jura and top Pinot Noir from Burgundy.

Madeira was 25 years old at the time. The penny dropped that wine was also a big part of Portuguese culture. He started reading books and discovered a Portuguese online wine forum where he could chat to many of the country's winemakers. It was this forum which brought him into contact with João Tavares de Pina and João Roseira, and also with another young Portuguese winemaker named Rita Ferreira Marques.

"I started to understand that this region that I love used to be very important for wine," he recalls. "But that was in the process of disappearing. I started to think maybe I can make a difference and help the region." Madeira became more and more obsessed with the decline of Dão's reputation and the feeling that it was dying. Finally in 2010, he decided to act. "I didn't have a cellar, I didn't have anything. I just had ideas," he says. And he'd never made wine in his life.

He befriended Luís Lopes, the consultant winemaker at Quinta da Pellada, the estate belonging to Álvaro Castro, a local pioneer and long-established winemaking icon. Quinta da Pellada is just a few minutes' drive from São Martinho, and Madeira started to hang around the cellar to learn.

Madeira's first vintage in 2011 was made with grapes from a neglected vineyard that he'd managed to rent. Castro allowed him to bring the grapes to Quinta da Pellada for fermentation, where he had Lopes on hand to teach him how to make wine. Madeira might not have had the experience, but he had a blueprint in his mind, formed from his experience back in Paris. He imagined pure, natural wines made with as little technology or intervention as possible.

Meanwhile, he'd commandeered the garage underneath his grandparent's old house. It became an ad hoc cellar, stuffed full of stainless-steel tanks and a few old oak barrels. He also started searching for vineyards he could rent or work, and would drive around the mountain villages looking for abandoned or semi-abandoned vines. Then he'd go knocking on doors and try to figure out who owned the plot and whether they would agree to let him rent it and take over the work. Sometimes he'd hear sob stories from wives whose husbands had died or who were no longer fit enough to get out into the vineyards.

Some old-timers still tend these precious old vineyards, but the viticulture is frequently brutally chemical. The grapes are then delivered to the local co-operative for a pittance. As vines get older, their yields tend to drop. Since co-operatives pay based on quantity and not on quality, working the old vines isn't a tempting prospect as the work gets harder and the already meagre financial returns diminish.

As Madeira points out, the co-operatives have skewed things in other ways too. They pay a premium for grapes from a stated single variety, and half the amount for grapes from a field blend – a vineyard where all varieties grow together, as has always been the tradition in Dão. Yet it's the wines from field blends that are often best at expressing Dão's unique character. Madeira is a firm believer in the natural balance and harmony that can be achieved with field blends and co-fermentations, where everything is not just grown together, but also harvested and fermented together.

The co-operative's premium has resulted in many old vineyards being ripped out and replanted just with Touriga Nacional or – even worse – Tinta Roriz. "It's a shit," exclaims Madeira, for whom there is little love lost for this Spanish import. Tinta Roriz is one and the same as Tempranillo. There's plenty of it growing all over Portugal these days, but Madeira feels it is not well suited to the climate. Compared with Dão's native varieties, it doesn't retain freshness or acidity so well.

Madeira has encountered plenty of resistance from locals who don't believe that a Frenchman – even if he is bi-lingual and entirely Portuguese by heritage – will look after their prized vines properly. In some cases, the unthinkable happens and vineyards are pulled out in return for EU grants or bulldozed to make way for housing. But Dão is not a wealthy region, nor a huge tourist draw, so many sites are just abandoned and left to rot.

Some of the plots that Madeira rescued are extraordinary. Nestled into rolling hills, perched atop granitic outcrops, many are invisible unless you know which tiny track to follow. In some places the ground-up granite and quartz creates soil as white as sand, making it look as if the vines have been planted on a beach. The vineyard that Madeira calls 'Vigna da serra' is his pride and joy. It's a compact plot of maybe half a hectare, with a few rows of wizened vines that are around 125 years old. The vines have twisted and formed into bizarre angles, as a result of negligent pruning. Their trunks are as thick as concrete posts, sometimes support-ed on rocks to stop them lying on the ground and rotting. Madeira couldn't identify all the different grape varieties, and neither could a specialist who came to visit. At least 30 different species nestle in the coarse granitic soil. Furthermore, all of these senior citizens stand on their own roots [35]

"It's a museum," laughs Madeira, except that this vineyard is now very much alive and in service. Madeira has nourished it lovingly back into health, renting a local horse to help gently plough the rows and planting fava beans to try to restore the nitrogen balance. The harvest from this special place is bottled as a wine called Centenaria. "It's like a grand cru," he explains. The wine is richly concentrated and dark fruited, with a depth of flavour that could never come from younger vines.

"In the beginning I was going to find vineyards and people. Then people started coming to me," says Madeira. Now he's known as the crazy guy who will take on your vineyards if you're 90 years old or just can't be bothered any more.

· · · · · · · · · · · · ·

35 Newer vines are almost always top-grafted onto American rootstocks, which are *Phylloxera* resistant.

From hobby to profession

It started out as a holiday pursuit, but by 2014 Madeira had amassed a total of 26 small vineyard sites spread around six different villages. He was spending every single weekend in Dão, before returning to France for his day job, and had even started work on building a dedicated winery.

The stress started to show. Madeira had his wife and young family to look after in Paris, not to mention his engineering job and the burgeoning collection of ancient vineyards in Dão that demanded his attention. "I was very, very tired and didn't have any time to rest," he says.

Finally in 2017, he convinced his wife that the whole family should move to São Martinho. Wine had become his life and he wanted to live from it. His grandparent's old house became a temporary home, and best of all Madeira now had his wife on hand to help with the vineyard work. Except that she promptly became pregnant with their third child.

Once the move was completed, Madeira ramped up a gear or two. He desperately needed more space, as his grandparent's garage had turned into a logistical nightmare, with barrels and fermentation vats spilling out onto the drive during harvest. An EU grant enabled him to complete the new winery, just in time for the 2018 vintage. A couple of kilometres outside the village, it's a modern and functional structure that reflects Madeira's more pragmatic engineering background – the mystique and romance are kept strictly in the vineyards.

Madeira hasn't been welcomed by everyone in the region and has had a few run-ins with the Comissão Vitivinícola Regional (CVR) do Dão, the body that regulates and certifies all wines from the region. During the first few years of his work, he documented everything on a blog written mostly in Portuguese, but with occasional deviations into English and French.[36]

Looking back, he feels it may have been naive. "At the beginning, I thought you could say everything, you could be totally transparent. But then I understood that what I was sharing with people, some started to use against me." Madeira has been criticised for everything from his choice of ground-cover crops in the vineyard to his decision to use a horse to work his oldest vineyard. He is now more wary of posting every detail, although the blog still receives very occasional updates.

. . . .

36 See vinhotibicadas.blogspot.com

Right from the start, Madeira's aim was to bring more focus to Dão and to help it recover its glorious reputation as a wine region. The labels for his wines reflect this, with the word 'Dão' emblazoned in far larger letters than his name. Madeira also prints 'Dão' on all of his corks, he says as a bit of additional promotion for the region. However, this altruism backfired on him in 2019.

Madeira produced a rosé from the 2018 harvest, which he bottled unfiltered without any added sulphites. It's a delicious wine, with pure fruit and a laser focus despite the lack of sulphur additions. But the CVR took exception to its slight haziness and refused to grant it the DOC certificate, meaning that the Dão region was no longer allowed to be mentioned on the label.

An inspector visited Madeira's winery and saw the already filled bottles waiting to be labelled. Spotting the word 'Dão' printed on the corks, they insisted that Madeira re-cork all 1,000 bottles using an unbranded closure, which was not only a time-consuming and frustrating exercise, but also one that risked spoiling the wines due to excess oxygen ingress during recorking. Madeira's take on this extreme bureaucratic pedantry shows more Parisian venom than Portuguese shoulder-shrugging. His anger does feel justified.

Madeira admittedly loves to cock a snook at the wine establishment from time to time. His top wine, a single vineyard bottling from one of his oldest plots, is named Palheira, a Portuguese word which translates roughly as 'hay barn' or 'small shed' where tools are stored. "A lot of wine labels are very show-offy, with names like Palazzio or Château," says Madeira. "So, for my best wine, I put the name of the simplest building you can find in the land."

These days, when Madeira goes to one of the wine fairs in Porto (or elsewhere), his table is quickly mobbed by young sommeliers and wine importers keen to taste his latest vintage and desperate to get their hands on his scarce production. And he does smile a little more than he did back in 2014.

QUINTA DA PELLADA

. . . .

As Madeira frequently acknowledges, he would have got nowhere without the help and support of Álvaro Castro, whose Quinta da Pellada estate is a ten-minute drive from Madeira, in the village of Pinhanços.

Castro has been described by Portuguese wine journalist Rui Falcão and many others as an ambassador for the Dão region. It's no surprise that he and Madeira became friends as the two have common aims: both want to return the region to its past glory, and both recognise the huge importance of its old vineyards with their treasure-troves of plant material and rare grape varieties.

Having trained as a civil engineer, Castro inherited Quinta da Pellada in 1980 and moved to the property from Lisbon, initially thinking that he'd just stay for a few months and see what would happen. He became happily subsumed by the challenges of viticulture and winemaking, a state of affairs that continues to the present day. In 1989, with the changes in legislation that allowed independent pro-ducers to bottle their own wines, Castro was able to start putting his own wines on the market. He began bottling wines from Quinta da Saes, a neighbouring estate also within the family's ownership.

While he has a quiet and unshowy personality, Castro is clearly someone with boundless curiosity. Walking through the labyrinthine cellars of his winery feels a little like being given a tour by a mad scientist. At every turn, there are seemingly random stacks of barrels with different blends, varietals and other experiments.

Since 2001, Castro has been assisted by his oenologist daughter Maria, who is taking the winemaking in a yet more stripped down, non-interventionist direction. Maria lives in Lisbon with her husband and family on weekends, but spends most working weeks living and working at Quinta da Pellada.

The house at the quinta where he now lives has been restored by Castro and, just like him, it is unshowy but has a beautiful period feel, giving some idea of what country life in Portugal might have been like several hundred years ago, albeit with modern comforts such as electricity and running water.

Castro collaborated with erstwhile friend Dirk Niepoort for many years, making a wine called Doda, which blends Douro and Dão grapes together. However, this collaboration ended with the 2013 vintage.

The family now not only owns Quinta da Pellada (with higher altitude vineyards responsible for most of their premium bottlings) and Quinta de Saes (in general, more entry-level wines) but has also purchased a plot from Quinta de Passarela, which is used in their Pape wine.

Castro and his daughter are now responsible for a total of 60 hectares and produce 200 to 300 thousand bottles per year. This makes them one of the more significant artisanal producers in the region. They place a great deal of importance on the vineyards, which have been fully converted to organic viticulture.[37] Sheep are used to keep the grass cover under control during the winter months, and to help fertilise the vineyards.

The relatively large vineyards at Quinta da Pellada, some of which are four or five hectares in size, are unusual in the region. Castro also has some prized plots of old vines more than 100 years old, some of which go into a small production wine named Muleta, meaning crutch in Portuguese and referring to the sticks or stones that support the vines.

Anyone lucky enough to be in front of a bottle of Muleta will be left in absolutely no doubt as to why old vines like these are so valued. The grape varieties are mainly Jaen and Baga, and the wine has an extraordinary sense of concentrated yet pure berry fruits. Although intense, it is refreshing and restrained. Vines of this age don't need to shout their message, but they do have amazing stories to tell.

Putting a value on the Dão's historic vineyards, rather than just seeing everything in terms of maximising yields and profits, is an ethic that's shared by the Castros and António Madeira, and also by a winemaking duo based a little further east.

Casa de Mouraz

15 October 2017 is a date that António Lopes Ribeiro and Sara Dionísio will never forget. The winemaking couple, better known to the world as Casa de Mouraz, were in bed at their house in Tondela, a small town on the eastern edge of the Dão region.

Their winery is situated in the hamlet of Mouraz, a seven-minute drive away, but their stock of bottled wines was in a rented warehouse a few kilometres further up the road. The phone rang late that night and it was a neighbour with bad news:

· · · · · · · · · · · · ·

37 Alvaro and Maria prefer not to show the organic symbol on their labels, although they have been practicing organic farming for the last 20 years.

"Your warehouse is on fire". Savage forest fires that had started further north in Galicia had reached Dão, thanks to Hurricane Ophelia and wind speeds of up to 100km/h.

As the night sky literally filled with balls of fire and the temperature soared to around 30°C, António drove to the warehouse to try to salvage what he could. It wasn't a pretty sight. The building was almost totally destroyed, and with it around 60,000 bottles of wine – a quantity that the couple would later describe as "uncountable".

The damage wasn't limited to their warehouse. Farming equipment and more than half of António and Sara's 20 hectares of vineyards were also burned. Some plots survived, with partly singed trunks or branches, but other vineyards were wiped out. One of the casualties was the vineyard in Botulho in Tondela, a plot with vines of more than 100 years old and a fascinating field blend with around 30% of white varieties. The final vintage of this wine, labelled Bot, was produced in 2017. Tasting the wine at the winery in 2019 was a bittersweet experience. Its peppery, herbaceous fruit was charming, quirky and lightweight, yet it was full of gravitas and structure.[38]

Several weeks went past before António could bear to return to the vineyards. "It's like some part of his body was burned," said Sara. "The vineyards were here since he was a young boy, it's part of his life". The couple launched a crowdfunding appeal in December 2017, together with a video of them sitting amongst charred vines reflecting on the damage. It makes for painful viewing, with António clearly shell-shocked and heartbroken.

A small house in the middle of the Mouraz vineyards also burned down. António was born here, directly above the simple winery and lagares where his father made wine. Like everyone, António's father sold most of his grapes to the local co-operative in Tondela but also made a small amount of wine that was sold and consumed locally. António and Sara had been restoring the house with the hope of making it their permanent home. It was just across the road from their small winery and surrounded by their vineyards. In retrospect, their temporary move to Tondela had been a lucky escape.

Like many of his generation, António was not encouraged to follow in his father's farming footsteps but rather to get a university education. He studied law at the University of Lisbon but remained smitten with the land and the idea of making

. . . .

38 Scribbled next to the tasting note in Simon's notebook is: "The last? A tragedy".

wine. He could see two possibilities – either he'd wait until retirement to make wine, or he'd do it immediately.

While he was still agonising over his career path, António worked for an art magazine in Lisbon. The magazine's publisher worked on a special project in 1980, a book celebrating a decade of contemporary dance in Portugal. The book brought António into contact with an outgoing, slight young woman with a mass of black curly hair, whose name was Sara Dionísio. Sara had studied sociology but worked in the field of contemporary dance, as both a performer and a teacher. Two decades later, she would abandon it all to move to Dão with António, where her creative spark would prove invaluable.

In the 1980s and 1990s, António spent many of his weekends back at home, during which time he'd seen his father give in to the use of synthetic herbicides. He felt passionately that it wasn't the right approach. "People thought you were lazy back then if you let grass grow between the vines," explains Sara. Now there's a different ethic at play, as organic and biodynamic growers realise that plant diversity and healthy competition for the vines is seen as far more important.

As António assumed more control of the family's vineyards in the 1990s, he convinced his father that they should convert to organic viticulture. It didn't happen without a fight. Ribeiro senior was still selling the grapes to the co-operative, and the conversion to organics meant an initial loss in quantity, and hence also income. But, by 1996, the Mouraz vineyards were certified organic. Not that the co-operative placed any value on the designation – the price for the grapes remained the same.

António and Sara moved permanently to Mouraz in 2001. They gradually purchased more small parcels of vineyards in the area and built a following for their stripped down, minimalistic winemaking. It's a style which brilliantly expresses the character and complexity of their old vineyards, some of which have up to 50 different grape varieties growing side by side. As Sara notes, "This is the old way of doing things. They made the blend in the vineyards, not in the winery. It's actually very intelligent!"

Along the way, their farming has started to incorporate more elements from the biodynamic canon. To reduce their reliance on copper and sulphur treatments in the vineyards, biodynamic preparations and herbal teas are used to prevent disease and to promote general vine health.

Working in collaboration with other growers, António also makes wine in the Douro and Vinho Verde. These ventures are bottled as António Lopes Ribeiro rather than Casa de Mouraz. A brief flirtation with a project in the Alentejo has been abandoned.

"It just wasn't us," explains Sara. "We are from the north. We like more freshness and more acidity in the wines." Still, the Douro and Vinho Verde wines were a lifeline for the couple when the fire nearly destroyed their livelihood in 2017.

António's character comes across as overridingly gentle. Sara says that he's very shy; hence the couple have evolved a division of labour in which she does the travelling to wine fairs and tastings, and handles visits to their winery. On the rare occasions when António does preside over a tasting table, it's a special experience. His smile can light up the room. Sara's frequent attendance at wine fairs around the world gave her increasing exposure to the developing natural wine niche, and to producers from France, Austria and beyond who inspired her. Where António's winemaking decisions tend more towards caution, Sara pushes for a more experimental agenda.

Despite 2017 being an annus horribilis for the couple, they embarked on a new chapter that year, making some wines that Sara would later christen Planet Mouraz. Here, Sara fully asserted her creativity and moved to the ultimate hands-off winemaking concept: zero-zero, not only eschewing additives such as selected yeasts or enzymes (which the couple never use in any case) but also working without filtration or any use of added sulphites.

Three new wines came out of these adventures. Each 'Planet' has a picture of one of the family pets on the label. Sara asserts with a cheeky grin that these are the winemakers: her dog Bolinha, Nina the cat and Chibu the goat. We were curious about what decisions Bolinha, a lovable white Maltese, had made. Sara replied knowingly that Bolinha is lazy, so he always decides to do nothing – so, no interventions!

The wines are a little funkier and wilder than most of the Mouraz bottlings, and with their bold labels are clearly designed to appeal to natural wine fans. Importantly though, they retain their sense of place and have something to say about Dão. Nina, for example, is a red/white blend that could be viewed on one level as a *glou-glou* wine – easy going, light and inconsequential. But the typical grip and herbal twang of the Dão asserts itself.

A charred vine at Casa de Mouraz

Connection to the landscape

Driving through the Dão region in February 2019, the effects of the June and October 2017 forest fires were still very clear to see. Entire hillsides and valleys lay bare and scorched, with charred trees and bushes at their edges. Instead of green, there was often just black and brown.

The scars are still visible at Casa de Mouraz, too. Vines that seem healthy at first glance have small patches of burned embers halfway up their trunks or branches. It's difficult to know how long these burns will take to heal, or what effect they might have on the long-term health of the plant. António and Sara are optimistic about the less badly scorched vines, but for those with more major wounds there's little hope.

For Sara, the disaster has highlighted an urgent need for people to take better care of the countryside. She laments the almost total lack of forest management in Dão. "It's going to happen again," she says, talking about the fires. "We still have all the conditions that this will keep happening, when no-one takes care of the countryside and with climate change bringing hotter summers".

The pain that the fires have caused António and Sara goes far beyond mere financial pressure. Their attachment to the land runs deep. There's a note in Sara's voice, a feeling of helplessness or inevitability, should this ever happen again. It's like watching a close family member get sick, and not being able to do anything about it.

Sara highlights another scourge on the Dão landscape as she drives us to one of the couple's more seriously fire-damaged vineyards. Heading down a rough dirt track, the truck weaves its way through a scrubby forest full of tall eucalyptus trees. Sara reminisces about her first visit here, two decades ago. "It was so beautiful. So many different trees, chestnut, oak, pine. Now it's almost all eucalyptus." she says mournfully. "We called this our paradise forest. When I look at this now, I want to cry."

Eucalyptus globulus, otherwise known as southern blue gum, is native to Australia. Originally brought to Portugal in the 19th century and planted to combat erosion, the species became hugely popular due to its use as pulp to make paper. The challenge is that *Eucalyptus globulus* is a highly invasive species, which needs no help at all to seed itself. Eucalyptus is slowly but surely taking over in unmanaged rural areas, which are plentiful in Dão. Worse still, when wildfires clear an area, eucalyptus is what grows back, rather than the less dominant natives.

By 2011, this Australian invader already represented 20% of Portugal's entire forested area according to forest engineer and researcher Vera Serrão, who has studied the effects across Portugal. It also creates a landscape full of dry and highly combustible material, making the likelihood of more devastating fires in the future much higher.

Sara muses, "If I had money, I would buy all this land in Dão just so I can get rid of the eucalyptus trees." It's not an idle thought as she and António have already acted on it as far as their finances allow. They've torn out eucalyptus and replanted with native trees and plants wherever they could. She stresses the importance of biodiversity and highlights the fact that all of their vineyards are interplanted with trees and bushes.

The destruction of a once idyllic landscape by the combined forces of fire and *Eucalyptus globulus* is a stark reminder of what can happen when custodians desert their land or just stop caring. Dão is already one of the most sparsely populated parts of Portugal, with a trend towards increasing depopulation that doesn't look set to change anytime soon. The hamlet of Mouraz doesn't even boast a regular café, let alone any shops.

Some 1,000 square kilometres around Serra da Estrela are now designated as a natural park and conservation area. The wine regions further down in the foot-hills don't enjoy any such official protection. They depend on impassioned and committed individuals such as those we've written about in this chapter for their survival. Responsible cultivation of traditional crops such as vines can do more than merely put a delicious liquid in your glass, it might just save an entire region from burning to the ground.

CHAPTER 5

BAGA

••••••••••

When Dinis Patrão decided to ramp up his business in 1962, it would change his home region Bairrada forever.

Patrão's investment was a €30,000[39] bulk purchase of one of the first synthetic herbicides to be imported into Portugal: a product known generically as paraquat and more commonly in Portugal by its trade name Gramoxone. His company developed into Bairrada's biggest supplier of chemicals to the agricultural sector. It was run from a warehouse in Poutena, a village about 20 minutes' drive from the town of Anadia, the so-called Capital do Espumante – or sparkling wine capital of Portugal.

Bairrada's many thousands of wine growers and farmers eagerly took to the herbicide. Patrão remembers that people stopped working the soil altogether and just sprayed industrial quantities of the product on their grass or weeds instead. Gramoxone is highly toxic and can cause heart failure, kidney failure, liver failure and lung scarring if even a small amount is ingested.[40] A commercial licence is now required for its use in the USA, but in 1960s Portugal its use was unregulated. "The supplier recommended the highest possible dose, and of course everyone used double that amount," shrugs Patrão.

Gramoxone and other products based on glyphosates got off to a slow start in Portugal. But Patrão recalls that it all exploded in the early 1970s, when a huge range of synthetics – insecticides, fungicides and herbicides – were embraced as part of the laughably named Green Revolution.

· · · · · · · · · · · ·

39 Converted from Portugal's currency at the time, the escudo. In today's money, this figure would be well over €200,000.

40 According to the Centers for Disease Control and Prevention (CDC) in the USA.

Business boomed and Patrão continued until his retirement in the early 2000s. But he'd begun to notice that there were severe detrimental effects on the environment from the use and misuse of Gramoxone and other similar products. "Many people just dumped the empty containers right next to waterways," he says. A river running nearby the family's small vineyard lost its population of eels and salamanders. Ladybirds vanished from the fields, and the vineyard landscape mutated to a uniform, barren carpet of bare earth.

Pollution and industrialisation are not exactly alien concepts in Bairrada. As part of the Região do Centro (Central Region), it has developed into Portugal's major manufacturing centre, with production of everything from cars to electronics and paper. The name Bairrada is derived from the Portuguese word *barro*, meaning clay, and clay is all around, both underfoot in the soil and in the many ceramic factories and businesses.

Boasting the crucial road, rail and sea transport links that are so lacking from neighbouring Dão, Bairrada is centrally positioned along a long stretch of Atlantic coastline, with easy access between its major metropolitan centres (Coimbra and Aveiro) to Lisbon and Porto. It's also relatively flat, again in sharp contrast to the mountainous and more inaccessible Dão. Perhaps it sounds as though Bairrada isn't much of a looker and certainly it is less dramatic than many of its neighbours. Even the region's major seaside town, Figueira da Foz, is a bit of an eyesore with its concrete high-rise buildings and overdeveloped coastline.

BUBBLES AND BAGA

The region's wine industry was dealt a crushing blow by the Marquis de Pombal in 1756. Even if his savage edict to cut down all the region's vines was only enforced for a few decades, it has left permanent scars on the soul of Bairrada's vineyards and their owners. Richard Mayson notes that "his sleight of hand has never been forgotten, and growers in the region still bear a grudge against those in authority."

Whilst the vineyard surface has certainly recovered since Pombal's attempt to wipe it off the face of the earth, Bairrada's vineyards are tucked away and often out of sight. Rough access tracks and an insider's knowledge of route finding are necessary to reach them. In this respect, the region feels similar to a steamrollered and flattened version of Dão.

Bairrada's maritime climate presents challenges for growing grapes. Cool temperatures and considerable humidity mean that mildew is an ever-present threat, which is one reason for the rapid take-up of synthetic fungicides when they became widely available in the 1970s. In addition to the troublesome climate, the region has historically been focused on a single thin-skinned red grape, Baga, which succumbs easily to the fungus *Botrytis cinerea*. It might be called 'noble rot' when it manifests in the vineyards of Sauternes or Tokaj, but *Botrytis* is far less desirable in Bairrada.

Even though Baga has dominated Bairrada's vineyards for well over a century, Portuguese viticulturist Dr Rolando Faustino suggests that it is not actually indigenous to Bairrada but more likely to Dão. Attempts to pinpoint Baga's true origins will remain fraught with difficulty, not least because Bairrada and Dão are commonly lumped together and just referred to as Beiras. To add insult to injury, the Comissão Vitivinícola Regional do Dão (CVR Dão) no longer lists Baga as an authorised variety, even though it is plentiful in the region's older vineyards.

Baga is a tricky customer. It's a very high-yielding variety, whose natural exuberance has to be curbed with careful pruning or green harvesting if there's to be any hope of quality over quantity. It has a tendency towards brutally high acidity and aggressive tannins, meaning that even Bairrada's best red wines historically required many years of cellaring before they were pleasurable to drink.

That said, it's a grape that can produce something quite sensational in the hands of a skilled winemaker. Baga has the same kind of backbone and potential to age as venerable varieties such as Barolo's Nebbiolo or Etna's Nerello Mascalese, with exciting, tart berry fruit and a smoky, herbal rasp (which Bairrada winemaker Filipa Pato suggests may come from the calcareous soils) as it matures.

Perhaps it was the region's rather un-user-friendly red wine that prompted the development of Portugal's sparkling wine industry, which has been centred on Bairrada since 1890. The Escola Prática de Viticultura da Bairrada (wine school) produced their first traditional-method wine that year. According to Luís Pato, there was a brief fascination at the turn of the century with planting and using champagne varieties[41] in the region, however in Bairrada they reportedly over-ripened and the resulting wines weren't deemed as elegant as their French cousins.

These days, Bairrada espumante is likely to be made from local white varieties such as Arinto, Bical, Cerceal or Maria Gomes. Baga is often used to make a blanc de noir style, in which its copious acidity becomes a blessing instead of a crutch.

· · · · · · · · · · · ·

41 Chiefly Chardonnay and Pinot Noir in Bairrada.

These very Portuguese bubbles have found a match made in heaven with the region's gastronomic speciality: *leitão assado da Bairrada* or spit-roasted suckling pig.

Anadia, home to the wine school which spawned Portugal's sparkling wine production, has become the hotspot for all things effervescent. It was also the location chosen by Sogrape in the early 1970s when they needed to create a new winery to scale up production of Mateus Rosé, something which has somewhat cemented the area's reputation for bulk production. By the 1970s, Bairrada also boasted a handful of under-performing co-operative wineries and a healthy sprinkling of other major producers bottling cheap wine for Portugal's African colonies. It hardly looked like somewhere that was going places when it came to quality wine.

A number of additional setbacks, including the Pombal diktat and *Phylloxera*, held the region back from having its identity enshrined into wine law. All this strengthened the implication that Bairrada was a bit of an also-ran. Until 1979, it formed part of the larger Beira Interior demarcated area, and did not have its own DOC.

That DOC was finally created just in time for the appearance of Baga's saviour, who would make his first wine a year later in 1980.

PIGS AND DUCKS

Mention Bairrada to anyone who has had even a passing dalliance with Portuguese wine, and the first name that comes to their lips will be Luís Pato. Whether he's a modernist, a maverick or just a pioneering spirit is much discussed, but whatever one thinks, his duck-emblazoned labels (Pato means duck in Portuguese) have transformed the way the wine world thinks about the region and Baga in general.

Luís grew up in a farming family in the lean post-war period. His father João Pato was a gruff, no-nonsense character who made wine mainly to sell in bulk to major bottling companies, who would transform it into espumante. However, he started bottling his own Baga-based red wines in 1970, a move that made him a pioneer at the time.

Luís trained as a chemical engineer and after military service in the navy in the early 1970s, started working in management for his wife's family business – a ceramics factory, typically for Bairrada. He was eager to apply his scientific mind to winemaking, but the father-son relationship wasn't one which allowed much in the way of discourse. João Pato lacked his son's education, and there was an unspoken rule that his farming and winemaking methods were not to be questioned.

Still, Luís found a way to experiment. His mother-in-law, who became a widow early in life, also had vineyards and a cellar. Luís made his first wine there in 1980 unbeknown to his father, who assumed he was safely ensconced in his desk job.

The 1980 vintage was unconventional to say the least. Luís's mother-in-law failed to secure harvest workers at the right moment, so the grapes were picked very late in October, by which time they were partially botrytised and overripe. Their potential alcohol was an impressive 16% which required the drastic solution of watering down the must. As Luís recalls, at the time no-one would have found it acceptable to drink a wine with more than 12% alcohol. Despite the dramatic interventions, the wine matured wonderfully.

Luís was a fast learner. As he often says, "I wanted to optimise everything!" He made wine every year from then on, and in 1984 went to London to present his 1980 Baga at a professional tasting in a hotel overlooking Hyde Park. Much to his surprise, the wine emerged triumphant, with many of those present proclaiming it better than the efforts of the more established producers.

He quit his job in the ceramic industry and briefly became a chemistry and physics teacher. But then in early 1986, Pato senior died. Luís could see that wine was going to be his future. He recalls that the harvest that year was horrible. Not only was it a rainy, washed-out vintage, but his father's recent death weighed heavily on the whole family.

But Luís finally had his chance to optimise. He replanted vineyards, adding white varieties on the sandier soils and moving Baga to the heavier clay soils where he'd figured out it would be more resistant to *Botrytis*. Recalling the one collaboration he'd had with his father – a sparkling wine made in 1981 – he asked other local winemakers how much yeast they would typically add to stimulate the second fermentation in the bottle. He was shocked to discover that no-one had the answer. They all worked by instinct alone, which was a totally unsatisfying prospect for the scientifically minded Pato.

Luís was nothing if not ambitious. He read everything he could to increase his knowledge. As he likes to remind people, he was trained as an engineer but not as a winemaker. A meeting with the wine critic Charles Metcalfe in 1987 proved to be key. Not only did Metcalfe write about the wines, but he also invited Luís to be a judge at the International Wine Challenge competition in London, a role he fulfilled enthusiastically from 1990 onwards.

"It became my tasting university," says Luís. He relished the opportunity to try wines from every corner of the winemaking world. When he was asked by a fellow judge how much he was being paid, he replied "nothing – I'm here to learn". He recalls judging side by side with UK wine legend Oz Clarke and many other luminaries.

The fickle nature of fashion in the wine industry was aptly demonstrated by how his fellow judges reacted in successive years. During IWC 1990, Luís tasted a wine that he found "quite strange", as he put it. It was an Australian oaked Chardonnay, which as he recalls "tasted of butterscotch and had 15% alcohol". The other judges lavished it with praise, and it won a medal. But by the following year, this rather obvious style was out of favour and similar wines were downgraded by the judges.

Luís had one driving vision above all – to prove that Baga was a superior grape variety capable of making truly fine wines. He made numerous tweaks and improvements to both viticulture and winemaking to try to tame the grape's less marketable tendencies. Destemming might sound like a no-brainer for today's winemakers, but it was hugely innovative when he first tried it in the mid 1980s and hugely effective in creating softer, less tannic wines that could be drunk younger.

João Pato had no money to buy oak barrels, but Luís invested in them as soon as he could. Again, this was a way to soften Baga's tannins and to produce wines that were still complex but also suited for earlier drinking. He vinified Baga in every way possible – structured and age worthy, soft, young and fruity; as a blanc de noir white wine; a cryogenically produced ice wine; and, most peculiarly, what he terms his 'noir de blanc': an ancient style that is perhaps more traditionally known as *curtimenta*[42] in Portuguese, produced in this case by the fermentation of white grapes with the skins of a red grape (Baga, of course) to lend a bit more 'oomph' to the proceedings.

Convinced that Baga might be able to grow on its own roots in the region's sandier soils, he planted a new ungrafted vineyard in 1988. The experiment was a success and the vineyard hasn't succumbed to *Phylloxera*, which is the ever-present risk for modern *Vitis vinifera* vines if they are not top-grafted onto resistant rootstocks from American varieties. The vineyard, called Quinta do Ribeirinho, is now vinified as Luís' top wine, Pé Franco.

. . . .

42 Somewhat confusingly, this term is also used by Portuguese winemakers to mean an orange wine (a white wine fermented on its skins). This is partly because the term 'orange wine' is not permitted on Portuguese wine labels.

Many of Luís's ideas were regarded with scepticism if not sheer disbelief in the region, earning him a reputation as a maverick. He fell out with the Comissão Vitivinícola da Bairrada in 2003 over changes in the wine regulations that would potentially shift the region's focus away from Baga. In protest, he declassified all of his wines to the broader Vinho Regional Beiras category. He would later get his revenge on the regional wine commission, leapfrogging over them to become vice-president of the nationwide promotional agency Vini Portugal.

The Pato Rebel wine was created by Luís in 2010 to show that Baga could produce something soft and aromatic, with a smidge of Touriga Nacional and Bical added to the blend. The label for this wine features Luís channelling his inner Einstein, tongue out and fingers waggling in defiant yet comic pose. He takes great pleasure in reproducing it live, something which has become a bit of a party piece.

Luís is a constant and playful experimenter and the winery's selection of wines just seems to keep growing. He's also made a special wine in honour of each of his grandchildren, and each one seems more unconventional than the last. Laranja da Madalena (2016), for example, is Luís' take on an orange wine, made as a Baga blanc de noir where the Baga skins are then reintroduced to the fermentation to create the macerated aromas and flavours.

It's not only Luís's engineer's brain that has propelled his successful career. He is an enthusiastic traveller and a true ambassador for Portuguese wine worldwide. With his bushy Tom Selleck moustache, mischievous twinkle and a grin that can be gently mocking but always warm, he cuts a figure like everyone's favourite grandpa who can walk into a room full of people anywhere and entertain them.

His take on the fads and fashions of the wine world is shrewd, questioning and no-nonsense. Regular riffs include a sceptical view of the natural wine world. Since 2012, he's made a completely natural Baga with no added sulphites and quips naughtily that "most natural wines have faults, so I decided to make one without them".

Luís's tireless promotion of Portuguese wine and Bairrada has taken many forms. The family's winery, and those of their colleagues in the region, are now part of a tourist trail that is becoming increasingly popular. Luís also involved himself in various promotional groups to help get the message out. The Independent Winegrowers Association (IWA) of Portugal was a groundbreaking early effort, which Luís chaired in the mid 2000s. Championing native grapes and the estate-grown wines of its six members (Quinta do Ameal, Quinta de Covela, Casa de Cello, Alves de Sousa, Quinta dos Roques and Pato himself), the IWA was one of the first independent attempts to promote Portuguese wine outside the country.

A rare bottle of Luís Pato's first vintage

Luís then became one of the vice-presidents at Vini Portugal, a role which he held for a decade (2007–17). He describes it wryly as "my civil service", but it was unquestionably a period when Portuguese wine began to blossom and to find a wider range of fans around the globe. He and his daughter Filipa are also part of Baga Friends, a small group of quality-minded Bairrada winemakers who focus on the Baga grape variety. They include António Rocha (Buçaco Wines), Dirk Niepoort (who has owned Quinta de Baixo in Bairrada since 2012), François Chasans (Quinta da Vacariça), Quinta das Bágeiras and Sidónio de Sousa.

The tourists, both Portuguese and beyond, don't just come for the wine. The area around the town of Mealhada (about a 20-minute drive from the Pato winery) is suckling pig central, with a clutch of competing restaurants that specialise in the lip-smacking dish. Luís doesn't eat a whole lot of *leitão* though –. "We've had tour groups here four days in a row," he said, somewhat wearily during our visit in autumn 2019 – and that means that every day the winery serves a suckling-pig lunch to its guests. Still, Luís is rather partial to the pigs' ears (the crunchiest part of the whole dish) and if his wife isn't policing too closely he can sometimes be seen quietly requesting them from the waiter.

Luís Pato presents a contradictory image to some. On the one hand, he's the tireless innovator constantly in search of better ways to do things with more optimisation, more modernism. On the other, he can be quite the traditionalist. He describes his winemaking as "working with the minimum intervention possible" and has increasingly backed away from the overt use of new oak. In contrast, he's not gone down the organic path in most of his vineyards, despite daughter Filipa successfully converting her 16 hectares to biodynamic farming.

Notwithstanding his farming methods, Luís doesn't lack green and sustainable credentials: the modern Pato winery has solar panels on the roof and a charging point in the car park for Luís's Tesla (the third electric car that he's purchased to date). Despite now being in his seventies, he hasn't lost his curiosity or his desire to experiment. In 2019, his youngest daughter Maria João collaborated on the creation of a new range of wines named João Pato AKA Duckman. The leftfield arty concept, complete with giant papier-mâché duck heads, is hers alone, while Luís has created a range of wines that perfectly encapsulate the modern trend to ultra-lightweight vins de soif. The João Pato wines are unapologetically natural wines, deliberately bottled unfiltered and unsulphured.

While Maria João and her dad get along, the relationship between father and eldest daughter Filipa is more complex.

Filipa Pato

· · · · · · · · · · · ·

Just like her father, Filipa studied to be a chemical engineer. And just like him, she ended up choosing to work in wine instead, admittedly after some serious thinking about wine versus ceramics (another of her passions).

Both father and daughter are single-minded characters who seem to clash. Perhaps reminiscent of the stand-off between Luís and his father João, Filipa also felt she had to seek out her own path. After she'd completed her degree at the University of Coimbra, she took off in 1999 with some contacts sourced from dad's little black book to travel and gain winemaking experience. She started in Bordeaux (still the classic choice for budding Portuguese winemakers) at Château Cantenac Brown, then spent a year in Argentina before finishing up in Margaret River, Australia.

Two years later, she was back in Bairrada and ready to go it alone. There was no question of working together with her father. Filipa had a different mission. Instead of working with the family's vineyards (her father currently has 55 hectares), she wanted to seek out and rehabilitate some of the many neglected or abandoned plots that have become increasingly prevalent in Bairrada. Rather than watch them be simply ripped out and replaced by kiwi plants (a popular choice in the region), she intended to take action.

"Normally to get started in the wine business, you either inherit vineyards or you're very rich," she says, "but it wasn't like that for me." Filipa began with bought-in grapes and rented vineyards, then started purchasing old plots as finances allowed. She made her first vintages in her grandmother's old winery in the village of Amoreira da Gândara (next door to her father's current winery) She was under no illusions about where her market would be, and it wasn't Portugal.

Her first wine was a wild fermented Arinto/Bical blend, made in 2001. She priced it attractively and secured distribution in Belgium. It caught the attention of a restaurateur in Antwerp, whose Italian-influenced restaurant was named Pazzo. He bought significant amounts of it to serve by the glass. Filipa was curious about her best client, so she and her importer went to visit the restaurant in 2003.

The owner and sommelier was a tall, jovial Belgian by the name of William Wouters. He'd been one of the first to introduce Portuguese wines to Antwerp and his wine list was somewhat revolutionary for the time. "We had maybe 20% French wines, and just one Bordeaux on the list," he recalls. "The typical fine-wine guys would come in and ask, 'Haven't you got anything decent?'"

Filipa's father's wines were on Wouters' list too, unsurprisingly. But she established a strict rule with her father, which is still observed – they never work with the same importer in any country, thereby avoiding direct comparison of their wines and ensuring their businesses remain fully independent from each other.

Wouters continued to be an excellent customer and Filipa continued to visit Antwerp. Love blossomed and the pair were officially dating by 2006. Filipa's life evolved into a seasonal game of two halves, spending much of the winter in Antwerp and the rest of the year in Bairrada. She relished the opportunity to leave Bairrada in the winter, having always hated its cold, humid atmosphere. "In northern European countries like Belgium, they are properly prepared for cold weather," she explains.

The relationship with William had wide-ranging effects on Filipa's professional as well as personal life. While in Antwerp, a constant stream of interesting bottles would arrive on William's doorstep and she tasted a huge range of wines. Filipa started to taste low intervention, or natural wines, and a pattern emerged. "The biodynamic wines were always the bottles that had more soul," she recalls. She and William also took the opportunity to visit a number of top estates in nearby France, notably the late Anne-Claude Leflaive, one of Burgundy's top biodynamic exponents.

Filipa was already working organically in her vineyards, but the inspiration from Leflaive and others pushed her further towards biodynamics. She continued to seek out and buy old vineyard parcels, working patiently to recuperate them. Although she often compares Bairrada, with its tricksy grape variety and small plots, to Burgundy, the cost of purchasing vineyards is a miniscule fraction of the eye-watering prices in the Côte de Nuits and Côte de Beaune, where prices per hectare can be in the millions.

The oldest vineyard in Filipa's portfolio, Missão, has vines of around 130 years old. This is not a vague estimation or idle claim. Filipa bought the vineyard from an octogenarian grower. Asked about its history, he replied, "My grandfather planted it!". With careful nurturing, the vineyard has been brought back from near dormancy (it produced only 50 kilos of grapes in the first year after Filipa purchased it) to a point where it yields enough to make one barrel of wine. It's bottled as Nossa Missão and produces a wine with an extraordinary feeling of delicacy combined with concentration and depth.

A big change came in 2014, when Filipa and William made the decision to move permanently to Bairrada. William got lucky because his head chef and the maître d' were willing to buy him out and take over the restaurant (they still run it today and Filipa's wines remain on the list). For Filipa, the fulltime move to Bairrada was necessary to fully immerse herself in biodynamic viticulture. Despite initial fears about the very strict limits on copper usage imposed by Demeter certification,[43] she persisted and now says with a shrug, "It's actually quite easy".

William had seen his restaurateur parents work themselves into the ground, only retiring at 65 with relatively little time left on the clock to enjoy life. He was delighted to have the option to downsize to a more family-orientated, rural lifestyle – and it is certainly quiet in Óis do Bairro, a village with under 500 inhabitants. William likes to joke that although the village has only two crossroads, he still managed to get a fine for a traffic violation. The local policeman takes his job seriously.

The partnership between Filipa and William is nothing if not equitable. Despite the name Filipa Pato being well established worldwide, she has insistently rebranded the entire project to "Filipa Pato & William Wouters". "I'm not in a monastery," she says, noting the importance of William's role. "We speak a lot and we discuss a lot. William has a completely different view of wine than I do, and that really helps."

Whilst William seems truly settled in Bairrada, when the couple built their home – right next door to Filipa's grandmother's house, where her father made his first vintage – he added a little reminder of his hospitality past. The family's house features a fully professional kitchen, with a gleaming stainless-steel pass that runs for about 10 metres along the whole length of the sizeable kitchen and dining room.

A lunch invitation chez Pato & Wouters is not to be sniffed at. William's background before he became a restaurant owner and sommelier was as a chef; he cut his chops cooking in his parents' restaurant and was once head chef for Belgium's national football team. Visiting on a sunny November afternoon, we were treated to a seven-course feast, whose presentation and quality easily compared with Michelin-starred establishments. Does Filipa cook as well? "Only when William isn't here," she laughs.

Filipa's relationship with her father remains somewhat opaque. Both winemakers now have an international following, albeit with slightly different audiences. "During the harvest, we never talk to each other", she says, "but after it's all done, we compare notes". Chatting about Filipa's plans to start using amphorae in 2013, she only half-joked when she said, "Don't tell my dad, or he'll wish he thought of it first!".

. . . .

43 Copper is typically combined with sulphur, forming a basic fungicide
    which organic or biodynamic growers are permitted to spray on their
    vines to combat mildew.

Vadio

· · · · · · ·

Unlike Filipa Pato, Luís Patrão didn't have a superstar winemaking father to spar with. His father Dinis Patrão had made wine at home in his spare time, but it did not leave the house. Luís was a bit of a tearaway when he was young. Aged 15, he played piano in a covers band and dreamt of breaking into the music business. During the harvest season, he worked at the local co-operative winery, the Adega Cooperativa de Vilarinho do Bairro, which like so many others became bankrupt and is now no longer in existence.

By his own admission, Patrão junior wasn't a particularly good student, as all his energy and enthusiasm was directed into music. But somehow over the course of four years working as cellar rat at the *cooperativa*, he picked up quite a bit about winemaking.

With his parents pushing him to go to university, Luís had limited choices as his grades were less than sparkling. He terms it a happy accident that he ended up studying winemaking in Vila Real (at the University of Trás-os-Montes and Alto Douro) from 1999. Luís took to his studies with gusto, and in 2004 was able to secure an assistant winemaker role with Esporão in the Alentejo. In the same year, as an experiment, he made 1,000 bottles of wine from the family's half-hectare plot in Poutena. The wine was only shared with family and friends, but it formed the genesis of a more serious project.

Luís's time at Esporão was transformational, in large part thanks to the vision of its new CEO, João Roquette, who took over in 2006. Roquette has a powerful ecological drive and set Esporão on a path to convert its entire 700 hectares of vineyards to certified organic farming, a monumental task that was completed by 2019.

It was an inspirational period. "Everything they do is done very professionally," he recalls, "so we had consultants and advisors who came to train the whole team." There were many learnings, notably that "organic farming is about everything else around the vineyard, not just the vineyard itself". The value of wild or rewilded land, cover crops, trees and animals were all factors that Luís absorbed.

He continued to work at Esporão until 2016, meanwhile developing his own winery back home in Bairrada. Vadio (meaning vagabond in Portuguese) was conceived in 2005, partly as a project where Luís could reconnect with his parents, as he was spending most of his time a three-hour drive south in the Alentejo.

Working at Esporão brought another surprise benefit. One of Esporão's Brazilian distributors visited the winery with his daughter Eduarda Dias. She and Luís met briefly. A year or so later, she moved to Portugal to do an internship. She contacted Luís by email and asked if he could help her to establish herself and to meet people. She'd clearly already met the right person and the two became a couple. They now live together in Lisbon, with a young family and Vadio to keep them busy.

The same warehouse that had previously housed Dinis Patrão's toxic chemicals was converted into a small but modern winery, and Luís set about acquiring more vineyards. Even though there was no shortage of old timers with unloved plots, it wasn't a simple matter persuading them to sell up. "It's cultural," explains Luís. "We only sell land when we don't have anything else left".

Purchasing a hectare here or a half hectare there required patience, legwork and countless phone calls and visits. But Luís now has around seven hectares of vines, and he's not done yet.

In contrast to Filipa Pato, Luís has in most cases replanted the older vineyards he acquired. There are just too many surprises lurking in old plots (unexpected grape varieties, unexpected diseases), plus, as he explains, some of the older vine-training methods expose the plants to a greater risk of mildew or *Botrytis*. Luís also had a specific reason for wanting to start out with the healthiest possible plants: from 2012, he decided to apply what he'd learned at Esporão and convert all of his vineyards to organic farming.

Luís smiles when he recalls the first conversations he had with his father about going organic. But Dinis was easily won over as he had seen at first hand the harm that synthetic products could do. Now he and Luís collaborate, with Dinis providing valuable help managing the vineyards while Luís is away at his new day job in the Alentejo.

Herdade de Coelheiros is an 800-hectare estate situated just north of the roman city of Evora. It mainly comprises cork forests, with a walnut tree grove, a lot of sheep and 50 hectares of vines. After its original owners floundered, it was bought by a Brazilian family who then employed Luís to head up their winemaking and vineyard team. Building on his experience at Esporão, Luís's new mission is to convert Coelheiros entirely to organically certified agriculture, making it, as he says, "an example for others in the Alentejo".

Tasting the wines at Vadio leaves no doubt that Luís is an assured and educated winemaker. He's also someone who wants to work in a minimalistic way. His wines are accessible and easy going, but there's a pure fruit focus to his style that conveys a clear message: it's the vineyard and the grapes that should do the talking, not the winemaker. Baga is, of course, his main order of business, but Luís also makes a delicious white blend, and a fascinating solera-based espumante.

Having seen the importance of biodiversity first-hand, Luís is now planning to purchase a small patch of woodland next to his Vale do Dom Pedro vineyard in Bairrada. It won't be cleared or planted with vines, but just kept as woodland to encourage wildlife. He's taken inspiration from his work at Esporão and applies it with vigour and drive in Bairrada. That said, he's very clear about the difference between his personal project and his work at Herdade de Coelheiro. "What I'm doing here [at Vadio] doesn't have a big impact," he says, "but doing this on a large scale at a property like Coelheiro can really change things."

Luís's mother has had more problems accepting the move to organic viticulture than his father. "Your vineyards look so messy," she complains, looking at the array of wild flowers, legumes and grass that grows between the rows. As Luís explains, his mum loves flowers, but she thinks they belong in the garden and not in the vineyard. She worries about what the neighbours will think. Luís's vineyards are still surrounded by conventionally farmed plots, with sterile earth in between the rows, which might look more orderly, but lack the signs of life and biodiversity that are clear to see in all of Luís's plots. After a decade of organic cultivation, the vineyards look stunningly beautiful – even if Luís's mother might not think so. The ladybirds are back in residence, as are the eels and salamanders.

Dinis notes that it's the co-operative mentality that forms the biggest block to Bairrada's growers reconsidering their farming methods. Many are still locked into the mantra of quantity over quality, and the idea of conversion to organics, with an inevitable slight drop in predictability or yields, just doesn't fly. More surprising are the other quality winemakers in Bairrada who continue to insist that it's impossible to be organic with the region's cool, humid climate. They clearly haven't taken a stroll over to Luís Patrão or Filipa Pato's vineyards in recent times.

Dinis Patrão

Caves São João

While Luís Pato was a pioneer when it came to making more accessible Baga wines, he certainly wasn't the first to popularise high-quality wines from the region. Caves São João is a venerable négociant-cum-winery whose name has become much loved by connoisseurs of mature bottles.

Created by three brothers, José, Manuel and Albano Costa, in 1920, the company originally focused on Douro wines and then shifted to Bairrada in the 1930s. Its two most iconic labels were created a few decades later: Frei João in 1959, for wines from Bairrada, and Porta dos Cavaleiros in 1963, for wines from Dão. The company purchased a Bairrada property, Quinta do Poço do Lobo, in the 1970s.

Caves São João have endured due to their extraordinary consistency of production and their ability to bottle traditionally made, high-quality wines throughout the dark decades when few other producers managed this feat. Many of their wines were vinified and purchased from co-operatives, but the brothers were extremely choosy and savvy about what they selected. According to Richard Mayson, the base wines for Porta dos Caveleiros were mainly sourced from Casa de Santar, one of the only private wineries in Dão which was able to continue vinifying and bottling its own wines during the latter half of the 20th century.

The Frei João tinto and reserva wines are made from close to 100% Baga and bottled with characteristic cork labels. These are wines that were always built for the long haul, but when they are mature they can really show the magic of Baga. The Frei João Reserva 1995 has spine-tinglingly sour acids and plenty of structure, plus earthy, herbal side notes. It's a magical wine, very much alive and just getting into its stride. The company has huge cellars with a large stock of vintages going back to the 1960s. When these old bottles turn up, as they are wont to do if you spend any amount of time in Portugal, they should be cherished both for their historical interest and, more often than not, for their drinking pleasure, too.

The Costa family are protective of their privacy; however, it is public knowledge that the winery came up for sale in 2020. Thus far, a buyer has not been found, so it's anybody's guess as to what the next chapter looks like for this venerable house.

CHAPTER 6

TALHA

••••••••••

In his emotive poem 'Cantar Alentejano', written around 1967 to honour the memory of Catarina Eufémia, Vicente Campinas wrote "O forgotten Alentejo, one day you will sing".

Oh Alentejo. Maybe you were forgotten then, but now your accessible, mainstream wines line supermarket shelves across Portugal and the globe. Your endless dusty plains are punctuated with gleaming stainless-steel tanks, massive wineries offering up robust red wines hewn from imported cultivars and irrigated vines. No-one stops to mention that your parched savannahs might be better suited to cork or olive trees. For the moment, this massive tract of southerly Portugal slakes the thirst of wine drinkers in their millions and celebrates its success as a modern wine powerhouse.

But peeking below the surface and beyond the corporate balance sheets, there are scars that still haven't healed.

If Catarina Eufémia were still alive today (she'd have celebrated her 92nd birthday in 2020), she would have painted a very different picture of her home region. Like many who were born and raised in the Alentejo during the Salazar years, she was poor and illiterate, working as a casual labourer whenever and wherever work was available.

When Catarina complained to her supervisor in 1954 that she and her harvest worker colleagues desperately needed a pay rise (they asked for two escudos a day extra, the equivalent of about 10 euro cents), he referred her to the police. Catarina had to repeat her request at the local station in Baleizão. She was slapped for her supposed insolence and, when she demurred, shot dead by the police officer. He not only fired three shots at the unarmed labourer, but also injured her eight-month son in the process. Catarina went to the grave, but her story became a cause célèbre for workers in the Alentejo.

Baleizão remains much as it always was, a small village to the south of the Alentejo. Its sparse, dusty streets are lined with squat whitewashed houses that are typical for the region. Their tiny windows peek out like half-closed eyes; in such a hot region, you need walls to keep out the sun rather than glass to amplify its effect. Like most of the Alentejo, the village is surrounded by vast plains planted with vines, olive and cork trees, and scattered with *herdades*. Poverty has always bitten hard here, with a stark contrast between wealthy landowners and those like Catarina who actually worked the land.

During the Salazar regime, preserving the status quo and the interests of big business was the order of the day. Anyone who complained or tried to rise above their station risked similar treatment to that meted out to Catarina. It would be nice to think that this barbaric system has been confined to history, but modern day Alentejo is still a region where massive inequality and near-slave labour persist. It's just that in the 21st century, the labourers are no longer Portuguese.

Migrants from poorer countries including parts of eastern Europe and Thailand often get trafficked into the country with the promise of well-paid agricultural work. The reality is very different, with gang leaders typically confiscating passports and paying well below the country's minimum wage – if they pay at all. In 2018, a trafficker was arrested for bringing in labourers from Eastern Europe. In 2020, the European Commission published a report with damning statistics for Portugal. It came second only to Malta when comparing the proportion of labour-trafficking victims reported during 2017–18.[44]

Much of this activity is concentrated around the fruit farms of the Alentejo, as evidenced by police raids on some of the raspberry plantations in 2019. As with any seasonal work that requires a cheap and plentiful workforce, grape picking is almost certainly not immune to this problem. Casual labour which is only required for a few weeks a year often tends to go undocumented. Meanwhile, the real money in the Alentejo has remained concentrated in the hands of outside investors and landowners from other parts of Portugal, or further afield.

This backdrop of inequality and deprivation may explain the perennially strong support enjoyed by Portugal's socialist and communist parties in the south. As David Birmingham explains in his book *A Concise History of Portugal*, Catholicism didn't penetrate the lives of poor Alentejo farm workers nearly as much as the communist party's promises to redistribute land to them.

. . . .

44 *Data collection on trafficking in human beings in the EU*, report published by the European Commission in September 2020.

It's not a coincidence that the now infamous revolutionary anthem '*Grândola, Vila Morena*' celebrates a town of the same name in the Alentejo. The song was written by Zeca Afonso in 1971 and on the face of it is just a simple celebration of Grândola. Salazar's government banned Afonso's other works on the basis that they showed communist leanings, but this apparently innocuous ditty escaped censorship. For that reason, it was chosen by revolutionaries in 1974 to be the signal to overthrow the Estado Novo regime. The song was played on national radio on 25 April 1974 at twenty minutes after midnight, and a military coup took place in Lisbon immediately thereafter. In typically understated Portuguese fashion, the so-called Carnation Revolution was a largely non-violent and bloodless affair.

• • •

Socialist or communist principles are not just political constructs in the Alentejo. A community-focused ideal is deeply embedded into the fabric of everyday life. It's still the case in many of the Alentejo's villages that friendship, food and wine are valued far more than hard currency. Family and the sense of community are what really counts.

Maria Josefa, 84 years old at the time of writing, still runs one of two cafes in the small village of Vila Alva, about 200km east of Lisbon. Marizefa, as she's known locally, only sells wine and other drinks (including some lethal local firewater) but she'll happily provide a plate, cutlery, olive oil, vinegar and salt to her customers if they bring their own food to the cafe. Everyone grows vegetables here and it's quite normal to see a customer enjoying a plate of their own freshly harvested tomatoes.

During one of our research visits to the Alentejo, our car broke down on a deserted stretch of highway. Dusk was approaching and it was eerily quiet and rather cold. The local breakdown company arrived to assess the situation, which turned out to be a sheared-off carburettor cap. "Can you make it back to the garage?" they asked. "We've got a guy there who might be able to fix it." So, driving at half-power, we coaxed the car a few kilometres to their HQ. Lacking the correct replacement part, the mechanic jerry-rigged a repair with duct tape and wire that would suffice to get us to our destination. There was no question of any payment being requested. Karma would ensure they were rewarded later.

Maria Josefa pours some local firewater at her cafe in Vila Alva

These are mundane examples. The key to the Alentejo's most profound community spirit isn't tomatoes or spare car parts, but rather, a clay pot. Locally known as *talha*, these large, free-standing clay amphorae (or more properly doliums) have been a fixture of village life since the Romans introduced the idea more than 2,000 years ago.

The wine produced in the region's small cellars (*adegas*) is shared copiously with friends and family, straight from the talha. It's almost never bottled, although locals will purchase and take out a litre or so in whatever plastic receptacle they have at hand. As winemaker Ricardo Santos explains, when you go to drink wine in a friend's cellar, payment is not expected – it would be the height of bad manners to suggest that money change hands. But they know you've got their back, either in this life or the next.

TRADITIONS OF CLAY
· ·

Ricardo now lives near Lisbon, but he grew up in Vila Alva. He recounts that decades ago his father used to walk through the village at the end of the working day, popping into his friend's adegas to shoot the breeze and taste a sip of wine. It could take him several hours to get home, as there were so many active cellars to visit along the route. Everyone used to make wine in villages like Vila Alva. And in many cases, they still do.

"There's a talha behind every door," is the claim in Vila Alva as well as in other nearby villages such as Cuba, Vidigueira and Vila de Frades. It seems hard to believe, but it's true. Flávio Carraça (Ricardo's cousin) who runs one of the two cafes in the village, walks across the street and rolls up the shutter of his father-in-law's garage to reveal a talha taller than a person tucked away behind his car. Sadly, it's no longer in use, although Flávio has his own cellar which is still active. Just up the street, Ricardo bumps into a friend who ushers us into his garden shed. Three knee-high talhas sit on the floor, full to the brim with wine.

The tradition here has barely changed in centuries. Grapes are foot trodden and crushed in a half-talha or sometimes in a small lagar. The crush then goes into the main talhas, with a small layer of grape stems added at the bottom. This provides an all-important natural filter, through which the wine will eventually drain.

The wine ferments spontaneously with ambient yeasts in the open vessel, with a cloud of CO_2 protecting it from oxidation and a little help from the winemaker who breaks up the cap of skins at least twice a day. This is a vitally important task. If it's not done often enough, the pressure from fermentation could build up to a point where the vessel simply explodes. An extra talha (called *ladrão* or 'thief') is typically buried underneath the middle of the cellar to catch the juice when this happens.

Talhas also have their own built-in temperature regulation system. Traditionally, cold water is sprayed over the thick stone braiding around the neck of the talha, which distributes it evenly over the entire body of the vessel. It sounds primitive, but it's remarkably efficient. Fermentation temperatures can be reduced from a dangerously high 40°C (where there's a risk that the wine ends up tasting stewed or cooked, and loses its fruit character) to a much more reasonable 20°C.

Once fermentation has finished, the talha will be sealed from the air with a thin layer of olive oil. Talha wine expert 'Professor' Arlindo Ruivo (of whom more later), says that the best wines were always sealed with the best olive oil, and that sometimes you could taste "a beautiful whisper" of the oil in the finished wine. This wasn't seen as a bad thing. Most winemakers also loosely cover the top of the talha with anything from a black bin-liner (functional) to a fancy embroidered cloth (Instagram- and tourism-savvy), to keep the flies out.

The wine isn't touched again until *o Dia de São Martinho* (St. Martin's Day, which occurs on the Sunday closest to 11 November). From this day on, it's deemed ready to drink straight from the clay. The winemaker will insert a wooden tap (the *batoque*) into the bunghole at the bottom of the talha and let the wine drain drip by drip into a strategically placed bowl known as an *alguidar*.

The slow drip... drip... drip... sound emanates happily from all the region's small adegas at this time of year. Patience is required, as the wine filters at a glacial pace through the layer of grape stems that have sat at the bottom of the talha for the last 60 days or so. If it's the branco you're about to taste, the colour will be a beautifully translucent amber. Tinto or *petroleiro* (a petrol-hued blend of red and white, known elsewhere in Portugal as *palhete*) span the gamut from light ruby to deep purple.

Tasting, as the locals call it (the dividing line between tasting and drinking can be delightfully fluid), takes place throughout the winter and until the wine runs out, which might be January or February depending on how thirsty the villagers happen to be. Adegas at this time of year morph into ad hoc bars, with small tables covered in gingham tablecloths. Anyone is free to stop by and have a glass or two. The glasses play to the idea that you are tasting – they're small, stemless and straight, looking more like something you'd fill with a shot of grappa than with wine.

Visit one of Vila Alva's larger cellars such as Adega Manual Fernando, and the scene looks like something from the last century. A group of old-timers sit in a dingy corner of the cellar, all wearing their traditional flat caps as they toast and chat. A younger group holds court out front, and one man grills sausages on the small open hearth. This is standard procedure when visiting your friend's cellar – bring something tasty to share. They're providing the wine, your responsibility is the snacks.

Zé is the host and winemaker, and he's being kept busy filling glasses as more guests arrive. All around the cellar, the talhas ceremoniously drip their precious contents into plastic trays and buckets. It could be a wildly popular tavern – except that there is no tab, and no money changing hands.

It's now Sunday lunchtime in Vila Alva, and the adegas buzz with life as people stroll back from the village church eager to taste the new wine and chit-chat. An unmarked door on the Largo da Fonte lies open. The small clay fragment of a talha mounted on the wall outside is the only clue to what lies within. This is Adega Marco 'do Panoias', and although it's small and modest, there is treasure within – the oldest surviving talha in the village, with a just-about-visible date of 1679 scratched into the fired clay on its neck. The squat vessel, also etched with a qabalistic-looking symbol representing its maker, is no museum piece. It's full to the brim with a thirst-quenching, delicious red wine, made from an intriguing blend of Tinta Grossa, Aragonez, Alicante Bouschet, Cabernet Sauvignon and Syrah, making it a true reflection of Alentejo vineyard-planting fashions through the ages.

Just across the square, Izalindo Marques has opened up his tiny adega, with six talhas squeezed chaotically around unused chairs and other bric-a-brac that presumably doesn't fit in his house. He lines up glasses of his spicy and tannic branco on a rough trestle table which takes up all the remaining floorspace. Bunches of drying grapes are strung from the ceiling, ready to snack on during the winter. The walls are lined with plastic flagons, ready to share the wine with thirsty friends.

REVITALISING THE ADEGA

Daniel Parreira is a young civil engineer who lives and works in Lisbon. He's urbane and speaks perfect English, but Parreira grew up not in the city but in Vila Alva. When he was a boy, Parreira thought that all wine came out of a talha – he'd seen his grandfather, his father, uncle and all their friends serving wine straight from the clay vessels. The illusion was only shattered when he turned 15.

His grandfather Daniel António Tabaquinho dos Santos was known as Mestre Daniel, *mestre* meaning carpenter in this case. His son (Daniel's father) continued to make wine at Adega Mestre Daniel but ceased production in the 1990s. Daniel junior still remembers the cellar when it was in active use. More than a decade later, he and his sister decided to restore the adega and turn it into a museum dedicated to the area's winemaking tradition. They also used the handsome space, with its typical lime-washed walls and wood-trussed ceiling, to host parties and other events. The cellar still boasted 26 talhas lining the walls. The imposing vessels, many over a century old, sat empty and unused.

Something was missing. The space just didn't feel the same without the smells and the sounds of wine fermenting. Ricardo Santos is a childhood friend of Daniel, and his father used to work for Daniel's grandfather, in the talha cellar. Ricardo has since developed his career as a winemaker consulting for a number of wineries in the region. He suggested the idea of bringing the cellar back into production. It would be a homage to Daniel's long-dead grandfather. His grandmother, very old and infirm but still alive, was delighted.

Daniel and Ricardo had to jump through some legal hoops, but once the bureaucratic demands were satisfied, they were able to start active production in 2018. But Daniel didn't just want to produce wine, he also wanted visitors to understand the history and the culture behind the wine.

He painstakingly researched and designed a map of Vila Alva which shows all of its historic adegas. By the 1950s, this village with its 800 or so residents had 72 known cellars that were all in use. Daniel only counted adegas that had at least three talhas. Otherwise, he'd have been counting just about every house in the village.

Only eight of these adegas are still active in Vila Alva. A further 14 cellars still exist but are dormant. The saddest statistic is the 50 cellars that have completely disappeared – their talhas gone, the buildings bulldozed or converted to more modern purposes. A century ago, there were more talhas in the village than residents; Daniel calculated a total of 1,046 of which only 200 remain today. The remainder were sold off to become garden ornaments, or to be installed at the centre of roundabouts, or worse still, ground up to become part of the road surface.

DISAPPEARING TALHAS

Why didn't anyone want to make talha wine anymore? Like so many questions relating to modern-day Portugal, the answer can be traced back to Salazar. The Estado Novo's introduction of large winemaking co-operatives during the 1950s and 60s signed the death warrant for talha winemaking and the culture that went with it.

Wineries such as the Adega Cooperativa Vidigueira, founded in 1960, were set up hand in hand with regulations to tightly control wine production. Growers who wanted to sell their harvest to the local co-operative were not allowed to sell or market their own wine. The co-operatives were designed to be efficient and cost-effective, and their impact was significant in the Alentejo. They more than doubled the volume of production in the region during the following decade.

Talha winemaking, in contrast to modern techniques, is labour-intensive, difficult to scale and highly skilled. Getting juice, skins and stems in and out of talhas is backbreaking manual work. Keeping the talhas cooled and avoiding pressure build-up requires skill and experience to avoid explosions! Then there's the tricky matter of inserting the *batoque* without losing too much wine. The talha winemaking tradition, being neither practical nor economically attractive, inevitably fell out of step with the modern age.

For the hundreds of growers in and around Vidigueira, selling their grapes to the co-operative was a no-brainer. It represented a guaranteed sales route and required very little effort to harvest and then transport the yield to the co-op's weigh-station.

With disposable income came new desires. As cars became increasingly popular and affordable, they prompted the sell-off of yet more talhas. If you were selling all of your grapes to the co-operative, why keep a cellar full of empty talhas when the space could be transformed into a more practical garage?

Talha winemaking didn't completely disappear – most families kept a small talha or two to continue making wine for everyday home consumption. They would often use the leftover grapes after larger estates completed their harvests, a largely consenting practice called *rabisco das uvas*. However, even if the tradition of making talha wine didn't die out, the skills needed to craft the impressive clay vessels all but vanished inside a generation. The newest talhas to be seen in the majority of the Alentejo's traditional adegas are from the early 1970s – and these are rare. Most talhas still in active service are between 100 and 150 years old.

The professor and his students

Mestre Daniel is the most entrepreneurial of the surviving talha cellars in Vila Alva. Daniel and Ricardo welcome tourists, who mostly come from Lisbon, and now bottle a limited amount of their production under the label 'XXVI Talhas'. This represents the 26 talhas installed in the cellar, although only half are currently in use. Their success rides a wave of renewed interest in talha culture which developed during the first two decades of the 21st century. It has its epicentre not in Vila Alva but in the nearby and equally small Vila de Frades.

Arlindo Maria Ruivo, better known simply as 'o Professor' in his home village, has arguably done more to keep the art of talha winemaking alive than anyone else in the Alentejo. A retired schoolteacher who turned 80 in 2020, he's been making his own talha wine since 1991. There are at least three previous generations of winemakers who went before him.

Tracking down the professor in Vila de Frades is as old-school as the man himself. "Everyone knows me", he says. "Just ask anyone in the village and they'll tell you where to find me." Luckily, it turns out that he also responds to phone calls. On a November morning, he's holding court in his favourite cafe, situated in the village market building and just a hop, skip and a jump from his adega. He's been out working the vines from 7am, which he still does every day apart from Sundays. Now it's time for coffee.

Speaking in a warbling high tenor, the professor's enthusiasm for his village's winemaking tradition is as infectious as his smile and charm. You know when he's excited because he starts rolling his Rs like a machine gun. He talks of talha wine as a precious liquid that must be not just tasted and smelled, but also enjoyed with the eyes and ears (drip, drip, drip!) – all the senses are involved. It's a wine made in the simplest, most natural way which allows the grapes to express themselves to their fullest extent.

His cellar is right in the centre of the village. Like most traditional adegas it's unmarked, except for one small detail, a single grapevine snaking its way up the wall by the door. Visit in the autumn and there'll be bunches of drying grapes hanging inside the cellar too. Called *penduras,* they are preserved by the CO_2 released by the fermenting talhas, which according to Arlindo sterilises the cellar and wipes out any bacteria or bugs that could munch the drying bunches. They're traditionally eaten around Christmas-time.

Adega Manual Fernando

The handsome stone cellar was built in the 17th century and has been in the family for longer than anyone can remember. Arlindo proudly recalls how his father-in-law made wine not just here, but also in a further seven rented cellars dotted around the village (sometimes this figure is reported as 14 rented cellars, it probably depends on the professor's level of enthusiasm on any given day!). He also notes that there were around 138 adegas operating in Vila de Frades during its heyday – quite an impressive number given that the population has always been stable at around 900 people. Similar to Vila Alva, there are only 10 cellars still operating.

Arlindo had never imagined that he'd be responsible for the adega, until 1991 when his father-in-law passed away following a two-year battle with cancer. As luck would have it, Arlindo had already completed 32 years of service as a schoolteacher, meaning he was able to take early retirement and devote his entire energies to the family's vineyards and talha cellar. As he tells it, the decision was easy to make, such was his passion for the unique qualities of the wine.

The talha tradition badly needed nurturing, too. 1991 was something of a low point, a moment when its survival was anything but assured. Arlindo wasn't going to let it die, even if at first he had very little idea how to make the wine.

There is some irony in Arlindo's role as the saviour of talha winemaking. His father-in-law was instrumental in founding the Adega Cooperativa Vidigueira (located in the neighbouring village), in 1960. This was the very institution that wiped out most of the talha tradition in the area, within a decade of its inauguration. The idea of the co-operative was well intentioned, to help raise the average price of grapes and wine in the region, and to be able to process the significantly increased grape yields that more intensive viticulture had enabled. Arlindo's father-in-law was saddened by the toll it took on the talha adegas, but times were hard. "There was no romance about it at that time, it was just a case of survival," explains Arlindo.

O Professor himself has continued to play a central role in the local wine industry as the president of the Vidigueira co-operative until the early 2000s. If this sounds like a case of poacher turned gamekeeper, it shouldn't be forgotten that Arlindo sells most of his grapes to the co-operative (like everyone else in the area), and with his 60 hectares of vineyards, that's a lot of grapes. In any case, having a prominent role in the local wine industry turned out to Arlindo's advantage when it came to rejuvenating talha culture.

The turning point came in 1997. A group of Arlindo's former students visited his cellar, and it wasn't just a social call. They had a suggestion to help promote the talha and gain more recognition for its place at the heart of the region's culture. "Why not organise an event – a grand tasting or a competition for talha wines?" they asked. These young men and women were not winemakers or industry pundits, they just loved their local tradition. And like Arlindo, they didn't want to see it entirely consumed by the stampede of commercial progress.

After thinking about it for a few days, Arlindo agreed and Viti Frades was born as an association of talha winemakers and an annual competition to select the best talha wine. For the inaugural year, the team contacted every winemaker and two-bit adega they could track down in the nearby villages – Cuba, Vila Alva, Vidigueira and beyond. Despite their efforts, a paltry five wines were submitted for the first competition. Arlindo had an inkling that it would take time. "*Calma, calma,*" he told his students – take it easy, be patient. He was right – by 2019 the December competition had grown to 140 submissions.

Vila de Frades and the neighbouring villages come alive during autumn. From early November, when the talhas are first opened, mysterious unmarked doors around the village suddenly spring open. The cellars fill up with friends eagerly tasting the new vintage, while street festivals and tastings allow everyone to get involved.

While researching this book in November 2019, we met Joaquim Oliveira, one of the linchpins of Viti Frades. We'd been told by Professor Arlindo's granddaughter to wait outside the offices of Viti Frades, right in the village centre; we didn't know for whom or what. Oliveira drove up to the kerbside, parked and got out of the car. "Are you the guys making a film or something about talhas?" he asked. We explained that we were writing a book and that we were keen to visit more of the village's traditional adegas.

Oliveira whisked us off to his friend's cellar, Adega Zé Galante, just around the corner. José Galante was busy filling some bag-in-box bladders with his fresh talha wines, but this was no oxygen-free industrial plant and there wasn't a bottling line or an ISO certificate in sight. As he chatted with us, he held a plastic demijohn in one hand, a funnel and the foil bladder in the other. It seemed like a novel way to achieve a bit of micro-oxidation!

We tasted a particularly delicious *petroleiro* from the talha, just as another friend arrived with a big sack containing bread, sausage and cheese for everyone. Now the party was getting started. Rafael carried on filling his bag-in-boxes, and also brought out some double-magnums of his wine just in case we were tempted by the prospect of a take-out. As it happened, we were.[45]

Oliveira shares the enthusiasm of his mentor, o *Professor*, and took us on a whistle-stop tour of several of the village's other talha bars and adegas. He mentioned that the local council, where he has his day job, is now putting together a UNESCO Intangible Cultural Heritage application for the talha wine tradition, modelled on the success of Georgia's recognition for qvevri wine. He also explained that the only problem with the talha wine is that it runs out before the year is up, especially now that tourists are starting to muscle in on the action. "When the talha wine's finished, we just drink the co-op's industrial wine until the next year," he said with a cheeky grin.

It's official
· · · · · · · · · · · · ·

The surge of interest in talha wine didn't happen in a vacuum. Arlindo also spear-headed the creation of an official designation, Vinho de Talha DOC, a wine classifi-cation which is a subset of the Alentejo DOC. Around 2002, he mentioned the idea of creating the classification casually to a lawyer working for the Alentejo's wine commission, the Comissão Vitivinícola Regional Alentejana (CVRA). The lawyer responded simply with a confused "Talha wine? What's that?", a sign of just how forgotten the talha tradition had become. A few years later, in 2008, he mooted the idea more formally to the CVRA. This time it was taken seriously.

In 2010, the Vinho de Talha DOC classification was ratified, with 2011 the first eligi-ble vintage for the certification. Perhaps official recognition of the talha tradition should have represented a watershed moment. but a decade later, it feels like a diversion. Because classified wines (DOC or Denominação de Origem Controlada in Portugal) have to be quality controlled before they can be put up for sale, this DOC only applies to wines that are bottled. It is irrelevant to all of the small adegas who continue their time-honoured social custom of offering wine to friends and family, direct from the talha. And this, after all, is the essence of the tradition.

Despite being one of the few producers who do actually bottle wines using the new DOC, Ricardo Santos admits with a sheepish grin that "this wine should really

· · · · · · · · · · · ·

45 Despite the primitive bottling conditions, the bottles held up and
were delicious a year later.

be drunk straight from talha. It shouldn't be bottled". It just tastes better and fresher from the clay.

The DOC has thrown up other challenges too. Its inspectors must record the exact amount of wine produced by each cellar, but no-one knows exactly how much their talhas hold. Not only are talhas handmade, with approximate capacities, but there is also the issue of skins and stems adding to the total volume. Therefore, DOC talha wines have to be racked off into a stainless-steel tank (or another vessel with a precisely stated volume) before they can be inspected, certified and bottled. It's a huge paradox that talha wine can only be given a certificate of authenticity if it first spends some time in a steel tank.

The rules for the DOC are fairly rigid. They dictate that grapes must be destemmed, although stems are allowed to then be added back into the fermenting must. This is the tradition in some parts of the Alentejo, such as Reguengos and Cuba, but varies elsewhere. The DOC also requires that the wine must stay in the talha, with its skins and any included stems, up until at least St. Martin's Day. The CVRA requires photographic evidence that the wine remains in the talhas during the specified period, from harvest until early November.

Producers have been extremely slow to embrace the classification. 2019 was the eighth vintage where wines could be classified as DOC Talha, and yet only 17 wineries chose to submit their wines. Most of those producing and bottling talha wines with DOC certification are not the traditional adegas, but larger more commercial entities who recently invested in antique talhas and started experimenting with the style. The big names include Esporão, Herdade do Rocim, Herdade de São Miguel (Casa Relvas) and, belatedly, the Adega Cooperativa Vidigueira who some-what ironically make a fine and very affordable vinho da talha branco.

GENERATIONS OF TALHA

Although he's produced thousands of litres of talha wine every year since 1991, Professor Arlindo has never sold a single drop. "It's just for family and friends", he says with a smile. He clearly has a lot of friends. Now, his wines are about to find a wider audience.

Arlindo's granddaughter, Teresa Caeiro, has joined the adega to work alongside *o Professor* while studying for her oenology degree. With an easy-going manner, she has her grandfather's charm and radiates enthusiasm. There's a mutual feeling

'Professor' Arlindo Ruivo with his granddaughter Teresa Caeiro

of fondness and respect for the work. While we talk, she busies herself checking some of the talhas, logbook in hand. Every measurement and observation is meticulously annotated in chalk on the clay. "Whatever you do, don't call them amphoras," she says sternly. "They're talhas, and that's not the same – it's just like the Georgians don't like their qvevris being called amphoras".

Teresa has masterminded the creation of a new line of bottled talha wines, branded appropriately enough as Gerações da Talha (Generations of Talha). As the 2019 vintage went on sale in 2020, it was a significant moment. "The first time we've ever sold a single bottle," says the professor. He seems quite amused by it all, whilst also delighted that his granddaughter is taking such an entrepreneurial attitude to the family tradition. And she's set to innovate in more ways than just getting the wine into a bottle.

Like many others, Arlindo decided to line his talhas with epoxy resin in 2014 – his production vessels now have a tell-tale grey epoxy collar clearly visible at the top of their necks. He claims that the gain in hygiene is a no-brainer and that the wine really doesn't taste any different. He cautions that if the wrong bacteria take up residence, it can mean a whole talha of wine has to be jettisoned.

There are plenty of winemakers who don't share his view. They include Ricardo Santos, Domingos Soares Franco (of José de Sousa) and André Gomes Pereira (Quinta do Montalto), who all insist that the true character of talha wine requires the vessels not to be hermetically sealed with epoxy, but to retain a minute amount of porosity so that micro-oxidation helps to age and soften the wine. Traditionally, talhas were not sealed with anything as watertight as epoxy. Instead they were lightly coated with a sticky paste known as *pês*.

This substance can feel a bit like Schrödinger's cat. An air of mystery surrounds its exact composition and many modern-day winemakers will state that no-one knows how to make it any more. Yet, talhas are still resealed from time-to-time, so someone clearly has the knowledge.

Professor Arlindo confirms that the paste is made from pine resin mixed with various other additives. Laurel is often added, as is olive oil. The mix is boiled until it solidifies enough to fill the pores of the talha. António Gato, who produces talha wine at his *tasca* (cafe-bar) in Arcos, recalls that there were once specialist *pesgadores* who would travel around the villages and reseal talhas with a pês made to their own secret recipe.

While Teresa offers up the explanations to justify her grandfather's decision to switch to epoxy lining, she's clearly on the fence. She walks into an especially dark, dusty part of the adega and points at four talhas that have escaped the epoxy treatment: "I'm going to try making wine in these, to see what the difference is," she says with a determined smile.

She's also got major plans to transform the vineyard work. The professor, like just about everyone else in the area, still works on the basis that synthetic herbicides and fungicides are the only way to keep yields at optimal and consistent levels. But Teresa has begun converting the farming to biodynamic viticulture. She's well aware that it will take years, but it could be a watershed moment if she changes the attitudes of her colleagues in and around Vidigueira.

THE SURVIVORS

Despite the wholesale destruction and disappearance of hundreds of adegas and thousands of talhas, a surprising number have survived. Talha culture doesn't just revolve around the adegas themselves, but also includes convivial spaces such as local restaurants or cafe-bars which produce their own talha wine. Your repast at País das Uvas, in Vila de Frades, or Casa Monte Pedral, in Cuba, will be accompanied with wine fresh from the talha,[46] brought to the table in a jug. It's the ultimate house wine, truly *da casa*.

These restaurants and *tascas* never quite died out, but until recently their regular customers and tourists came for the food and barely remarked on the wine. The historical significance of the giant clay jars was neither explained nor grasped.

Casa Monte Pedral is situated in Cuba's old adega *cooperativa* building, and consists of three sizable dining rooms, two of which have talhas lining their walls. Another restaurant País das Uvas is located on the same site as Adega Honrado, a grand cellar with a high ceiling that now also serves as a talha museum. The wine produced at these establishments is authentic, sometimes a little rustic, but always tasty and the perfect accompaniment to the cuisine.

Many smaller cafes and bars from Evora to Arcos still have talhas sat in dusty corners, but more often than not they have been empty for decades. Still, in the classic villages of production, adegas are gradually being revitalised, as with Mestre Daniel in Vila Alva. The revival is in full swing.

. . . .

46 This is theoretically only possible in season, should the restaurant run out of wine before the following harvest.

The largest talha cellar of them all already underwent its own revival decades ago. And it doesn't belong to o *Professor*. Heading east from Vila de Frades and Vidigueira, the town of Reguengos de Monsaraz is another talha hotspot. Here, you'll find Casa Agrícola José de Sousa Rosado Fernandes. Its historic cellar today contains 118 talhas, although not all of them are still in one piece.

By the 1980s, José de Sousa was one of the Alentejo's most prestigious wineries. It is unique amongst the major players in having had a more or less continuous tradition of making wine in talha. It's just that most of the world had absolutely no idea that they were drinking talha wines when they uncorked the winery's classic red blends. If you were lucky enough to have enjoyed a bottle of Rosado Fernandes, Tinto Velho or Garrafeira from José de Sousa's golden era (up until around 1965), you were in fact drinking a wine made entirely in talhas using the same traditional method as in hundreds of humble adegas.

The winery fell on hard times following the death of its eponymous owner José de Sousa in 1969, passing first to his widow and then in 1982 to her brother, a well-heeled doctor who had absolutely no interest in wine. By the 1970s, a new and lacklustre winemaking team no longer took proper care of the talhas and the quality of the wines plummeted. The final straw came in the autumn of 1984, when three of the winery's employees died in an accident that showed just how careless they had become.

A huge underground tank at the winery was used to collect grape skins and stems after pressing. They were then sold to make brandy. One of the workers climbed down into the tank without checking if there was any oxygen inside – a schoolboy error, given that fermentation doesn't necessarily stop just because the skins are separated from the juice. Instead of oxygen, the worker was enveloped in a cloud of carbon dioxide (the by-product of fermentation) and suffocated instantly. Two of his colleagues followed blindly into the tank to try to save him, sealing their own fates.

The doctor decided to sell, and offered the estate to various large companies, including José Maria da Fonseca. The doctor had offered the estate at a bargain price. JM Fonseca took the opportunity to expand into the Alentejo. It was a region that held sentimental sway with the group's owners, the Soares Franco family, who are originally from the region.

Domingos Soares Franco was tasked with managing the José de Sousa winery. Fresh from a winemaking education at University of California, Davis, he hadn't originally intended to work for the family business or even to stay in Portugal. But as he puts it, "My father just said, 'I need you'."

Domingos had left Portugal under a cloud, in 1975. Graduating in the year of the revolution, he found himself persona non grata. The new socialist/communist regime, the Movimento das Forças Armadas, wanted to break up or nationalise major companies such as JM Fonseca. Company directors and other visible corporate executives were in the firing line.

Domingos had wanted to study winemaking at a Portuguese university, but this was denied due to the black mark against his family. He'd also tried to apply to winemaking schools in Bordeaux but was told he'd need to stay in Portugal for a further year and learn to speak French. When an opportunity presented itself, he went instead to the US. After six months' further high school, he successfully applied to UC Davis and became the viticulture and oenology department's first ever Portuguese student.

It was 1986 when he first opened the doors of the newly acquired José de Sousa winery – or at least what was left of it. There was an unexpected discovery – the historic cellars contained what Domingos describes as "12 clay pots", marooned in a space that could hold 10 times that number. "Something clicked in my mind at that point," says Domingos. "I decided I wanted to become a clay-pot winemaker."

Domingos knew of the existence of the talha wine tradition but had no idea how the winemaking worked. It was a world away from everything he'd learned at UC Davis. But he knew in his soul that the tradition was important and believed in it enough to seek out old-timers and experienced winemakers who could help him get the cellar back into production. The process wasn't straightforward, as not only did he need to build the skill and knowledge of his team, but he also had to find some more talhas.

By 1986, most of the Alentejo's historic talha makers were long gone. The only way to replace the missing denizens of the cellar was to source them second-hand, from homes, garden centres or antique dealers. The process was slow, but between 1987 and 1988 Domingos acquired 120 additional talhas, including 20 from another winery that was right next door.

The team needed time and experience to know how to properly treat these vintage acquisitions. The water-cooling technique proved to be key, as did management of the pressure that builds up during fermentation. The importance of punching down the cap of skins (which is pushed up to the top by the CO_2 created during fermentation) wasn't initially recognised, leading to a number of self-detonating pots. Domingos recalls driving into the winery on one occasion when he heard an explosion that was so loud that he assumed it must be a bomb. Some of the more spectacularly destroyed talhas remain in the cellar, offering a visual warning of what can go wrong.

By the mid-1990s, José de Sousa had started to recover lost ground. Its premium talha-fermented red is no longer called Tinto Velho or Garrafeira, but has now been renamed as José de Sousa Mayor. It's still foot trodden (but in lagares, rather than in a half-talha), and it's still made with a high proportion of the once extremely unfashionable Grande Noir variety, which Domingos feels is key to the blend. However, it's also aged in oak barrels following the talha fermentation.

Staff at the winery haven't always been so enthusiastic about Domingos' dogged adherence to this old Alentejo tradition. Paulo Amaral, who joined José de Sousa to manage both vineyards and winemaking in 2005, spent his first few years cursing at how impractical the talhas were and how difficult they were to clean. But by 2015, the team was confident enough to launch the Puro Talha range, consisting of wines made entirely in the clay pots without any further ageing in barrels. For perhaps the first time in history, the back label and the winery's marketing now actively talk about the talhas. What was once an embarrassment has become a selling point.

THE NEW HOLY GRAIL

If it was hard for Domingos Soares Franco to find 120 replacement talhas in the late 1980s, it would now verge on impossible. With the new-found interest in the Alentejo's heritage of clay, talhas have become extremely desirable for major wineries in the region and beyond. And since almost no-one makes them anymore, the supply of antique 19th-century examples is starting to dry up. Those that remain are sold for increasingly high prices, if the owners want to sell at all.

Potters with the skill and experience to construct and fire large talhas suitable for making wine are now so thin on the ground that rumours abound that there is no-one alive who knows how to do it anymore. While not far from the truth, there are still a few craftsmen who learned the old way from their fathers and grandfathers.

In the Alentejo, António Mestre is a potter based in the village of Reja (near Cuba and Vidigueira). Mestre learnt his craft from previous generations of his family but had never made talhas larger than about one metre high. Mestre uses a potter's wheel in combination with the older coil-pot method and is now, after considerable experimentation, making talhas of up to 800–900 litres. His order book is full, and he sells both locally and internationally. However, he admits that he has no-one lined up to take over; his children live abroad and he hasn't found the right person to mentor.

Another António, António Rocha, has taken an entirely different route. He was a construction worker until the 2008 financial crash. Portugal stopped constructing and Rocha lost his job. He wasn't likely to get another one, being in his 50s and close to retirement age, but he certainly wasn't ready or financially able to retire. He decided to teach himself to fire pottery, starting with terracotta roof tiles, which are now his bread and butter. But a chance request from a friend to replace a small, broken pottery jug got him started on fashioning talhas. Rocha could see that talhas were suddenly becoming fashionable and there were plenty of stories of the nearby wineries scouring the villages to buy up any antique examples they could find.

Rocha exudes energy. He's diminutive in stature, with a builder's tan and the strength of an ox. Working out of a large shed by the side of a motorway junction outside Vidigueira, Rocha first set about building his own outdoor wood-fired kiln. It looks like a giant rabbit warren, tunnelled into a patch of ground behind his workshop.

He has slowly expanded the capacity of the kiln, and now it's big enough to be able to fire his first experimental talhas. Rocha had no-one to show him how the historic 1000-litre talhas were constructed. He's also struggled to find the right type of clay, which has to be watertight once fired. His first two-metre-tall talha was too porous for making wine, but he now has some more successful examples ready to sell. Essentially, he's trying to reverse engineer clay pots that were made by master craftsmen over a century ago.

Ironically, one of the most experienced remaining talha makers isn't based in the Alentejo at all, but in neighbouring Ribatejo, on the other side of the river Tagus (Tejo in Portuguese). José Miguel Figuereiro lives and works in the village of Asseiceira, near Tomar, and says that there are at least 300 years' history of making talhas in his family.

Figuereiro always wanted to follow in his father's footsteps even though neither of his parents wanted him to do so. Born in 1971, he left school when he was just 12 and started hanging around the workshop. His father insisted that "this is nothing for you, nobody wants talhas any more, you should go and study". But Figuereiro was adamant that all he wanted to do was work with clay and in the end his father relented, saying, "OK, if you're not going to school, you better come and learn. You start at 9am and you finish at 6pm!" Figuereiro made his first talha in 1984 aged 13, and his mother said, "We're not going to sell this one". It's still proudly displayed in the family home.

The market for talhas was already dying by the 1970s. Figuereiro recalls that a significant part of his father's business was buying back old talhas that his grandfather had made, from winemakers who no longer needed them. They were then resold to customers all over Europe as garden ornaments. He recalls trailers piled high with hundreds of the smaller 100-litre vessels.

The history of the area around Tomar is steeped in pottery. Up until 50 years ago, Figuereiro says there were still some Roman-era kilns that had survived. Locally, his village is even called "the land of clay" and he adds that two centuries ago, anyone with his family name would have automatically been a potter. Somewhat bizarrely, in the land of clay the preferred medium for ageing wine is wood. Figuereiro laughs as he admits, "In this town where we make some of the best talhas, we make wine in barrels."

Figuereiro had 10 employees until the financial crisis hit Portugal. In 2009, he had to let them all go. He was already the sole surviving talha maker in the area. The other five potters who were still in business by 1985 had since given up. Figuereiro narrates this with a sense of inevitability – he's a cheerful character who seems to take anything in his stride. Why didn't he just give up, like everyone else around him? "This is in my blood, it's what I love to do".

Now the business is a two-man affair, meaning that he cannot feasibly construct a talha larger than about 600 litres as more than two people would be needed to move it in and out of the kiln. At its height, Figuereiro's workshop used to make 150 talhas a week. Now, production is down to about half that amount and most are small, ornamental examples that will never hold much more than a bunch of flowers. He's seen a change, though: "Twenty or thirty years ago, people still wanted talhas for wine, but then they forgot about that tradition and were just using them for decorative purposes." But then from around 2018, he started seeing more interest in talhas to make wine again.

Two years earlier, Figuereiro had received one of the most surprising requests of his career. A young and passionate winery owner by the name of André Gomes Pereira contacted him in 2016 and asked, "Please make me the biggest talha you possibly can, and don't line it with epoxy – I want to do it the traditional way". The usually chatty Figuereiro was temporarily rendered speechless. It had been 30 years since he could remember lining a talha with pês. "We used to do it when my father was still making talhas for wine," he recalls. But he switched to epoxy lining once people just wanted talhas for their gardens.

Talhas in 'Professor' Arlindo's adega

José Miguel Figuereiro resealing a talha with pês, at Adega Mestre Daniel

"It's been a long time since I did this and I'm not really sure where to get good pês", Figuereiro eventually responded. He didn't realise that the person standing in front of him had a more direct connection to pês than just about anyone else in Portugal. Pereira lives about 15 minutes' drive from Tomar. His family owns Quinta do Montalto, which Pereira took over in 2002, but most of their income comes from a business specialising in pine-resin products. The family can trace itself back through five generations of winemaking and four generations of pês production. Pereira wasn't going to struggle to source the paste; he just needed Figuereiro's skills as a potter and his experience in applying it to the new talhas.

Pereira had taken charge of the winery after his uncle passed away. His uncle was passionate about the vineyards and had converted Quinta do Montalto to organic farming all the way back in 1997, which was almost unheard of in Portugal for vineyards. He wasn't such a good businessman though, as Pereira explains. "He couldn't keep up with the paperwork and all the new bureaucracy after Portugal joined the EU."

Pereira's initial task was to save the winery from the jaws of bankruptcy. But along the way, he became obsessed by a quest for authenticity which ultimately connected him to the talha-tradition and brought him to Figuereiro's door.

The area around Quinta do Montalto and the village of Ourém is the source of a curiosity which Pereira abbreviates conveniently to "medieval wine". Medieval de Ourém is a tradition that dates back to the 12th century, when a Cistercian monastery named Tomareis was established in the area.

Everything about Medieval de Ourém is topsy-turvy when compared to modern winemaking. Both white and red grapes are fermented in barrels, at first separately and then blended together to complete the fermentation. The proportion is surprising too, being more or less the exact opposite of the more common *palhete* or *petroleiro* style (mostly red grapes with a small proportion of white). For medieval wine, the proportions are 80% white and 20% red. Nonetheless, it is a style that has structure and colour aplenty. At Quinta do Montalto, Trincadeira grapes form the red part of the equation, with Fernão Pires making up the white part. The result is a spicy, red-berry flavoured wine that has the freshness and zing of a white, plus a serious tannic grip.

This fascinating style seems to have been prevalent in only two locations, according to Pereira, around Ourém and also in Valdepeñas in Northern Spain. Pereira says there used to be some 2,000 producers of medieval wine in Ribatejo, but the style was killed off by EU labelling restrictions, which typically don't permit red/white grape blends to be marketed as quality wine. This meant that from the 1990s, the medieval wine could no longer legally be labelled with its region, vintage or grape varieties. For this niche style, it was the bureaucratic kiss of death.

Pereira felt that such a unique tradition was worth fighting for, so not only did he continue to produce it at Quinta do Montalto, but he also fostered a producer's association for the few remaining winemakers who still believed in the medieval wine. Together, they petitioned for the creation of a regional classification that would effectively give the wine back its commercial passport. After almost a decade of fighting, they were successful in 2005. The DOC Encostas d'Aire was created as a sub-region of Lisboa (Lisbon). This DOC specifically allows not just red, white and rosé wines to be produced, but also the previously verboten red/white blend Medieval de Ourém.

The producers' association for Medieval de Ourém was itself a member of the broader Associação dos Vinhos Históricos de Portugal, an 'association of associations' for various regions in Portugal seeking to achieve similar recognition. The team of winemakers who wanted to create the DOC Talha classification in the Alentejo turned to this organisation in 2008, seeking advice on how they could proceed. This brought Pereira into contact with talha culture. He mentions with some regret that the final version of the DOC Talha ordinance to be approved looked very different to what he and some of the other producers had envisaged. His implication is that the interests of some of the larger wineries resulted in a loosening of some of the requirements.

Specifically, Pereira says that it is absurd that the DOC talha regulations allow the use of talhas coated in epoxy. He feels that the whole point of using a talha is to benefit from its subtle micro-oxidative properties. Pereira's interest in all things talha was, in any case, piqued by his collaboration with his colleagues in the Alentejo. He was curious if it was still possible to make new talhas and coat them traditionally with pês, hence his request to José Miguel Figuereiro. Figuereiro agreed to make five 400-litre talhas. One broke during firing, but the duo were able to seal the remaining four with pês that Pereira sourced from his cousin in Spain. He mentions that the same mixture is used in some parts of Spain to coat the inside of bagpipes.

The process of sealing talhas requires considerable manpower, dexterity and skill. The talha is first up-ended and warmed very slowly over an open fire. Figuereiro says he only knows when it's hot enough by touching it. The pês mixture is then poured inside, and the talha is rolled around the workshop to evenly distribute the paste. If the pês doesn't have the right proportions of resin, olive oil and beeswax (the core components), or if the lining is too thick, there's a risk that its flavour will be imparted in the final wine. Figuereiro has tasted enough examples of wines that have been ruined in this way. André Gomes Pereira has a hunch that the reason why pês often seems to have been flavoured with herbs, bay leaves or honey was to cover up any undesirable taint that the pês itself might leave in the wine.

Despite his apprehensions back in 2016, Figuereiro seems to be on a roll with the process now. He notes with pride that he recently resealed a talha from 1783, brought to him by a customer. Figuereiro's skills are becoming more and more in demand, because right now he's one of very few craftsmen with the skills and the will to make talhas suitable for wine production and to coat them with pês. Among others, Daniel Parreira and Ricardo Santos have asked him to help them reseal some of their vintage vessels.

Some winemakers, such as Pedro Ribeira (Herdade do Rocim/Bojador), still feel that the larger 1,000-litre talhas are optimal for fermentation. With both Figuereiro and António Mestre able only to fashion smaller sizes, the market in second-hand larger talhas remains strong. Furthermore, the two talha-makers have full order books and little ability to scale up their businesses to meet the growing demand.

Until Figuereiro expands his workforce or António Rocha fine-tunes the formula of how to make large talhas, there's a logistical problem as more and more wine-makers in the region want to get onboard with the talha renaissance, yet the supply of century-old clay pots is fast diminishing. Not only that, fewer and fewer old-timers are willing to sell their antique talhas. The Alentejanos have finally realised they're sitting on a goldmine.

CHAPTER 7

TERRA

· · · · · · · · · · ·

Cabo da Roca can feel more like a box-ticking exercise than a tourist attraction. From a small car park crammed with tour buses, a scrubby footpath leads to a plain stone cross erected in the middle of a small dirt circle. A low stone wall stops passers-by from falling into the Atlantic. If it's a clear day, they're rewarded with a sea view of unending deep blue nothingness. When the weather's good, visitors linger to take a selfie before they wander off to explore the cliff paths or the nearby lighthouse.

The draw to this slightly featureless spot is that it's the western-most point of mainland Europe. Due to its exposure, it's also one of the windiest. Just a 45-minute drive northwest from Lisbon, the point sticks further out into the Atlantic than any other part of Portugal's long coastline. Getting buffeted around by the gusts for a few minutes is a good way to understand what it might feel like to be a tree or a vine in such conditions. Grape vines and apple trees grow just a few minutes' drive away, but neither is easy to spot because they adopt the position of least resistance in strong winds. They lie flat on the ground.

The vineyards that are scattered around the sand dunes form an historic wine region named Colares, famed for fresh Atlantic wines with extreme longevity. Once upon a time, it had the reputation of being the Bordeaux of Portugal. It is mentioned often in Portuguese literature from the 1800s and enjoyed a golden age in the early 20th century. But how the mighty are fallen. The lure of prime real estate took hold from the 1960s on, and the vast majority of the region's vineyards were torn out and replaced with holiday homes. Today, most people know the region as the Sintra-Cascais Natural Park. Colares is merely an obscure microdot on Portugal's wine map, yet the story of its survival is almost as curious as its wine.

GRAINS OF SAND

. . . .

Francisco Figueiredo survived the region when it was at its lowest ebb. Born in Lisbon, his parents moved to the national park in the early 1990s and Figueiredo got to know the area. He had thoughts of moving to Dão to make wine, but a chance encounter set him on a different course. In 1999, Figueiredo had one final part of his winemaking education to complete: his thesis on vine irrigation. He conducted vineyard trials in the Alentejo as part of his research, and there he met another young wine professional named José Vicente Paulo.

Paulo had recently become the executive director of Colares' co-operative cellar, the Adega Regional de Colares. He suggested that Figueiredo might like to come to work during the harvest. Figueiredo did just that, and fell in love with the unique vineyards and the wines. He continued to work for the Adega as a cellar hand and became chief winemaker in 2003, a position he's held ever since.

When Figueiredo and Paulo started working together at the end of the 1990s, the Adega's future was balanced on a knife edge. Conceived with the might of government intervention behind it, the Adega was effectively owned by the state until Portugal joined the EU. In 1994, ownership was returned to the co-operative's members, but they might have felt they were handed a poisoned chalice. The co-operative had failed to pay any of its growers for the previous five years, racking up a sizeable debt. Furthermore, as it had only sold wine in bulk since 1934, the Adega had no brand of its own to market and nothing it could readily sell or monetise.

The Adega was conceived in a different age. Created in 1931 to safeguard the quality of the wine, which due to huge popularity had fallen prey to fakery, the Adega's original remit was to be a trusted source of the region's liquid gold. The Salazar government strengthened that mission quite significantly in 1938, granting the Adega a winemaking monopoly and making membership mandatory for any grower in the region who wanted a route to market.

It's a detail that's seldom remarked, but today's wine lovers who open a prized bottle of Colares Visconde Salreu 1974, Viúva Gomes 1969 or Chitas 1955 are drinking a wine that was produced by the co-op. Not that there is any shame in that. Notwithstanding a slight dip in quality in the 1970s and 80s, the Adega has always made authentic, high-quality wines. Unlike co-operative cellars in other parts of Portugal, the Adega Regional de Colares maintained a traditional and largely non-interventionist winemaking style. Although its lagares were eventually retired in favour of stainless-steel tanks, the wines have always been patiently aged in traditional hardwood barrels and vinified without the use of cultured yeasts or other additives.

During the 1930s, the Adega operated at full capacity, producing around 1.1 million litres of wine each year. At any one moment, there would be around 700,000 litres of wine ageing in the 50 or so large mahogany barrels in its long and impressive barrel hall. The négociants, such as Viúva Gomes, Paulo da Silva (Chitas) and others that have long since closed their doors, would come to select wine from their favoured barrels, which would then be further aged in their cellars before bottling under the various proprietary brands.

Even though the 1930s saw Colares at its peak, the downward trend began in the same decade with the collapse of the Brazilian market, itself a casualty of the 1929 financial crash and the Great Depression. After the second world war, the region's growers started to be tempted by options other than working their land. It was hardly a surprise. When Figueiredo describes the vineyard work in Colares as "heroic viticulture", it is no exaggeration. The sandy soils in the Sintra environs have been both Colares' saviour and its nemesis at different points in history. The sandy topsoil can be as deep as five or six metres in some parts of the region, although one to two metres is more normal. Either way, it's deep enough to prevent *Phylloxera*, the scourge of European viticulture, from taking hold. The louse cannot reach the roots of the vine through such a depth of sand. The challenge is that new vines have to be planted in the clay soil underneath the sand, meaning that a large trench or pit must be dug.

Digging several metres down into sand is a perilous activity when it has to be done manually with buckets and spades. Photos from the early 20th century show workers with baskets on their heads. It was a basic form of insurance – if the sides of the trench collapsed in, the basket shielded the worker and gave them a few precious minutes to scramble out before they suffocated.

Once the vine's roots are safely anchored in the clay, it's then nurtured through its first few years, while the sand is periodically piled back into the trench. As it grows, the vine spreads out horizontally. No training or trellising system would be a match for the high winds that rip through the dunes. The winds are so strong that they prevent most small insects from being able to fly, which in turn keeps the vines free from many airborne diseases. Even with the vines sat flat on the ground, bamboo windbreaks are needed to provide some shelter. All of this makes the vineyards barely recognisable to anyone used to the orderly rows and guyot-trained vines of Bordeaux, Napa or the Alentejo. The vines cohabit with apple trees that are also trained flat on the ground. Their sporadic placement makes the vineyards look like an abandoned vegetable garden or a wild moorland reserve. The only clue that this is viticulture comes in the summer, when short wooden canes called *pontões* are used to lift branches and grape bunches far enough off the floor that they don't succumb to mildew. Needless to say, harvesting in such conditions is back-breaking work. Yields, too, are tiny.

The Colares region had 1,800 hectares of vineyards planted on its sandy soils in the 1930s, but once property development and second homes became popular in the 1960s, the vineyards were quickly decimated. The meagre returns from growing grapes in this hugely labour-intensive manner lost any appeal when the land could be sold at a high price to a developer. Simultaneously, the world fell out of love for Colares. By the time Figueiredo and Paulo had taken over the running of the co-operative, the lean, salty, low-alcohol signature of Colares' wines no longer held much appeal. Instead, fashion had moved on to riper wines. The era of oaked Chardonnays and Robert Parker wines was in full flow, and Colares definitely hadn't been invited to the party.

By 1999, the year that Figueiredo first came to help during the harvest, there were just 12 hectares of Colares vineyards still in existence, an area far smaller than a single Bordeaux estate. Added to the parlous state of the Adega's finances, it was a grim situation. As Figueiredo tactfully puts it, "A small revolution had to take place."

With most of its capacity unused and barrels lying empty, Paulo realised the Adega needed another way to make money. He reimagined the barrel hall as an events venue, a role that it continues to fulfil today. Up to 600 people can congregate in the space. In the same year, Colares found an unlikely saviour. The municipality of Sintra finally woke up to the reality that its historic wine region was about to die, when its largest remaining vineyard looked set to be concreted over. Nine hectares of vines had been planted by grower Tavares & Rodrigues in the late 1980s, but the company, whose wines were bottled under the brand 'MJC', lost heart in the project. Their backer, global drinks giant Allied Domecq, then threatened to sell the plot to developers. The city council searched desperately for an organisation that would take on the vineyard project. A Lisbon-based cultural foundation named Fundação Oriente came to the rescue. The organisation had been set up as the beneficiary of a massive gambling licence for the ex-Portuguese colony of Macau. The licence is no more, but the foundation's coffers were full.

Figueiredo admits that when he started working at the Adega, he was quite pessimistic about its ability to survive. Despite the intervention of Fundação Oriente, it felt as though all the odds were stacked against Colares. With Portugal's accession to the EU had come plentiful funding for new vineyard planting. But the EU's VITIS funding scheme for upgrading and converting vineyards had a sting in the tail:

the money was only available for vineyards that were planted on EU certified (for which read American) rootstocks. And written into the Colares DOC regulations was a condition that the wine must come from ungrafted vines, in other words planted on their own roots. The DOC was supposed to protect Colares' grand tradition, and celebrate its triumph over the *Phylloxera* plague, but these conditions, enshrined in 1908, seemingly locked the region in a double bind. Figueiredo recalls this dilemma with clear frustration: "It was completely stupid; it prevented any major investments for the region that most needed help". A further kick in the teeth was another piece of EU pedantry, that doesn't permit a grape variety to have the same name as a region. Malvasia de Colares is unique to its namesake yet cannot be declared as anything more than Malvasia on the label.

Paulo spent a decade petitioning the EU to try to get the VITIS funding rules changed. Finally, an exemption was granted in 2016 that allowed Colares to benefit from the scheme, which had already been running for 30 years. While it didn't exactly prompt a flood of new plantings, green shoots started to appear. Colares pulled back from the brink, and now has around 26 hectares of vineyards and 27 growers. Figueiredo also did some research which debunked a popular notion, that all of the eligible land had been paved over. He discovered that there was still around 350 hectares of available land that could be planted with vines. The issue was not availability, but rather fragmentation. It was divided between around 2,000 different owners.

Figueiredo has a certain stoicism, and he's clearly a bit of a fatalist. Despite the region's uncertain future, he's remained stalwart and persistent, putting the quality of the Adega's wines on a consistently high footing. He does admit, in his quiet and understated manner, that he now feels rather more positive than he did in 1999. And there are good reasons for his change of heart. The city council finally brought in regulations to curb the developers, although they are arguably nothing like strong enough. Currently, any landowner within the park area who owns less than a single hectare is not permitted to develop the land. Clearly, this wouldn't stop a cunning developer acquiring adjacent plots and then combining them, but so far the ruling seems to have quelled the conversion of vineyards into bricks and mortar.

Despite the restriction, prices for the land within the Colares DOC, which only covers the sandy soils, remain very high. Figueiredo and Jorge Rosa Santos, winemaker at the nearby Casal Santa Maria estate, both talk of prices between €60,000 and €100,000 per hectare. It's a huge barrier for anyone brave enough to want to become a Colares grower. As Figueiredo notes, it's also between five and ten times more expensive than comparable land just a few kilometres further inland, where the soils change to clay and the Colares DOC ends.

Still, even if Figueiredo and his colleagues aren't out of the woods yet, the appreciation for the wines has changed out of all proportion. Figueiredo started to see increased interest in Colares from around 2015. Suddenly, younger sommeliers from the US or Scandinavia were beating a path to the Adega's door. Sales rocketed up, and the geek end of the wine market started buying up old vintages with a passion. It marked a cyclical change and perhaps a generational shift in wine taste. As recently as 2012, famed Californian winemaker Jerry Luper was quoted on the subject of Colares. He expressed considerable disdain and doubt about whether the region was worth preserving, saying, "Nowadays, we don't accept as 'exceptional wine' a product that under natural conditions cannot achieve more than 11 percent alcohol." But almost a decade later, a new generation of natural wine lovers craves wines that are lighter, fresher and easier on the system. Furthermore, if the 1990s were about homogenisation and globalisation of wine, the 21st century has embraced the curios and unicorns of wine to a far greater degree.

The vast majority of Colares wine, historically and now, is red. Made from its native grape Ramisco, which is found almost nowhere else in Portugal, red Colares is tannic and slightly briny with bracing Atlantic acidity. It is typically aged for at least seven years before it's put on the market. The Adega's Ramisco picks up liquorice and cedar notes from its long passage in the mahogany barrels. The far rarer white Colares, made from Malvasia de Colares, has a similar acid streak and pronounced saltiness. It can be quite generous and fruity when young, and even a little aromatic. It is never overbearing or overripe. But it's how these wines develop, and their extraordinary longevity that tends to get Colares fans so excited. Their structure and acidity seem to gift them near immortality, especially in the case of the reds.

THE WIDOW GOMES

Proof of this immortality can be sampled from historic bottles of 1930s Colares. Most of the surviving bottles from these vintages can be found in the cellars at négociant Adega Viúva Gomes in the village of Almoçageme. The business was established in 1808 by "the widow Gomes" as the Portuguese name translates. The building has a stunning frontage entirely covered in traditional Portuguese *azulejos* or tiles. It is no less impressive inside, with a high ceiling and exposed hardwood beams. The space feels rather empty, although a clutch of large mahogany barrels proudly occupies half of the main hall. The interior doors and glassed panels with dark wood frames are reminiscent of a Victorian train station.

Viúva Gomes was passed around a bit, belonging to José Maria da Fonseca in the early 1930s. At that time they also owned what would later become the Adega Regional de Colares building. JM Fonseca soon lost all interest in Colares and sold up to Portugal's largest olive oil producer, Azeite Gallo. The cellar limped on but ceased trading in the 1970s. More than a decade later, José Baeta went looking for a wine business he could buy. The Baeta family had been in food distribution for decades, and their primary business was supplying small grocers and minimarkets. But by the 1980s, the market started to dry up as large supermarkets opened up. Baeta decided to quit the food business and just focus on wine. Purchasing a Colares négociant business wasn't the most obvious choice, but that's what he did in 1988. It also happened to be the year that his son and future winemaker Diogo was born.

The attractive building came with a bonus: its cellars were full of wines from the best and highest yielding vintages of the century. There were thousands of bottles from 1931, 1934 and the late 1960s. Baeta had stock he could start selling immediately. He also forged an agreement with the Adega Regional and started bottling new vintages from the 1990s. But there was a challenge. No-one wanted to buy the wines. Baeta had to sit it out for well over a decade before things changed. By 2012, he was sick of staring at all the stock in the cellar, and had begun to worry about the longevity of the 1969 Colares Malvasia. He released the entire stock at a bargain price and it was eagerly snapped up.[47]

Baeta then started seeing the same effect that Figueiredo had noted in 2015. Suddenly there were wine geeks worldwide who wanted old vintages of Colares. Baeta started rationing his remaining stocks. He equates the change of heart with a move from traditional wine critics writing for newspapers, who he says never liked the high-acid Colares style, to the rise of wine bloggers who started writing about obscure corners of the wine world such as Colares.

When we visited in 2019, a member of Baeta's staff was diligently labelling small lots of wine and preparing them for sale. As she carefully glued the labels to the bottles and added the wax seals, the vintages were visible: 1969, 1967, 1965 and a precious few single bottles of 1934. Baeta no longer has any of the 1931 left and he is down to the last 150 or so of the 1934. He gets regular offers to buy the entire stock, which are always rebutted. Instead, he's resolved to sell off minute allocations each year. It is well worth tracking down a bottle, as the wine is quite extraordinary. It still has spellbinding freshness and a noticeable grip. It's hard to imagine how many decades this Ramisco needed before it entered its drinking window.

. . . .

47 Ryan bought a few cases at the time and conceded that the wine was a bit of a lottery. One in five bottles was transcendental but serious oxidation had marked the rest.

Hand labelling 1965 Colares at Adega Viúva Gomes

While Colares grapes grown on the *chão de areia* (sandy soils) remain scarce, the region does have more plentiful and more conventional vineyards on *chão rijo*, or clay soils.[48] These cannot be used to make the Colares DOC wines but have to be bottled within the broader Vinho Regional Lisboa classification. Diogo Baeta masterminded a new phase in the history of Viúva Gomes with the planting of its own vineyards. As well as an entry level Malvasia from clay soils, he also created the Pirata range of wines. These are made in a more hands-off, natural style, using only wild yeasts and bottled without filtration. Pirata Malvasia provides a wonderfully salty expression of this Atlantic, cool-climate region, despite not being on the hallowed sandy ground. After three years of searching for the right site, and dealing with the considerable bureaucracy, Diogo also planted a new vineyard on *chão de areia* in 2019. Totalling a mere 3,000 square metres (0.3 hectares), it is minute, but nonetheless it's an important reversal of the times when Colares really did look like it would be swallowed up by concrete.

THE STATE OF PLAY IN 21ST-CENTURY COLARES

Three producers now vinify and bottle their own Colares, something which has been permitted by law since 1994. They are Ramilo, Casca and Fundação Oriente, who have resurrected the MJC label of the vineyard's original owner. Both the first two producers price their DOC Colares at a super-premium level, reflecting the tiny quantities. Casca buys in grapes while Ramilo have their own DOC Colares vineyards.

Adega Viúva Gomes, Adegas Beira Mar – Paulo da Silva (Chitas) and Casal Santa Maria all purchase wine in bulk from the Adega Regional de Colares for further ageing. The one exception is the Malvasia de Colares from Casal Santa Maria, which is made from crushed grapes purchased from the Adega Regional.

The Adega Regional de Colares produces around 10,000 litres per year of DOC Colares wines, meaning that between 12 and 14 of its barrels are now filled every year. Francisco Figueiredo cannot imagine a future when the winery ever operates at capacity again.

• • •

Just half an hour's drive from Colares, round to a more sheltered part of the bay is the coastal town of Carcavelos, these days more or less a suburb that's become subsumed into the capital's urban sprawl. With beautiful beaches and big waves beloved of surfers, it attracted luxury hotels and apartment blocks

· · · · · · · · · · · ·

48 The literal translation of *chão rijo* is 'hard soil'; however, this is the term that is used locally to differentiate the inland clay soils from the sandy soils.

from the 1960s and on. But Carcavelos was once a revered wine region, talked about in the same breath as Colares, Bucelas and Setúbal. Now it provides a grim reminder of where Colares might have headed. Carcavelos' last historic producer, Quinta do Barão, was wiped out by road expansion in the 1990s. A parcel of 12.5 hectares was replanted in Oeiras in the 1980s, on land that was part of the Marques de Pombal's estate. The municipality took over the management of the vineyard in 1997 and now bottles a Carcavelos 'Villa Oeiras' from those vines. The wine is aged in the cellars of Pombal's palace. Other than this heritage project, occasional bottlings from old stocks appear on the market, and the Quinta da Ribeira de Caparide estate still makes table wine; however, a Carcavelos has not been released for over 15 years.

Carcavelos is admittedly an even more niche style than Colares. The wine is perhaps most similar to madeira. Made traditionally from a field blend that can include white and red varieties, it's fortified to around 20% alcohol and then aged oxidatively in barrels. The end result has the complexity and mellowness of an old tawny port, but with the fresh acidic streak of a Sercial or a Verdelho from Madeira. It is doubtful that Carcavelos will ever achieve the kind of comeback that Colares managed in the past decade, mainly because virtually all the undeveloped land is earmarked for further building. Furthermore, fortified wines have fallen out of fashion to a far greater extent than any other style.

MADEIRA
· · · · · · · · · ·

Perhaps someone forgot to tell the Madeirans about those changes in fashion. In terms of wine, the island is still almost entirely focused on the production of its eponymously named fortified wine. Production is tiny in global terms. Each year, between three and four million litres of madeira wine are produced in total, less than one twentieth of the annual production of port and not even a quarter of the volume of a single major Rioja winery.

Madeira has been Portuguese territory since 1420, although the island was allegedly first discovered in the late 14th century. The site of a number of dormant volcanoes, Madeira is lush and temperate. Tempting though it might be to think of it in the same breath as the more southerly Canary Islands, or the distant Azores, Madeira is distinct from both. The subtropical, humid climate suits the cultivation of bananas, vegetables and fruit of all kinds. Passion fruit is a speciality. But it's not a particularly easy place to grow grapes. Due to cooling westerly winds and

Terraced vineyards or poios cling to Madeira's cliffs

cloud cover which lingers over the centre of the island, the growing season is short and the temperatures never reach extremes in either direction. The white grape varieties that have traditionally been grown on the island – Sercial, Verdelho, Bual, Terrantez and Malvasia amongst others – often struggle to ripen to more than 9% potential alcohol.

As author and fortified-wine obsessive Alex Liddell ponders in his book *Madeira: The Mid-Atlantic Wine*, the unfortified madeira wines from the 17th century might sometimes have been made from late harvested grapes or were deliberately oxidised. If they were harvested at a normal ripeness level and fermented out to dryness, the resulting wine might well have been thin and acidic. Then came the alchemical discovery of *vinho da roda* in the second half of the 17th century. With more regular shipping trade between the island and the Indian subcontinent, merchants noticed that madeira actually improved after a few months of exposure to heat and being battered around in the hold of a ship. For the next 150 years, barrels of madeira were sent to be deliberately mistreated on the long sea voyages, before returning transformed into the oxidised style that became their signature. The process of fortifying the wines to reach between 17% and 20% alcohol developed over the same period. Then in the 19th century came the development of the *estufas*, heated tanks or concrete vats where madeira could be quickly and conveniently 'cooked', replicating the much more expensive and lengthy process that had previously taken place at sea. Needless to say, wines subjected to the rather crude *estufagem* process tend not to be of the highest quality. Long, slow barrel ageing in naturally warm warehouses on the island, called *vinho canteiro*, is these days the preferred technique for the best wines.

Madeira is very much a wine that's made in the cellar, not in the vineyard. Tasting some of the few examples of Madeira table wines is enough to reinforce this point. The fabulously complex, nutty and salty amber or brown liquid that madeira fans know and love bears no relation to the raw materials, or even necessarily to the base wine. The ageing process is all. But here lies the rub: the vast majority of all madeira wine sold every year is the most basic, heat-treated three-year-old version.[49] Typically made from the high yielding red grape Tinta Negra Mole, which has dominated vineyards since *Phylloxera* decimated the traditional varieties, three-year-old Madeira sells in large quantities to markets such as France, Germany and Belgium. But they're not drinking it. Instead, it is mostly destined for

· · · · · · · · · · · ·

49 According to IVBAM. Additionally, Paulo Mendes (ex-director of Madeira Vintners) maintains that three-year-old Madeira makes up around 85% of sales by volume.

the saucepan. Before 2002, the export of bulk wine was permitted, and made up as much as 40% of the island's total madeira production. Now, bulk wine has to be deliberately denatured, usually by the addition of salt or other seasonings, before it can be sold to catering companies as a food product rather than a beverage.

Madeira wines start to get interesting at the relatively premium level of the 10-year-old category. These are invariably single varietals, focused on the four main historic varieties Sercial, Verdelho, Bual and Malvasia, although the theoretically lowlier Tinta Negra was granted entry into the varietal club in 2016.[50] A 10-year-old madeira, somewhat confusingly, is a blended wine that merely has to have the expected character of madeira with an average age of 10 years. There can be dramatically older or younger wines in the blend. Just like tawny ports with an indication of age, the average age of a 10-year-old madeira doesn't have to be 10 years. The same is true of the progressively rarer and more expensive 20-, 30- and 40-year categories. These are often truly wonderful wines, but they represent a miniscule slice of the market, perhaps as little as 5% by volume.

Still more niche are the single vintage madeiras, called *colheitas* when bottled with between five and 19 years of barrel ageing, or *frasquieras* when bottled after at least 20 years in *canteiro*. Due to long and slow ageing, fortification and deliberate but controlled oxidation, madeira wines are pretty much indestructible. Wines that have been aged for a century or more in barrels, or a combination of barrels and then *garrafeira* (demijohns) to prevent excess evaporation and concentration, are magical to taste. Not only is there gravitas from just thinking about the year written on the label, but the wines retain extraordinary freshness and sometimes seem fruitier at 100 years old than they do at 20.

Yet these are not the experiences enjoyed by most madeira drinkers. Just as glasses of stale cream sherry probably turned generations against Jerez's fortified jewel, so a sip of most cheap three- or five-year-old madeiras would be unlikely to convert most wine lovers to the joys of the beverage. This is madeira's blind spot: how can it create new audiences when most drinkers no longer come into contact with the good stuff? In times past, quality madeira was an essential feature of any dinner or high society event, but in a more hectic age obsessed about the health risks of alcohol it can seem like an anachronism. The industry itself also feels stuck in time, with its distributed model of anonymous growers and branded producer-shippers. In an age where wine lovers want a greater connection with the idea of authenticity, and the source of a product – the person who grew the grapes – madeira

. . . .

50 Before 2016, Tinta Negra was not allowed to be mentioned on the label at all.

The official IVBAM seal on a barrel of ageing madeira wine

has stubbornly resisted this path. The idea of truly boutique or small production madeira, where the same person tends the vines, vinifies and ages the wine, and ultimately puts it on the market simply does not exist.

During the past century many of the island's shippers or *partidistas* (non-exporting producers who only sell wholesale to other shippers) went to the wall and many others consolidated. There are now just eight companies who produce and sell madeira wine. Blandy's, one of the oldest British firms to establish itself in Madeira, has absorbed many other brands including Cossart Gordon, Leacock and Gomes. It now trades under the name the Madeira Wine Company, a legal renaming from the Madeira Wine Association which was a partnership until Blandy's acquired the controlling share. Justino's is the largest volume producer and since 1993 has been wholly owned by French drinks giant La Martiniquaise, who will also automatically take over the management of Henriques & Henriques when the current CEO Humberto Jardim passes away. Pereira d'Oliveira is the most historic firm which remains completely independent,[51] and is quite unique due to their policy of only producing and selling high-quality *canteiro*-aged madeiras. They have never traded in bulk wine or basic three-year-old madeira. A visit to their atmospheric lodge in Funchal is highly recommended, if nothing else just to marvel at the wines dating back to 1850 that can still be purchased. Significantly smaller, but also independent, is H.M. Borges, a quality madeira producer with an attractive lodge minutes away from IVBAM's offices.

The three remaining producers are, by Madeiran standards, newcomers. J Faria & Filhos set up in 1949 with a focus on producing fruit liquors and rum, but only started marketing madeira (initially produced by partidista P. E. Gonçalves) from 1998. Most of their modest range is sold on the island or in mainland Portugal. Barbeito came into being officially in 1948, while Madeira Vintners is the most recent, established in 2012.

· · · · · · · · · · · · ·

51 Blandy's aka the Madeira Wine Company is part owned by Symington Family
    Estates, although the port wine firm reduced their share from a majority
    holding to just 10% in 2011.

Barbeito: the first attempt at innovation

The website for Vinhos Barbeito offers up a surprising factoid, for anyone who digs a little deeper than the homepage. Alongside three members of the Barbeito family are listed the names of a Canadian businessman and a Japanese company owner. Since 1991, Barbeito has been 50% owned by the Kinoshita corporation, for whom the Canadian Sebastian Teunissen used to be a director.

The acquisition came about because Barbeito was struggling in the 1980s. Mario Barbeito started the business in 1946, initially not producing but just buying up old stocks from other partidistas. Barbeito's profession was accountancy, and he wisely bet the farm on the future value of old madeira wine. The company's stocks date back to the 18th century. His daughter Manuela ran the company from the 1970s but shifted the focus to bulk wine production. It might have seemed like a good short-term decision, but it brought the company close to ruin by 1988 as it no longer had any point of difference with the other more established shippers.

Ricardo Freitas, Manuela's son, started out his career with a history degree from the University of Lisbon and then worked as a history teacher. But he joined the struggling family business in 1991, and a solution was broached to its financial woes. Despite his mother's considerable trepidation, Ricardo insisted that the company stop selling bulk wine. Correspondingly, the company needed to be refinanced. Kinoshita had been Barbeito's Japanese importer since 1967, and the two families enjoyed a close relationship that went beyond business. The deal was struck. Meanwhile, Ricardo immersed himself in the winemaking side of the business. Since the 1990s, his considered and one might even say intellectual approach has been hugely innovative.

Ricardo developed a recognisable style across the whole range, where high acidity is something of a trademark in the wines. Although the company had an atmospheric property in Funchal, it was cramped and not fit to fulfil Ricardo's ambitions. In 2008, Barbeito moved to new premises high up in the hills of Câmara de Lobos. With more space has come more experimentation. Ricardo now vinifies some wines in lagares, a technique which had not been practiced on the island for over a century. Some white varieties are fermented with stems and skins. Wandering around the company's spacious canteiro cellars is fascinating. Chalked descriptions on the barrels point to many curios. They include the now very rare Malvasia Candida, a variety originally imported to the island from Greece, some even rarer Terrantez and a couple of barrels of certified organic madeira. Ricardo notes that organic viticulture is extremely challenging due to the threat from *Oidium*. An interest in the island's history promoted him to reintroduce Bastardo as a variety in 2004. The red grape has become a house speciality, with a number of premium bottlings including a '50-year-old', a new and fabulously expensive category that Ricardo pretty much invented.

In an industry as traditional as madeira wine, Barbeito is the bright young thing, arguably the only one of the established houses which has eye-catching and modern branding and the only one which really has product innovation at its core. But for a few short years, it looked as though Barbeito might have a challenger.

Madeira Vintners:
Not just made by women

If anyone ever tried to shake up the madeira wine industry, it was Paulo Mendes. The Madeira-born management consultant started his career, post-MBA, in Lisbon but then decided to move back to the island after he and his wife had their first child. Seeking a new job, Mendes was initially sceptical about a position offered at the Cooperativa Agrícola do Funchal (CAF). The co-operative is not a member organisation, but rather a chain of shops offering farming and agriculture products to customers. It also provides advice and consultancy to farmers and grape growers. And in 1999, when Mendes took on the role of executive director, it was close to bankruptcy.

Mendes turned it around so spectacularly that by 2008, as he puts it, "The cash was piling up". Meanwhile, he had fallen in love with madeira wine and started scheming a way that CAF could get involved by investing some of its surplus profit. He hit on the idea of the co-operative setting up its own madeira winery. Mendes was not going to let the IVBAM's strict rule that any new potential producer must have a minimum of 120,000 litres of madeira wine stocks get in his way, and promptly set about trying to buy some stock of old wines. He wrote polite letters to all of the producers on the island. Most ignored the letters and the two that did reply declined to sell any of their stock. The CAF then started to look into acquiring H.M. Borges. The deal failed at the due diligence stage when agreement could not be reached over the valuation of the Borges' historic lodge in the centre of Funchal.

Still not thwarted, the audacious Mendes took the chance to get educated in wine. He studied for the University of California, Davis Wine Marketing and Winemaking degree online, and also completed an MBA in wine marketing at the Bordeaux

Business School. Then in 2012, he got his chance. The year produced a massive harvest and IVBAM agreed to an exemption to the old stocks rule for CAF to set up as a madeira producer on the basis that they could absorb some of the extra grapes. Mendes had befriended Ricardo Freitas, who agreed to let CAF make their first vintage at the new Barbeito winery. It was a quid pro quo deal, as Freitas was concerned about the bountiful vintage. He couldn't afford to buy all the surplus grapes, but neither did he want to cut off some of his top growers who might not then offer him their grapes the following year. So, Freitas and Mendes hatched a deal that suited them both and Madeira Vintners was born in 2012. There was such an oversupply of grapes that year that Mendes ended up purchasing double the amount that he'd original intended and made a second batch of wines at the IVBAM-owned winery in São Vicente on the south side of the island. It was an experience that he did not relish, saying that it was "far too full of mould for my liking".

Mendes has strongly held beliefs that the madeira wine industry has grown complacent with its entry-level product. "Most three-year-old madeira is sub-optimal," he says, adding "if you come to madeira during harvest and look at the state of the grapes being delivered to the wineries, you can see the problem." Mendes maintains that the historic madeira producers always have the option to blend with some of their older stock, to correct or cover up defects. He cites many issues with grape quality, notably that *Botrytis*, aka noble rot, is a big issue in Madeira, as soon as the harvest date slips by a few days or weeks. For Madeira Vintners to be successful without possessing any old wine stocks, he reasoned that it had to have a point of difference. The young wines – three- and five-year-old madeiras – would need to be exemplary and of a higher standard than anything else available on the market.

Great wine starts with great grapes, so Mendes set about building solid working relationships with a small number of handpicked growers. From 2013, he signed three-year contracts with 20 suppliers who he felt could deliver above average quality. The approach was radical. The idea of a fixed contract that required exclusivity between the winery and the grower was unheard of, with virtually all the other producers on the island buying grapes on the cash market via agents. For the 2013 vintage, Madeira Vintners also upgraded to a brand new and very modern winery, thanks in part to a million euros in EU matched funding. Mendes conceived the winery to be able to vinify small lots separately, with many smaller stainless-steel fermenting vats. He also prioritised hygiene, which is, as he says, "the most important advancement in wine in the last century". Most importantly, he used a sorting table to triage incoming grapes, discarding, he says, between 5% and 10%. The technique, which is standard in many other high-quality wine regions worldwide, is not widely used on the island.

The first signs of discord between Mendes and CAF's board started to manifest themselves during 2013. Mendes discovered that one of the island's oldest partidistas was up for sale. Artur de Barros e Sousa wanted to sell for what Mendes felt was a bargain price. He says it was "less than the price of the average apartment, and less than the wholesale price for their stock." Mendes considered buying the business himself, but CAF vetoed the idea on the basis of a conflict of interest. He convinced the chairman of CAF's board that the co-operative should acquire the firm for its valuable old wine stocks. But something went wrong with the deal. Mendes kept being told that negotiations were in progress, until finally he heard from an outsider that Artur de Barros had been sold to its neighbour d'Oliveira.

During 2014, Mendes created a flurry of publicity for Madeira Vintners. Portuguese, English and Swedish journalists visited the winery and wrote about his new approach. Mendes had barrel samples for them to try, although it would take another year before even the basic three-year-old madeiras could be bottled. But CAF's board became increasingly unhappy with the approach that this self-styled "arrogant consultant" was taking. They wanted Madeira Vintners to function like a traditional madeira house, exactly the opposite of what Mendes maintained was necessary. By the end of 2014, the board's chairman José António Coito Pita decided he wanted to exert more control and take up an executive position. In early 2015, the board passed a motion that transformed the structure of the co-operative and its subsidiary Madeira Vintners. From March 2015, the board became fully executive and Coito Pita assumed a more hands-on role. Mendes knew this spelt the end for his innovative strategy. As he reflected later, "It would have turned CAF into a two-headed monster", referring to himself and Coito Pita. Mendes quit in March 2015 and left the building 24 hours after his announcement.

However, Mendes had started to put a team in place before his departure. One of his hires was a young winemaker named Lisandra Gonçalves. Born on the island, she knew wine was the career she wanted from a young age, despite the protestations of her mother who thought she should become a nurse. Gonçalves worked a harvest in the Alentejo, and then travelled to New Zealand and Provence for further work experience. She started working at Madeira Vintners in 2015. Another key member of the team from the start was Suzanne Pedro, a French-Portuguese woman who had worked at CAF as their financial controller since 2004. With the recruitment of two additional agronomists, Micaela Martins and Cristina Nóbrega, the team hit on a new marketing strategy. As Pedro recalls, it wasn't a conscious decision at first, but they realised that the core team had become all female after Mendes' departure – so why not continue to recruit on that basis and make it a point of difference?

Senhor Amaro

Madeira Vintners now markets itself as "Wine made by women". The concept hasn't endeared itself to everyone in the madeira wine trade. Luís d'Oliveira struggles with the idea, saying that he thinks writing "made by women" on the back label is "a mistake". Certainly, it's open to dispute given that the core team relies on a much larger number of vineyard and winery operatives who span a mix of genders. In general, the industry seems slightly suspicious about this new and overtly modern intervention into a business that has remained resolutely traditional and conservative for centuries. Still, the wines that Madeira Vintners has released so far are delicious. Mendes' vision for quality appears to have paid off. The three- and five-year-old wines have exceptional clarity, focus and pure fruit character which is unusual if not unheard of in the entry level offerings from the more established houses. Furthermore, the decision to fortify them to the lowest permitted level, 17% alcohol, makes for a lighter and fresher style which is charming. Tempting though it might be, it's dangerous to associate these delicate and refined qualities with notions of femininity. The currently released wines were bottled in 2016, produced under Mendes' watchful eye and largely to his specifications.

It'll be fascinating to follow the progress of Madeira Vintners as the current team get their feet properly under the table. Gonçalves is clearly excited about the first 10-year-old wines which will be released in 2022. However, according to Mendes, the board has done its best to reverse many of his original initiatives. Notably, the contracts with growers to guarantee the best quality fruit were not renewed. Pedro, Gonçalves, Martins and Nóbrega have their own battles to fight, but there is real potential for this upstart producer to create something that is unique in the world of madeira wine.

Mendes has since forsaken the wine world and, in addition to creating a successful craft brewery in Lisbon, continues to work as a management consultant and owns a small distillery on the island, something he describes as a retirement project.

Vinho seco and table wine
· ·

Just as most of the Douro's winemakers and growers don't really drink port, the last thing that would pass the lips of a Madeiran grape grower would be a bottle of madeira wine. *Poncha*, a dangerously thirst-quenching cocktail of the local sugar-cane-based rum, freshly squeezed lemon juice and honey or sugar, is the de facto choice in local bars. The islander's growers all make their own simple table wine, called *vinho seco*. Its sale to the public is strictly forbidden by IVBAM, no doubt to protect the valuable tourist market for madeira wine. Yet arguably, *vinho seco* is the authentic Madeiran wine, the equivalent to the rustic macerated white wines of Lazio or Umbria, or the Alentejo's traditional talha wines served straight from the clay. It is undoubtedly a very humble beverage, usually made in an amateur fashion and just for home consumption. It is often made from American grape varieties such as Isabella or Jacquez, often referred to as 'direct producers' or just '*americano*' by locals.

We sampled a *vinho seco* made by a talkative and effusive pensioner named Senhor Amaro, who farms a tiny 0.2-hectare plot of Tinta Negra vines planted on a precipitous slope in the Câmara de Lobos area of the island. Senhor Amaro explained – in very heavily accented Portuguese – that he bought the land in 1977 when it had been completely abandoned. He planted the vines for pleasure, and the vineyard certainly didn't produce a proper income at the time. Now it's his retirement project. He and his wife live on-site at the top of the slope, in a small house which is more or less a cave built into the side of the hill. His Tinta Negra wine was a translucent purple in colour, cloudy and slightly sour, but with an intriguing floral character. It is produced in his minute cellar in primitive conditions, but the couple enjoy drinking it and happily serve it to friends and passers-by. The wine would not be so out of place it was served in a natural wine bar. Perhaps it was rustic and simple, but it was 100% authentic.

The vineyard, like most on the island, is stunningly beautiful. In March, there was a carpet of bright yellow *erva azeda*[52] mixed with fava beans and grass. The vines are trained on high pergolas to offer protection against mildew. Climbing the steep steps from the bottom to the top of the plot is exhausting enough, never mind undertaking physical work or the harvest. Nonetheless, his vineyard is a walk in the park compared to many on the island. Small and steep stone terraces called *poios* line the hills and snake their way up many of the island's *fajães* or cliffs. Those cliffs are no joke either, in some places plunging over 500 metres down to the Atlantic. Standing on the platform at Cabo Girão, at almost 600m above sea level, terraced vineyards can be seen cut into the sheer rock in locations that seem completely inaccessible without the aid of a helicopter. It brings a whole new meaning to the term "heroic viticulture".

The island has dipped a toe into the Atlantic when it comes to serious table wine production. In 1999, IVBAM built a winery in São Vicente in 1999, as a solution to help budding winemakers who lacked funds or land on which to create their own wineries. The facility functions much like a co-operative winery, except that

. . . .

52 *Oxalis pes-caprae*, or African wood-sorrel.

each grower can choose from a few parameters concerning how their wine is made. After two decades, there are still only a dozen growers on the island who have taken up the option. They include several of the major madeira shippers. The winemaker in charge of production is João Pedro Machado. An earnest, slightly nervy and bearded young man, João Pedro gave the impression that the winery operates under a fairly restrictive set of possibilities, during our visit. He explained that the winery gets seriously hectic during the harvest season. Because each grower's harvest needs to be vinified separately, it's common for him to have more than 30 different fermentation vats on the go in the autumn. Some wines are made in minute quantities, sometimes as little as 200 litres.

The winemaking follows conventional and rather interventionist lines, with all fermentations completed using selected yeasts, and the vast majority of wines chaptalised to increase their alcohol by 1% to 2%. João Pedro says with a slight sense of resignation that there is no way he could manage all the different micro-vinifications if he allowed them to proceed using less predictable spontaneous fermentations. "I want to be able to sleep at night!" he adds. Due to financial and logistical constraints, the winery itself doesn't own any oak barrels, however João Pedro does use oak staves which are added into fermentation or ageing vats when growers want to have some wood influence in their wines. Additionally, three or four of the growers have invested in their own barriques, which are all clearly branded in the cellar.

The wines are a mixed bag. When white grapes ripen naturally to a mere 9% or 10% alcohol, chaptalising them and then vinifying the wine in a clinical and bone-dry style doesn't appear to do them many favours. The wines often feel thin and lacking in character. Reds, typically made from grapes grown in the island's warmer microclimates, seem to fare slightly better. Ilha and Terras do Avo are two producers who both make noteworthy wines, the former a varietal Tinta Negra and the latter a blend. The largest still-wine producer, Barbusano, makes a sparkling wine which is crisp and refreshing if not a whole lot more.

Given the huge hype and excitement around wines made from other volcanic regions – think Etna in Sicily, the Greek island of Santorini or the Azores – Madeira's table wine output so far is a little disappointing. But it has to be seen in context. Thus far, none of the growers has their own winery, with the exception of Blandys who make their own range of table wines under the brand Atlantis[53]. Furthermore,

. . . .

53 The Atlantis wines do not differ dramatically from the other table wines produced at São Vicente. The rosé, for us, is the highlight of the range.

most growers still put their focus into producing generous yields that can be sold to the madeira wine producers. Just 2% of the island's grapes are utilised for table wine production, and most see this as a side project at best. The wines are sold locally to tourists, with very little in the way of exports.

There is potential for so much more. There's a story to tell, and it involves volcanoes, sub-tropical islands in the Atlantic, and heroic viticulture on photogenic stone terraces. There are interesting local grape varieties, some of which barely exist elsewhere. And there's an opportunity to create light, naturally low-alcohol wines, something increasingly seen by a younger generation of wine drinkers as a positive, not a negative. Perhaps what's missing from the Madeira table wines equation is the maverick grower who would dare to be different. Where is the Josko Gravner, the Luís Pato or the Frank Cornelissen of Madeira? Sometimes, a single impassioned winemaker is all that's necessary to challenge established ideas and shock an industry into upping its game.

One grower on the north side of the island, Terra Bona, has created a small estate which is purely focused on table wines and not on selling the grapes for madeira. At the time of writing, their small winery is just a building site. It's difficult to say if Terra Bona could be the catalyst, the pioneer that drags Madeira table wine into a more artisanal and terroir-driven space. But the island's table wine industry cries out for someone to shake it up and make the most of its extraordinary natural assets. It's tempting to compare Madeira with the islands of the Azores. Although wine cultivation was almost completely killed off in the Azores by *Phylloxera*, it has recovered over the past few decades. On the island of Pico, a decent-sized co-operative makes good wines, but more thrills are to be had with some of the output from a growing clutch of independent producers, notably the Azores Wine Company and Adega do Vulcão. The difference? Pico doesn't have a fortified wine industry that ties up all the grapes or stifles innovation.

Island life proceeds at its own laidback pace. For most of Madeira's growers, the grape harvest is a convenient cash-cow and a good reason to spend time in their bucolic vineyards. Life is good, and the madeira wine shippers pay a high price for the grapes. Madeira wine is there for the tourists, *poncha* for the bars and *vinho seco* for home drinking. The connoisseurs in the US and UK continue to wax lyrical about sensational antique madeiras, as indeed they should. But there's an ever-present risk that madeira might follow in the footsteps of other historic fortified wines such as marsala or commandaria, becoming little more than a cooking ingredient and a footnote in wine history. The winds of change lightly gust against the shores of the island, but almost no-one listens to their message.

CHAPTER 8

BOM DIA!

• • • • • • • • • • • • •

Three decades ago, winemaking or working in the vineyards was not an aspirational career. During the 1990s, Portugal's agricultural sector drastically shrunk, unable to compete with more efficient food producers in the European Union. Tourism began to transplant farming as a more profitable industry, and it tempted the workforce away from the fields. For ambitious young Portuguese, university education became the norm. Many emigrated to richer EU nations, in search of better opportunities and decent wages. Depopulation of rural areas and migration to Lisbon and Porto continued apace. Both cities built reputations as some of Europe's leading technology hubs, and the country became an attractive destination for tech companies to headquarter themselves. Low wages compared to the richest EU nations were a key part of the package.

But after the 2008 financial crisis, and the knock-on effects in Portugal of a significant regime change in 2011, the political and economic climate changed again. With neoliberalism and austerity biting, many chose to look outside the conventional professions or sources of income. More importantly, the millennial generation could take advantage of an opportunity that their ancestors never had: setting up as an independent winery was not only possible, it could even attract EU funding. Small family estates where grapes were historically surrendered to the local co-operative started to transform into boutique wineries. Post-1986, there was more than one way to enter the wine industry. Where budding winemakers previously had to work their way up the ranks at a large co-operative winery or a major producer such as Esporão or Sogrape, now it was possible to travel the world and then set up an independent business. If your family had a few hectares of vineyards, so much the better. If not, there was no shortage of abandoned vineyards to rent or grapes in need of a buyer.

Nowhere has this trend become more visible than in the Lisboa region, formerly known as Estremadura. Sometimes, when a region stays so long in the doldrums, and becomes so relentlessly cast in the mould of cheap, bulk wine, opportunity knocks. Lisboa is this place – Lisboa the wine region, not Lisboa the city. The area extends almost as far north as Figueira da Foz, Bairrada's overdeveloped beachside resort town, and heading south, well into Lisboa's ever-expanding urban sprawl.

It's a part of Portugal that has been dominated by large co-operative wineries since the 1950s, to an even greater extent than Dão. Their stock in trade for decades was producing cheap plonk for sale to Portugal's old colonies, notably Angola. That market has been in terminal decline for years, but the model remains much the same. The statistics tell Lisboa's story: less than 10% of the region's considerable output is bottled as a DOC wine, with almost everything classified in the more lowly Vinho Regional or plain table-wine categories. Partly, this is because many of Lisboa's historic sub-regions, such as Bucelas, Colares or Carcavelos, are on the critical list in terms of output and remaining vineyard area. But in general, the picture they paint of a region with little at the quality end is accurate. And it's been this way for a long time. In his 1992 *Portugal's Wines and Winemakers* book, Richard Mayson has little good to say about the region that was then known simply as "Oeste". He writes, "Most of the wine from these lush Atlantic vineyards goes into anonymous blends, sold in the plastic-covered five-litre *garrafões* that can be seen in roadside taverns or tascas all over Portugal or anywhere in the world where there is a Portuguese community."

But slightly under the radar, the region has started to fill up with quirky new wine-making projects during the 21st century. While the quantities they produce are minuscule compared to the co-ops, estates such as Humus, Vale da Capucha, Vinhos Cortém and Casal Figueira have done far more to put the region on the global quality wine map. All of these growers work organically or biodynamically in their vineyards. It is almost impossible to find a similar cluster anywhere else in Portugal.

Humus & friends

. . . .

Rodrigo Filipe is a man of few words, but many smiles. His dark, tanned physique is just one sign that his favourite place to be is out in the vineyards, not talking to journalists! His family's estate, Quinta do Paço, is tucked away in the hills of the Óbidos sub-region, a cool and windy part of Lisboa. Rodrigo's father started bottling wines in 1988, but only as a hobby. He planted the oldest three hectares that Rodrigo still farms in 1991 and then found that he was overstretched. Rodrigo came back from university to help out in 2000 and discovered quite accidentally that making wine was his future.

If anyone has pushed the envelope on 'zero-zero' winemaking in Portugal, it's Rodrigo. Lacking a formal winemaking education, he read his father's old wine-making books and attended some local courses. But all the advice to "add this" or "correct that" just didn't satisfy him or his palate. Visits to friends in Spain and France exposed him to the possibilities of more minimal intervention winemaking. By 2007, Rodrigo had converted the estate to organic farming. The Humus brand was born the same year[54], suggested by his wife as a catchy and relevant name. In 2008, he made his first experiments vinifying and bottling without adding any sulphites, and also stopped using selected yeasts for fermentation. Rodrigo is the first to acknowledge that it's not all been plain sailing, and we've certainly tasted the odd unstable wine from his range over the years. But he persisted, and his thirst-quenching and characterful wines with their bold and primal branding have found a wide audience – mostly, it goes without saying, outside Portugal.

Rodrigo is nothing if not creative, and his creativity reached its peak when he first wanted to make an orange wine. Lacking enough white grapes for the experiment, he hit upon the idea of a blanc de noir made from his Touriga Nacional, to which he then added the leftover skins from some Sauvignon Blanc and Arinto grapes that were busy fermenting to become his standard white wine. The result, first produced in 2016, is delicious and different, with a peppery kick that slices through the wine's smooth texture.

Despite the isolated position of Quinta do Paço, Rodrigo has built a mini network of like-minded growers and friends. One of those is Luís Gil, who started out working with Rodrigo but now also has his own winemaking project, Marinho. Two vintages in, the results are extremely promising. Just a few minutes away is another quirky estate, Vinhos Cortém. Utilising land which had been fallow for 30 years, Cortém was created by Englishman Christopher Price and his German partner Helga Wagner, who farmed organically from the start.[55] Both are escapees from the world of film and television sound recording. The pair planted a somewhat bizarre selection of mainly red grapes, with everything from Jaen to Cabernet Franc to Petite Syrah. They also have small plots of Viognier and Sauvignon Blanc, from which they make an orange wine. Their wines, made very simply without any oak or technology, are excellent. Like Rodrigo, they started out without any formal winemaking knowledge, instead turning to their neighbours

· · · · · · · · · · · · ·

54 Previously Rodrigo and his father bottled wines under the name Encosta da Quinta.

55 Price and Wagner sold the winery in 2019, but continue to live on the property.

in the village, and to colleagues elsewhere in Portugal for advice. The estate does not always get the attention it deserves, perhaps one suspects due to the labels which look a little dated.

Casal Figueira

· · · · · · · · · · · · · · · · ·

Heading south-west from Cortém, Casal Figueira is a project that is almost the polar opposite. Here, instead of international grape varieties, the focus is entirely on neglected local cultivars. António Carvalho began his career working at his parent's estate in 1995 and was an early convert to biodynamics. His future wife Marta Soares, an artist and painter, arrived at the estate in 1999. She was looking for workshop space and a quiet place to paint and contemplate. She became fascinated with Carvalho's "litany of working in the vines", and the pair fell in love. Soares abandoned her plans to go to New York to continue her art career and instead embraced winemaking and working as what she describes as "a cellar hand" with Carvalho – although she did also continue painting.

What started out as a rural idyll quickly became beset with problems. The raw, authentic wines that Carvalho was making were out of step with the market, and the couple filed for bankruptcy in 2003. After a year living and working in Spain, they returned to Carvalho's family estate after his father passed away. But financial problems again consumed the project, forcing the sale of the house and land in 2007. Adamant that they wanted to continue living in the area and making wine, Carvalho and Soares went looking for other options. She recalls that their options were limited. "We had no money!" she says. But eventually, through family connections they discovered some very old vineyards on the north and south slopes of Serra de Montejunto whose owners were willing to collaborate. The northerly plots were planted with Vital, a white grape variety traditional to the region, but somewhat unloved and commonly just hidden away in blends.

The drama wasn't over. The couple made their first vintage of Vital in 2008, but the following year Carvalho suffered heart failure and died while he was foot treading red grapes. The event was shocking, although Soares admits he had some health issues at the time, despite being just 43. But, as she says, "It was incredibly sad, but it wasn't a tragedy". She describes Carvalho as "a very obstinate man but a very passionate man who lived life to the absolute maximum". Furthermore, as she notes, "He died doing something he loved". Whilst Soares has time to reflect on his death now, back in 2009 she had no chance for contemplation. "The juice was pressed and was about to start fermenting," she says. "It took me about three minutes to decide that I had to continue making the wine."

Soares threw herself into winemaking, utilising the decade of experience she'd had working with her husband. She admits that the challenges of looking after their two young children, making wine and keeping her painting career alive were significant. But, as she reflects, "In art there is freedom, but in wine there is not – nature doesn't wait for you". So, the painting sometimes had to wait if the cellar needed cleaning, the grapes needed harvesting or the wine needed racking. Adapting to winemaking on her own, she started to trust her instinct more. Carvalho had been a trained winemaker, but all of her knowledge was built up just through observing and doing. She smiles that "António really hated machines, but as an artist I don't have a problem with them". So there is a bit more automation in her cellar now, compared to 2009. That said, she continues to make wine with the minimum of intervention. The end results don't just do justice to the beautiful vineyards on the mountain's slopes, they also honour her husband. Her top Vital bottling is named 'António' in his memory.

As Soares sits in her cellar after a hard day's work, clad in a leather jacket and smoking a cigarette, she still looks and talks like an artist. While she's more than comfortable talking about wine, ask a question about art and there's a glint in her eye and a noticeable stepping up of the intellectual gears. Her latest series of works, titled 'Pinturas arrancadas à noite' (Paintings torn out at night), represent "the marks that people leave on things". She describes them as "a kind of print" of the walls and locations that she sought out. She draws a comparison with the generations of people who leave their marks on old vineyards. It's clear that she continues to find release and freedom in art. But for Soares, the Lisboa region also has a kind of freedom. She compares it to the Douro, where estates tend to be grander and steeped in history. "Lisboa used to be a bulk wine region, so it's much easier to find vineyards here without that heavy heritage of the family farm," she says.

Vale da Capucha

· · · · · · · · · · · · · · · · · ·

There is, nonetheless, no shortage of heritage. Pedro Marques, who makes wine with his brother Manuel under the name Vale da Capucha, understands both the benefits and the challenges. His family's 13 hectares of vines were purchased by Pedro's great-grandfather in the 1920s. His grandmother managed the winery for decades, focusing mainly on bag-in-box wine. Pedro's mother wasn't attracted to the business and didn't feel that it was financially a good bet, so his grandmother carried on running things with the help of her brothers. Finally, in 2007, Pedro and Manuel hatched a plan. "We wanted to cut with the past and do something that was better for the land," explains Pedro. They were set on converting the vineyards to organics, but first they had a different problem to solve.

When the pair officially took over the vineyards, they realised that what they'd inherited was dominated not by native varieties such as Vital or Castelão, but instead made up of 50-year-old hybrid grapes which had been popular in the 1950s and 1960s. "Shit, it was a mess," says Pedro, looking back. They spent two years replanting the entire estate. Meanwhile Pedro went to California to study winemaking, and then spent time travelling around Burgundy and Beaujolais to gain further experience. He remembers with some amusement that most of the French winemakers knew nothing about his homeland. "Ah, they produce wine in Portugal?" asked one vigneron somewhat quizzically.

Back in 2007, the brothers had two goals for the replanting. First, they wanted to move away from the dominance of red grapes in the region and plant white varieties instead. But secondly, Pedro was in love with the idea of bigger, more full-bodied red wines. Going with the fashion of the time, he planted some Touriga Nacional and Tinta Roriz – a decision that he now looks back on with regret. His travels through Burgundy and Beaujolais would later develop his love for a lighter, more cool-climate style of wine, something that makes sense in a region with Atlantic breezes and classic clay-limestone soils. Now, more than a decade later, he's planting the area's traditional and much lighter Castelão. "We're going back and searching for the tradition that used to be here," he explains.

Wandering around the slightly chaotic cellar at Vale da Capucha, filled with a piled-up jumble of barrels, stainless-steel and fibreglass tanks, Pedro confides that the hardest part of the winemaking for him is deciding when to bottle. He's nothing if not patient though. His first experiment with a *curtimenta*, or orange wine, in 2013 led to five years of experimentation before he finally bottled a solera-style blend from the first three years. The result, Branco Especial, has a complexity and assuredness that it definitely wouldn't have possessed if he'd rushed the wine onto the market a year after the harvest. Needless to say, it's a wine that doesn't fit into any existing classification, so it ends up being bottled as Vinho de Portugal, the lowliest category, a table wine without any regional indication. He concedes that, in any case, Vale da Capucha's wines are rejected by the Torres Vedras DOC "just about every year". Pedro's wines sit in stark contrast to most other winemakers in his appellation. While the norm in the region is to ferment wines at a cold, controlled temperature with selected yeasts, Pedro's wines are wild fermented and allowed to complete their malolactic fermentation naturally. They're then usually aged much longer before bottling and release than the more mainstream examples that pre-dominate. He describes the tasting panel as "Pavlovian" and makes the point that his style of wine is simply outside their frame of reference.

Another bugbear is the permitted grape varieties. Pedro struggles to hide his frustration that Torres Vedras allows international varieties such as Chardonnay or Sauvignon Blanc to be bottled as varietal wines, but not the Portuguese Gouveio which he planted. Here's the rub: Vale da Capucha's wines now have an appreciative global audience, most of whom have never heard of the theoretically prestigious Torres Vedras sub-region. Pedro and Manuel are not allowed to make any reference to it on their labels when the wines are rejected by the appellation's tasting panel.

OUTCASTS AND NÉGOCIANTS

Those who were not lucky enough to inherit vines via their families have found other solutions. Vinhos Aparte is a group of three friends from the Lisboa area, who since 2018 make wine from small plots of native grapes that they purchase from growers in different parts of Portugal. Their 'classic red' is a blend of Touriga Nacional grown in Torres Vedras and Alfrocheiro from Dão. Essentially, they are what the French would term a *micro-négoce*, with a punk attitude to their wine-making and marketing. Daughters of Madness is the project of American Luke Schomer and his Portuguese wife Joana Ruas. Two vintages in, they work with rented vineyards and bought-in grapes, sourced from around Cadaval. João Tereso, who makes wine under the label Chinado and divides his time between life as a sound engineer and tending vines, works with a mix of family-owned but previously abandoned plots and some rented vines near Alcobaça. All of these projects are just a couple of years old. Lisboa has become a hotbed for experimentation, and home to many winemakers who found it was the perfect place to realise their dreams.

Luis Seabra

The *micro-négoce* model can be found all over Portugal. Luis Seabra didn't inherit a family estate or an old plot of 100-year-old vines, but built a long career as a winemaker nonetheless. After starting out in Vinho Verde, he worked as a senior winemaker at Niepoort until 2012. Then he decided it was time to stop working for other people and put his own name on the label. Seabra ferrets out interesting parcels of vines and grapes in the Douro and Vinho Verde, and has rented some vines in Dão since 2018. His winemaking style shows the same kind of elegance and preference for lighter wines that can be found at Niepoort.

Seabra likes discourse. He has strongly held views about his craft and long discussions about philosophy or technical details are very much the norm. Luckily, they often take place with the accompaniment of delicious food, as Seabra is an exceptional cook and an amicable host. He's openly sceptical about the idea of natural wine, or at least the way that it is marketed, yet makes no secret of the fact that he consults for one of the natural-wine world's darlings, Suertes del Marqués in Tenerife. Always pragmatic, Seabra has plenty of respect for old traditions such as foot treading, but at the same has no room for romantic ideas in his winemaking. In the cellar, he doesn't do anything interventionist, yet he has the skilled and steady hand of someone who is trained and experienced. Seabra's wines have a laser-like precision to them, always expressing their origin more than the winemaker's hand.

Since 2014, he's also lent his skills to a rebooted Douro estate. Quinta da Costa do Pinhão has to be one of the Douro's most idyllic locations, just a stone's throw from Sanfins de Douro, but at a slightly lower altitude. The vineyards here are graded 'A' for port production, and the grapes were historically sold to Niepoort and other major shippers. Miguel Monteiro Morais inherited the estate from his grandfather in 2007 and although he continued to sell the grapes it didn't take long before he got the winemaking bug. Morais holds a PhD in engineering from Cambridge University and teaches civil engineering at the University of Aveiro.

Morais renovated the old winery at the quinta, and together with Seabra started to make wine from 2014. As the winery was designed purely for the production of port wine, it lacked any of the equipment to make white wine – significantly, there was no press. Morais and Seabra decided to respect the history of the quinta and the estate's single white wine is fermented with its skins, in the same way that red and white ports are made. Morais has chosen not to highlight it on the label – something that would be bound to fall foul of the IVDP's certifying board – but his branco is very definitely an orange wine.

If the idea of orange wine sounds like something weird or hipsteresque, Morais has proven that it can have a completely different face. His example has a flinty, concentrated and almost Burgundian quality. The red wines sit in the same Douro new-wave category as Conceito or Folias de Baco. High alcohol or toasty oak is not on the menu. The oldest vineyard at the property, Peladosa, was a candidate to be ripped out as it is shockingly unproductive. But Morais could not bear to do so. Instead, the precious few kilos of grapes are vinified into a single vineyard bottling of the same name. It's a stunning and nuanced wine which shows that premium Douro wines don't have to be big, bold and high in alcohol. Instead, spine-tingling energy and freshness are the watchwords.

Morais and Seabra both do their best to work within the confines of the IVDP's strictures, and thus far all of the Quinta da Costa do Pinhão wines managed to get the DOC Douro classification. Morais is proud of his Douro heritage and it means something to reflect that on the label. But not everyone takes this view. On the southern edge of the Douro, straddling the Baixa Corga and Cima Corgo, is a small estate that doesn't fit the mould.

Near the town of Lamego, the Douro starts to change as it yields to the neighbouring Távora-Varosa appellation. The terrain becomes more forested, the soils are granite rather than slate or schist and the altitude climbs to 600 metres or more. It's here that the Ramos family has a small house and a 3.5-hectare parcel of vines that were planted in the early 20th century. Pedro Frey Ramos is one of seven siblings, and he decided to move to the deserted house in 2012 when he was 25. The house had belonged to his grandmother, but over the years became nothing more than an occasional stable for horses.

Pedro became interested in wine mainly because he wanted a career that allowed him to travel and to spend more time "in nature". He says it was never wine per se that was the draw. Following an internship in Argentina in 2004, he set up in business with his brother Diogo. Calling themselves Tavadouro, to show the split across two wine regions, they not only made wine from their family's various vineyard parcels, but also offered winemaking consultancy to other local growers. But Pedro Frey found he was spending more and more time in his least favourite places – the cellar and the office. After he moved from Lisbon to his grandmother's rundown property, a different future began to take shape: he could make wine from the property's vineyards under his own name.

Pedro made the first vintage of what would become his Frey Blend label in 2013. Two years later he left Tavadouro with his brother remaining in charge. Frey Blend properly came into being in 2016, and Pedro has built its sales in his own unique fashion. Meanwhile, he travels every year to Melbourne, Australia, to make wine with some friends in the Melbourne area. He also flies into Chianti for a couple of days each year where he also consults for a winery.

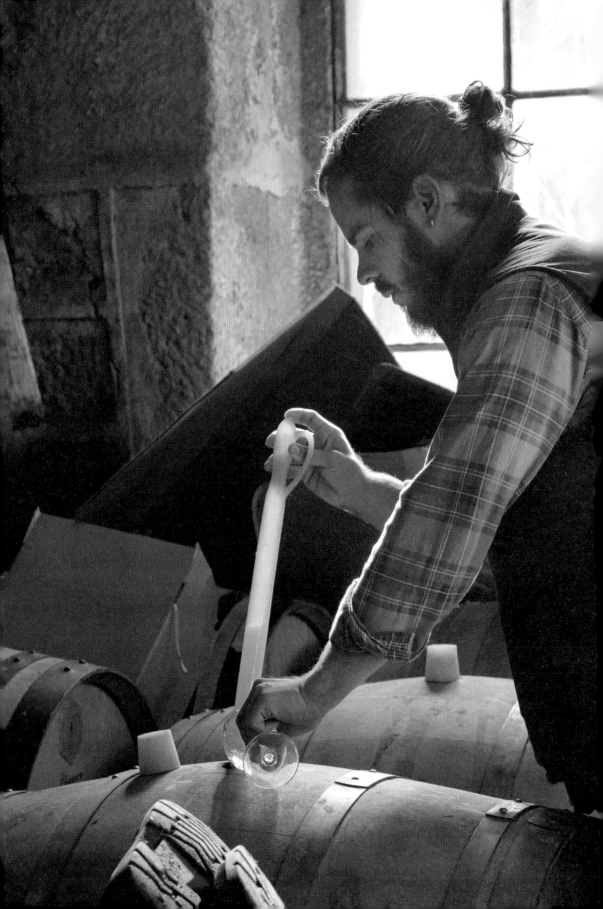

Pedro's house feels a bit like a 1970s hippy commune – at least, the decor probably hasn't been updated since then. He greeted us one October morning, wearing
shorts and two odd sports socks, and apparently slightly worse for wear. Gesturing
to a table full of empty bottles he smiled, "I wasn't alone last night". It had been
a busy autumn and Pedro ended up harvesting almost all his grapes on his own.
In a normal year he relies on a stream of friends who visit to help out during the
harvest, but in 2019 he'd been caught short. For some, the thought of harvesting 3.5
hectares of grapes would seem like a herculean task. But Pedro says he got up early
each morning and went at it. If nothing else, it was a good reason to be outdoors,
which he clearly loves. "This is my dining room," he says, pointing at a rough and
ready wooden table and bench just in front of the house. A few metres away, an old
iron bedstead with a tatty floral cover sits apparently abandoned under some trees.
"That's the guest bedroom," smiles Pedro. "Well, actually it used to be my bedroom."
A campfire and more ad hoc seating complete the bohemian look of the garden.

Everything happens outdoors chez Frey, and although he doesn't look like a sports-
man, Pedro has a badminton court which lurks on the edge of one of his vineyards.
He's also a keen golfer, and has a tee set up prominently on one of the vineyard
paths. He takes a swing and his dog crouches at the ready to run after the ball and
retrieve it. Pedro admits he's lost a few balls. Back at the house, a small basketball
hoop is set up next to a wall.

The winery is a tiny one-and-a-half-storey stone building with a selection of used
French oak barrels piled up in its porch and a line of stainless-steel tanks inside.
A pair of rubber boots are slung onto the barrels. It looks like chaos, but tasting
samples from the tanks makes it very clear that Pedro knows exactly what he's
doing. The wines are rich and complex, certainly quirky at times but never clumsy.
Although he often makes blends once he's figured out where the wines are
headed in their development, Pedro recalls one night when he was alone in the
winery "working and drinking" as he puts it. He points to a now empty tank and
recalls that, after tasting, he became so excited by the wine that he decided it had
to be bottled there and then. He stayed up all night and bottled all 1,000 litres by
himself. When Pedro writes "handcrafted" on his labels, he really means it. The
bottling machine is a small, manual affair. Corking, labelling and waxing are also
done by hand.

As we taste a very light rosé which has yet to be bottled, we laugh that stylistically
it doesn't seem to have much to do with the Douro. The wine has 10% alcohol
and Pedro expects he will bottle it without any added sulphites. It is wonderfully
thirst quenching and moreish. We struggle to spit. Pedro reflects, "It's not a Douro
style, but I'm not really sure what the Douro style is." He adds that "We had a style

more than 50 years ago, but then there was a big influence from Bordeaux and that's what all the winemakers grew up with today." Pedro doesn't even attempt to get his wines classified as DOC Douro, and routinely bottles his entire output in the basic IVV (table wine) category. It doesn't seem to bother him that he can't mention the region, the grape varieties or the year on the label. The labels tell their own quite savvy marketing story: "*vinha de altitude em solo de granito*", vineyards at altitude on granite soil. Underneath, written in English, is "Handcrafted, naturally grown, wild fermented, unfined wine". The wines are confidently priced and sold via a typically non-standard network of Pedro's friends and colleagues in other countries, plus the odd regular importer here and there.

Pedro's work is no secret to the IVDP, and their technical director Bento Amaral concedes that he wants to find a way to include the less traditionalist winemakers in the DOC. His approach is cautious, and he adds, "We have to change something but they also have to follow some rules. But not everything produced in the Douro can be certified as DOC Douro." Amaral's words are heartfelt, and he clearly worries about alienating a new generation of winemakers, but the IVDP is a juggernaut that needs many hands to help change its course. Thus far, the perceived mavericks of the Douro and many other Portuguese regions often end up with a face-off where they either produce more conventional wines or forsake their DOC, as with Pedro Frey.

WHEN QUALITY BECOMES A FORMULA

Perhaps the riff of upstart winemakers being rejected by their region's classification body can seem repetitive. But it has to be said that, at the time of writing, it is particularly entrenched in Portugal. The regional commissions who act as the gatekeepers for what is supposedly quality wine seem frozen in time. And that moment is not today's time, but rather a few decades ago. As the British wine writer Andrew Jefford explained in an online debate[56] with typical lucidity, the concept of appellations with stylistic guidelines and tasting panels dates from a period when quality was not a given in wine. They were never intended to be arbiters of style.

. . . .

56 See 'The Great Debate: Natural Wine with Andrew Jefford and Simon J Woolf' at winescholarguild.org/the-definition-of-natural-wine-france-s-vin-methode-nature-page-01

In Portugal, as in France, many of the DOCs date back to the 1930s. Back then, winemaking education was in its infancy. Degree courses in winemaking or oenology, such as those offered by UTAD in Vila Real, came much later. With scant understanding of the science of winemaking and limited technology to work with, problems such as oxidation or bacterial infections could easily occur even in the largest and most professional wineries. The original role of tasting panels was to weed out wines that were clearly faulty or substandard. Nowadays, there is very little wine put up for sale that is seriously faulty, although there is plenty that is pedestrian and dull. Tasting panels have evolved into the style police. Each appellation, or DOC in Portugal, has developed an idea of what it considers to be typical for its regional grape varieties and wine styles. Wines that are submitted for the highest quality level, DOC wines, must measure up to their region's idea of typicity, as well as being fault-free.

The challenge is that typicity itself is a nebulous concept. The Douro has evolved a certain style of table wine over the past few decades that now sets the benchmark. Douro red wines are expected to have deep colour, ripe fruit and, more often than not, detectable oak influence. This, according to the IVDP, is what the Douro represents and by extension what the customer expects when they purchase a bottle that has 'Douro' written somewhere on the label. But there is not just one Douro, and as Rita Marques and Tiago Sampaio (amongst many others) have demonstrated, there are plenty of exceptions where the Douro's terroir can yield light-coloured, delicate wines that just don't fit the tasting panel's formula. Tiago Sampaio's Renegado is his homage to an old tradition in the valley, yet not only is it routinely rejected by the tasting panel because it doesn't fit a modern idea of what Douro wine is supposed to be, it now cannot even show the name of the town where it's made.

The IVDP's ruling is that because 'Sanfins do Douro' contains the hallowed term 'Douro', it cannot be mentioned on the label. Sampaio could theoretically just write 'Sanfins', but instead chooses to put the name of the nearby town Alijó. It's a ludicrous situation when a wine that represents a much older and more authentic tradition cannot say its name. Sampaio is not an uneducated winemaker who puts sub-par bottles on the market. He, like many of his colleagues, has huge pride in his home region. Sampaio is not an emotional or melodramatic character, yet the sadness in his eyes when he explains that he can't declare his origin on his own wine label is clear to see. His wines are denied their passport to promote the Douro on the grounds that they do not fit the template. But the template isn't even half a century old.

Marta Soares doesn't even attempt to have her wines classified as DOC Óbidos (which would theoretically be possible according to the location of the vineyards), but instead submits her bottles for the broader Vinho Regional Lisboa classification. But even here, she explains that the wines are regularly refused, and for reasons that she describes as "subjective", such as "we did not like the taste of the wine". Soares notes that she once resubmitted the same wine, after initial rejection, but under a different name. The second time, the wine was passed by the same tasting panel. Soares' suggestion is that the CVR tasting panels are neither objective nor fit for purpose.

Many of the winemakers profiled in this book have regular run-ins with their local CVR bodies. It has become a new norm that any winemaker who thinks outside the box or does what they think is best for the wine rather than for getting the DOC, risks their hard work being thrown out from the appellation. No-one feels this more profoundly than António Madeira, who endured a new and crushing rejection from the CVR Dão in June 2021 just as this book was nearing its completion. Madeira posted eloquently about the decision on social media and his frustration is crystal clear:

> Yesterday was a sad day.
>
> Yesterday I heard that my white Vinhas Velhas 2019 was rejected by the CVR Dão tasting panel who scored it 52 points out of 100.
>
> Vinhas Velhas is a wine that my clients, including some of the most highly renowned sommeliers around the world have recognised as one of the great white wines not only of Dão but of Portugal, reminding them of the famous producers of Puligny or Meursault.
>
> I have no doubt that if this wine was produced by a respected Portuguese house or a more press-friendly winemaker, it would sell for an indecently high price.
>
> My mum asks, "Why can I find two-euro PDO[57] wines at the supermarket, when yours are rejected?"
>
> Good question.

· · · · · · · · · · · · ·

57 PDO is the generic European term for products of denominated origin, for example DOC wine in Portugal.

I think I've reached breaking point. I've been highlighting Dão on my labels, promoting my grandparent's region in the best restaurants on the planet. In return, I am treated without the slightest consideration.

I'm considering abandoning any attempt to classify my wines as PDO, and just declassifying to IVV.[58] It was never what I wanted, but then maybe I wouldn't have to feel debased and humiliated every time I send wines for certification.[59]

It might seem pompous for Madeira to compare his wines to top white Burgundies, but the comparison is fair. Vinhas Velhas Branco has been a highlight from his range for years. It speaks of an ancient vineyard, with ripe and concentrated fruit, yet has the kind of elegance, chalky texture and harmony that certainly wouldn't be out of place amongst the grand crus of Beaune. But more to the point, it could never be a Burgundy because the wine has so much to express about Dão. The field blend, the combination of ripeness with an earthy, herbal undertow and the texture are typical of their region. The tasting panel marked the wine down for oxidation, but one suspects they were comparing it with a line-up of simple, young wines made with industrial yeasts, cold fermentation and prodigious use of filters and fining agents to produce the sort of beverage that supermarkets find acceptable.

What do these exchanges between supposedly maverick winemakers and conservative classification boards demonstrate? When many of Portugal's best ambassadors are shot down in flames for trying to update and improve a tried-and-trusted formula, there is a problem. Portugal's wine industry has a long history of regulation, which in many cases enabled it to progress and achieve greatness. Pombal's somewhat brutal reforms of the port industry ultimately allowed it to grow and prosper. The regulation of Colares' wine in the 1930s stemmed the flood of adulterations and imitations which could have ultimately derailed the region. Yet the spirit of enforcing boundaries and restricting possibilities has started to hold Portugal back. The rules, regulations and stylistic requirements that once helped drive quality now stifle innovation and diversity in winemaking and wine styles. Worse yet, they alienate some of Portugal's most innovative winemakers from the organisations which supposedly exist to support them.

. . . .

58 Table wine, the lowest classification possible.

59 This is an excerpt from António's full post, which has been edited for brevity and translated from the original Portuguese.

It wouldn't have been too hard to canvas strong opinions about DOCs and their restrictive practices at Simplesmente Vinho 2020. Since the heady days of 2013, the event has expanded five times over, and now features over 100 wineries, most of which are small, independent operations. João Roseira receives many more applications but has curbed the numbers at a level that can still be accommodated in the event's new venue. Like its predecessor, Cais Novo is right on the river, but has a few more mod cons and fewer mice running around. While seven years ago the fair was a bit of an insider tip, now Simplesmente attracts wine lovers and professionals from far beyond Portugal's borders. Visitors to Porto each February talk about "the wine fairs" in plural, and many try to attend both Essência do Vinho and Simplesmente Vinho to get the full picture of what's going on. In order to keep up, Essência do Vinho has massively increased the diversity of its seminars and side events to include less mainstream wine styles of the sort that would more commonly be found at Cais Novo. It's a great demonstration of the impact that Simplesmente Vinho has had.

Wine fairs such as Simplesmente Vinho don't just serve a function for wine lovers, journalists and importers to meet and greet their favourite growers. They also provide a valuable opportunity for the growers themselves to come together, to swap stories and to taste their colleague's wines. Working in the vineyard and the cellar can be a solitary business, and many growers relish the chance for some sociability and a chance to talk shop. Back in 2013, many of the individuals profiled in this book worked in relative isolation. Some questioned if they were on the right path. Now there is a community that supports them, and a public that relishes what they do.

No-one is under any illusions. Life is hard, finances are tight and the regulatory bodies still struggle to understand "authentic wines made without makeup". But as the fair opens and hundreds of visitors stream in, eager to sample the wines and to meet the growers who made them, it looks like it's going to be a good day – a *bom dia*.

Foot treading at Quinta do Bom Retiro

Glossary

Adega: cellar or winery building. This term often forms part of the name of a producer, for example Adega do Vulcão or Adega Viúva Gomes.

Adega cooperativa: a co-operative winery, formed of members who submit their grapes to the winery for transformation into wine, which is then sold under the co-operative's brand or brands. The concept is similar to the French *cave coopérative* or Italian *cantina sociale*. Such wineries became popular in the 1950s in Portugal as a means to improve efficiency and the average quality of wines from an admittedly low base.

Aguardente: Portuguese generic term for strong distilled spirits. For the purposes of fortifying port or madeira, the *aguardente* used is always grape based.

Barco rabelo: the traditional wooden barge which was used to transport port barrels down the Douro river to Vila Nova de Gaia.

Benefício: the licence which allows a grower to produce a specified amount of port wine each year.

Biodynamic farming: A system based on the philosophies and lectures of Rudolf Steiner. It focuses on soil health and vitality, and treats the farm as a holistic unit where humans, animals and plants exist in harmony. No synthetic products are used and field or vineyard treatments are made with preparations which were described by Steiner in his 1924 lectures. Preparation 500, based on buried cow manure and preparation 501, based on silica, are the most commonly used. Copper and sulphur may also be used to treat vines against mildew and other diseases. Biodynamic farming and viticulture are certified by the Demeter organisation, which has independent certifying bodies in each country. For Portugal, the relevant organisation is SATIVA.

Casa: house.

Chaptalisation: the practice of enriching grape must with additional sugars, normally in the form of rectified concentrated grape must, so that the final alcohol level is increased. Chaptalisation is still common in mainstream winemaking, particularly for wines made in large quantities where the buyer wants to ensure that the final alcohol level of the wine is consistent from one year to the next. The process is named after its inventor, Jean-Antoine Chaptal.

Colheita: literally meaning 'harvest' in Portuguese, this term has various legal meanings depending on the wine region. A *colheita* port is produced from grapes from a single year (or harvest) and is aged for a minimum of seven years in barrels. *Colheita* madeiras must also be from a single year and aged for a minimum of five years before bottling. The term *colheita* is sometimes written on table wines, where it has no special meaning other than to draw attention to the vintage, for example '*colheita* 2021'

Curtimenta: literally the term means to preserve or prepare for preservation, but in wine terms it refers to a skin-fermented white wine, or orange wine to use the popular term. The term *curtimenta* has been trademarked in Portugal by winemaker Anselmo Mendes and cannot be used by any other Portuguese producer as a brand name for their wine. The term may however be used as a descriptor on the back label.

CVR: acronym for Comissão Vitivinícola Regional, or regional wine commission. The CVRs in each region regulate and authorise the sale of regional wines with DOC or Vinho Regional classifications.

Denominação de Origem Controlada (DOC): The highest quality tier in Portuguese wine classification, at least theoretically. DOC regions typically have strict regulations about permitted grape varieties, yields and even stylistic indicators for how the resulting wines should taste, smell and look. Wines that a producer wishes to label as DOC must be submitted to a local classifying body who taste the wine before deciding whether to approve its classification.

Direct producer: a common name for hybrid (qv) grape varieties, due to their ability to produce grapes without the grower undertaking any vineyard treatments.

Espumante: sparkling wine, typically made using the Traditional Method (qv)

Field blend: the practice of co-planting multiple grape cultivars together in a vineyard and typically harvesting and fermenting all the varieties together.

Fortification: the process of adding distilled alcohol (typically grape brandy, or its Portuguese equivalent *aguardente*) to fermenting must to arrest the fermentation, preserve some residual sugar and raise the alcohol level of the finished wine.

Frasqueira: a madeira wine produced from a single year and aged for a minimum of 20 years in casks before bottling. Such wines can be bottled as *colheitas* if they are bottled with between 5 and 19 years of cask ageing.

Grafting: the practice of splicing together two plants. With respect to grape vines, this is typically done with a rootstock from one cultivar and the top part from another cultivar. Grafting is usually done to ensure that the rootstock is resistant to *Phylloxera*, but on occasion a producer will 'top-graft' as a way of changing the grape varieties in a vineyard without needing to plant new rootstocks or to wait as long for the plants to grow to maturity.

Green harvesting: the practice of thinning out grape bunches in early summer to reduce yields and increase the quality and concentration of the remaining grapes. Green harvesting is a particularly important technique for those grape cultivars which tend naturally to overproduce, such as Baga or Tinta Negra. Higher yields can often lead to grapes with more pronounced tannins or a reduced flavour profile.

Herdade: ranch or homestead. This term is most commonly encountered in the Alentejo. A typical *herdade* consists of a low-built, whitewashed farmhouse and other farm buildings, surrounded by olive groves, cork trees and other crops.

Hybrid: a modern grape variety created by crossing two different *Vitis* species, for example *Vitis vinifera* and *Vitis riparia*. Hybrid crossings are typically bred to have better disease resistance than pure *Vitis vinifera* cultivars, or for survival in adverse conditions such as extreme cold.

IVDP: acronym for the Instituto dos Vinho do Douro e do Porto, the body which regulates and classifies both port wine and table wine from the Douro region. The IVDP has its headquarters in Régua, and offices in Porto. The IVDP's paper seal can be seen on all port wines and DOC Douro wines which are put up for sale.

IVV: acronym for the Instituto da Vinha e do Vinho, the Portuguese public vine and wine institute. Wines which are not classified under the more stringent Vinho Regional or DOC categories are instead submitted to the IVV and labelled as table wines. These wines will only bear the descriptions 'Vinho do Portugal', 'Tinto', 'Branco' or similar, and are not permitted to make any reference to their region, grape variety or year on the label.

Lagar: a large open stone or metal basin in which grapes can be crushed (typically by foot) and fermented.

Low intervention: alternative term for natural winemaking.

Must: the mixture of crushed grapes, juice and, in some cases, skins that will be used to ferment and produce a wine.

Natural wine: popular but largely unregulated term which describes a loose set of philosophies around winemaking. At its core is the aim to use the minimum possible intervention in winemaking and to make wine without any additives. Natural winemakers typically ferment their grapes without the addition of selected yeasts, enzymes or yeast nutrients, and often without any temperature control. Wines are usually bottled without filtration or fining. Minimal amounts of sulphur dioxide are sometimes used during the winemaking process or at bottling, but most so-called natural wines will have total sulphur dioxide levels of 70mg/L or substantially less. The term natural wine is unregulated in most countries. However, in France the INAO has approved a voluntary labelling scheme to which growers can submit their wines.

Oidium tuckeri: a fungus which causes downy mildew to infect grapes. *Vitis vinifera* vines have been susceptible to the disease since it was accidentally introduced to Europe in the mid-19th century. The mildew can be treated either with synthetic fungicides, or in the case of organic or biodynamic estates, with a mixture of copper sulphate and sulphur dioxide which is commonly known as Bordeaux mixture or *calda bordalesa* in Portuguese.

Orange wine: popular but unregulated term for wines made from white grapes that are fermented with their skins and, in some cases, then aged for further periods of weeks or months with the grape skins. The term 'orange wine' is not permitted to be written on Portuguese wine labels, hence the use of the term *curtimenta* by many Portuguese producers.

Organic: a farming system in which no synthetic products are used in the field. Organic farming and viticulture are subject to strict certification should the grower wish to display an organic logo on their products or labels. Organic certification schemes also prescribe lower maximum limits for total sulphite levels in wines.

Pé franco: Portuguese term for an ungrafted vine.

Pét-nat: abbreviation for the French term 'pétillant naturel', meaning naturally sparkling. A pét-nat is produced by bottling the wine before fermentation has finished. As fermentation completes, the resulting CO_2 is trapped in the bottle creating a lightly sparkling wine.

Pês: A paste made from resin, olive oil and beeswax which is heated and used to lightly seal the inside of a talha. Historically it was often flavoured with other additions including herbs and honey.

Phylloxera vastatrix: an insect, similar to an aphid, which infects both the leaves and then the roots of Vitis vinifera grape cultivars, via a complex four-stage 18-month life cycle. The insect is native to North America, and many American native grape cultivars are resistant to it. Phylloxera was accidentally imported into Europe in the late 19th century and resulted in the near destruction of all viticulture in many regions. The only protection from Phylloxera is to top-graft Vitis vinifera vines onto American rootstocks, a practice which is now the norm worldwide.

Port lodge: historically, the sales and shipping headquarters of a port house in Vila Nova de Gaia. Until 1986, growers and wineries were not permitted to export port wine unless it was shipped from a warehouse in Vila Nova de Gaia.

Port wine: a fortified wine made from grapes grown in the Douro valley. Port is normally fortified with aguardente to a strength of between 19% and 22% alcohol. Depending on the desired style, the port will then be aged either in barrel or bottle before sale. Most port wine is produced from red grapes, however white ports also have a long history of production. Rosé or pink port is a new innovation.

Quinta: estate or farm. This term is often used in Portuguese wine labelling to designate a wine made from a single estate.

Ruby port: the simplest and usually cheapest style of port wine. Ruby ports are young and fruity, and bottled within a year or two of the vintage. They are designed to be drunk immediately.

Solera: a fractional blending system which is best known in the Jerez region of Spain. A solera consists of wines from different years which are blended together to produce the final wine. Newer vintages are fractionally blended with wines from older vintages, so that a consistent blend results. The average age of wines in a solera system will gradually increase over time.

Table wine: we use this term in the book to specify non-fortified wines, and thus to differentiate them from fortified wines, for example port or madeira. 'Still wine' is an alternative term which is used to make this distinction.

Talha: Portuguese term for a freestanding clay pot which is used for fermentation and storage of wines. *Talhas* are similar to the Roman vessel named dolium, being flat-bottomed and ovoid shaped. They do not traditionally have lids, and instead a thin layer of olive oil is poured on top of the wine to avoid oxidation after fermentation has finished. *Talhas* have a bunghole near to their bottom that is plugged until the wine is ready to consume. At this point a wooden tap known as a *batoque* is inserted.

Tawny port: a port wine aged for many years in wood barrels. Tawny ports can have an age indication such as '10-year-old' or '20-year-old', which is actually an indicator of style more than it is of the average age of the wines. Tawny ports lighten in colour and show an oxidative character as they age.

Traditional method (sparkling wine): a sparkling wine made according to the same method that is used in Champagne. The term 'champagne method' or '*méthode champenois*' is no longer legally permitted outside the Champagne region itself. The wine undergoes a standard first fermentation, and is then bottled with a *liqueur de tirage*, a mixture of additional yeasts and sugars that cause the wine to referment in the bottle and thus create bubbles due to the trapped carbon dioxide. Traditional-method wines are then disgorged, meaning transferred into a fresh bottle, to remove the dead yeasts.

At the disgorgement stage, a *liqueur d'expedition* or dosage may be added to increase the sugar content to balance the wine.

Vineyard treatment: the application, usually by spraying, of either synthetic or elemental substances.

Vinhas velhas: old vines, a term which is sometimes used on labels but which has no legal definition.

Vinho branco: white wine.

Vinho generoso: Portuguese term for fortified wine.

Vinho licoroso: Portuguese term for fortified wine.

Vinho Regional (IG or IGP): the middle-quality tier in Portuguese wine classification. Vinho Regional wines come from more widely demarcated areas than those used for DOC classifications and are subject to less stringent controls. However, producers wishing to use a Vinho Regional classification still need to submit their wines to a regional tasting panel, and approval is sometimes denied. In these cases, the producer must then label their wine as table wine (IVV).

Vinho tinto: red wine.

Vintage port: a port wine which is bottled after six to 24 months in barrel, and then aged further in the bottle. Vintage ports are typically intended to be aged for a decade or more before consumption, however the ageing becomes the responsibility of the purchaser rather than the producer!

Acknowledgements

Many winemakers and other experts gave their time generously for this project. In particular, we would like to thank Francisco Figueiredo, Pedro Marques & family, João Menéres, José Perdigão, João Tavares de Pina & Luisa Lopes Tavares, Alexandre Relvas, Amílcar Salgado, and Luis Seabra & Natalia Jessa for their hospitality.

Bento Amaral, Tiago Caravana, Rodrigo Costa Felix, Dorli Muhr, Dra. Claudia Milhazes, Gaspar Martins Pereira, Olga Lacerda, Paulo Russell-Pinto, Johnny Symington, Paul Symington and Sonia Nolasco all considerably enhanced our understanding of Portugal, its wines and its culture.

Our appreciation of the Alentejo's talha culture and the challenges of fabricating and maintaining these venerable clay pots was transformed thanks to José Miguel Figuereiro, Joaquim Oliveira, André Gomes Pereira and all at XXVI Talhas.

We are very grateful to Paula Jardim Duarte, Nadia Meroni and Maria Gorete de Sá at IVBAM, for their assistance in organising a research trip to Madeira amidst the challenging conditions of a pandemic.

Diogo Ribas Amado and his team at Prova not only transformed Porto's wine scene, but also ensured that we always had something thought-provoking in our glasses. Oscar Quevedo provided a valuable insider's view of the Douro, and supported and encouraged us at every stage of this project.

Without the indefatigable energy and commitment of João Roseira, it is quite possible that none of this would have happened.

Ryan would like to thank Gabriella and Mica for their patience every time dad had one more photo to take or interview to do, his parents who always support him no matter how crazy they think his latest idea might be, and Portugal for warmly welcoming his family and allowing them to call it home.

Simon would like to thank Elisabeth for her keen eyes and understanding, and everyone who offered words of encouragement or enthusiasm about this project along the way. It really helped.

KICKSTARTER SUPPORTERS

We could not have realised this book without the generous support of our 518 Kickstarter backers, whose names are listed below. Thank you for believing in us and in Portugal.

Chris Abbott ★ Sarah Abbott ★ Joshua Abell ★ Diogo Abreu ★ Sérgio Abreu ★ Danny Adler ★ Fabio Adler ★ Carlos Afonso ★ Sarah Ahmed ★ Antonin Aidinian ★ Hilary Akers ★ Mohammed Albaker ★ Jesaja Alberto ★ Steve & Patti Allen-LaFleur ★ Alvier J. Almeida ★ Bento Amaral ★ Cornell Anderson ★ Patti Anderson ★ Kjartan Sarheim Anthun ★ Safiye Arifagaoglu ★ Allard Arisz ★ Eric Asimov ★ Gökhan Atılgan ★ Sina Balke-Juhn ★ Justin Bandt ★ Paul Bangert ★ Ari Barker ★ Chiaki Bascands ★ T Baschetti ★ Alastair Bathgate ★ Mikael Östlund Bekele ★ Mikael Bellander ★ Simone Belotti ★ Roland Benedetti ★ Bill Bennett ★ Nea Berglund ★ Maria Valéria Bethonico ★ Mariëlla Beukers ★ Joshua Beyer ★ Gurvinder Bhatia ★ Donna Billingham ★ Andrew Bird ★ Simon Bishop ★ Eileen Blairlafleur ★ Marije Bockholts ★ Thomas Bohl ★ Mark Bolton ★ David Bombaça ★ Fredrik Bonde ★ Carolyn & Rowan Bosworth-Davies ★ Mike Boyne ★ Stuart & Vanessa Brand ★ Luciana Braz ★ Alex Bridgeman ★ Chris Britten ★ James Brocklehurst ★ Ilya Brodsky ★ Sarah Broughton ★ Andy Brown ★ Marcel van Bruggen ★ Jason de Brum ★ Helen Gallo Bryan ★ Milan Budinski ★ Nils Bugge ★ Jeff Burrows ★ Nicole Byrd ★ Mikey C. ★ Rayna C. ★ John Caiger ★ Benjamin Perus & Charlotte Campbell ★ Christopher Cannan ★ Mariana Cardoso ★ Faye Cardwell ★ Anna Carreira ★ Karin Luize de Carvalho ★ Nuno Ricardo dos Santos Carvalho ★ Tiago Carvalho ★ Casa de Mouraz ★ Umay Çeviker ★ Gloria Chang ★ Remy Charest ★ Mark Chenhall ★ Nick Chisnell ★ Paul Chisnell ★ Isabelle Chow ★ Hp Chu ★ André Cis ★ Davide Cocco ★ Marcel de Cocq ★ Moshe Cohen ★ Colibri Curioso ★ Annie Collins ★ Neil Colman ★ Comida Independente ★ Conceito Vinhos ★ Helen J. Conway ★ Frankie Cook ★ Stephen Cooper ★ Heather Corcoran ★ Emanuelle Dalla Costa ★ José Luís Costa ★ Vasco Sousa Cotovio ★ Gregory Crawford ★ David Crossley ★ Terence das Dores Cruz ★ Rhona Cullinane ★ Giles Cundy ★ Ebba Dahlquist ★ Seamus Daly ★ Jeff Davis ★ Daxivin ★ Steve de Long ★ Ralph de Wijnmissionaris ★ Cathinca Dege ★ Daniela Dejnega ★ Juliana Dever ★ Pedro Nelson Dias ★ Sjoerd van Dijk ★ Toby Dillaway ★ Polina Disilvestro ★ Jonathan Distad ★ Ian Dobbs ★ Peter Dobos ★ MA Duarte ★ Janja Dugar ★ Gavin Duley ★ Laura Durnford ★ Klaus Dylus ★ Mardee Eamilao ★ Kevin Ecock ★ Serena Edward ★ Donald Edwards ★ Keith Edwards ★ Thomas Eickhoff ★ Eklektikon ★ Mark Ellenbogen ★ Tomas Emidio ★ Jesper da Silva Endelt ★ Becky Sue Epstein ★ Magnus Ericsson ★ Simon Ernst ★ Esporão ★ Annemarie van Ettekoven ★ Exotic Wine Travel ★ Selene F. ★ Joe Fattorini ★ Anita's Feast ★ Júlio Fernandes ★ Tiago Ferreira ★ Francisco Figueiredo ★ Tom Firth ★ Rick Fisher ★ Andraž Fistravec ★ Zé Fontainhas ★ Ove Fossa ★ Robert Frankovic ★ Caroline Franzén ★ Erika Frey ★ Pedro Frey ★

Hannah Füllenkemper ★ Ricardo MoBro Gandara ★ Garage d'Or Norway ★ Anders Håkon Gaut ★ Rosemary George ★ Deborah Getlin ★ Robbin Gheesling ★ Ghvino.nl ★ Jemima Gibbons ★ Graeme Gladwinfield ★ Janet Gold ★ Colin Goldin ★ Nicolas Goldschmidt ★ André Pintado J. Gonçalves ★ Lynn Gowdy ★ Tom Green ★ Darrell Greiwe ★ Maggie Grimm ★ Michael Grisley ★ Sarah May Grunwald ★ Elisabeth Gstarz ★ Thomas Gubanich ★ Paulius Gudinavicius ★ Chris Gunning ★ Lianne van Gurp ★ Carrie Guthrie ★ Rebecca Haaland ★ David Hagen ★ Jenni Hagland ★ Denis Hakes ★ Andrew Hall ★ Kate Hall ★ Peter Handzus ★ Liam Hanlon ★ Frédéric Hansen von Bünau ★ Julia Harding MW ★ Carl Haynes ★ Jacob Head ★ Chris Hefner ★ Richard Hemming MW ★ Caroline Henry ★ Herdade do Rocim ★ Herdade dos Grous ★ Meg Herring ★ Katrin Heuser ★ Peter Hildering ★ Andrew Hisey ★ Dave Hora ★ Daniel ter Horst ★ Molly Hovorka ★ Xavier How-Choong ★ Niels Huijbregts ★ L Humphreys ★ Louise Hurren ★ Cathy Huyghe ★ Justin Isidro ★ Diederik van Iwaarden ★ Jay Jackson ★ Karen Jenkins ★ Ales Jevtic ★ Vidar Kenneth Johansen ★ Anna Jorgensen ★ José Maria da Fonseca Vinhos ★ Asa Joseph ★ Jakub Jurkiewicz ★ Nikolaus Kaiser ★ Jason Kallsen ★ Janet Kampen ★ Edgar Kampers ★ Chuck Kanski ★ Valerie Kathawala ★ Charles Kelly ★ Jane Keogh ★ Fintan Kerr ★ Mary Kirk ★ Jan Matthias Klein ★ Matthew Klus ★ Marijke van den Berg & Frank Kneepkens ★ Mia Kodela ★ Roger Kolbu ★ Michaela Koller ★ Eero Koski ★ Aleš Kovář ★ Anne Krebiehl ★ Frank Kreisel ★ Frederik Kreutzer ★ Per Kristiansen ★ Jan Kruse ★ Peter Kupers ★ Heidi J. Kvernmo ★ Niels van Laatum ★ Minaë Tani & William LaFleur ★ Laurie Lafontaine ★ Theo Laigre ★ Fabien Lainé ★ Ellen Lainez ★ Harry Lamers ★ Daniel Lamy ★ Dennis Lapuyade ★ Alice Lascelles ★ Bruce & DiAnn Lawson ★ Cathy Lee ★ Stephane Lefevre ★ Isabelle Legeron ★ Tim Lemke ★ George L. Leonard ★ Lillian Leong ★ Diane Letulle ★ Judith Lewis ★ Richard Lewis ★ Lisa Lieberman ★ Alison Lienau ★ Vinostito ★ Susan R Lin MW ★ Andrew & Tamar Lindesay ★ Matt Lindon ★ Ben Little ★ Angela Lloyd ★ Wink Lorch ★ Karen Low ★ David Löwe ★ Lusocape Wines ★ Chris Lynch ★ João M. ★ Carole Macintyre ★ Ewen Macleod ★ Ben Madeska ★ Vasco Magalhães ★ Vladimír Magula ★ Vladimír Magula ★ Alessandro Mambrini ★ Aaron Mandel ★ Tim Reed Manessy ★ Anton & Lela Mann ★ Anna Mantchakidi ★ Alan March ★ Julien Marchand ★ Shaphan Markelon ★ John Massey ★ Daniel Matos ★ Hadia Mawlawi ★ John McCarroll ★ Stephen McClintic ★ Elin McCoy ★ Robert McIntosh ★ Peggy McLaren ★ Niav McNamara ★ Nicole L. Mead ★ Gert Meeder ★ Ron Meijer ★ Maria Susete Melo ★ Hugo Miguel Santos Mendes ★ Vitor Mendes ★ Paul Metman ★ Karol Michalski ★ Samuel Middleton ★ Tom Mikkelsen ★ Simon Mills ★ Tze How Mok ★ Filip Molnár ★ Matt Monk ★ Ana Catarina Morais ★ Miguel Monteiro Morais ★ More Natural Wine ★ Luca Moretti ★ Morris Motorcycles Racing Team ★ Kim & Coleen N. ★ Bernard Nauta ★ Carolyn Nemis ★ Leah Newman ★ Aga Niemiec ★ Menno Nieuwenhuyse ★ Sonia Nolasco ★ Boris Novak ★ Ryan O'Connell ★ David O'Mahony ★ Jim & Kim O'Malley ★ Michael & Connie O'Sullivan ★ Tobias Öhgren ★ Ana Sofia Oliveira ★ Lauren Oliver ★ Irene Oostdam ★ Josje van Oostrom ★ David Oranje ★ André Ornelas ★ Yolanda Ortiz de Arri ★ Greg Ossi ★ Ivan Ota ★ Dennis Ouwendijk ★ Patrick Owen ★ Filippo Ozzola ★ Sara Pais ★ Daniel Parreira ★ Sharon Parsons ★ Samuli Pasanen ★ Jennifer

Patterson ★ Abigail Pavka ★ Samuel Pernicha ★ Antti-Veikko Pihlajamäki ★ Adrian Pike ★ Adriana Pinto ★ Bruno Pinto ★ Marco Piovan ★ Tao Platón ★ Virgílio Porto ★ Karina Pozdnyakova ★ Meghna Prakash ★ Charles Pretzlik ★ Christopher John Emmerson Price ★ Matt Price ★ Nick Price ★ Paula Prigge ★ Henry Pringle ★ Helen Prudden ★ Noel Pusch ★ Oscar Quevedo ★ Quinta do Montalto ★ Quinta do Noval ★ Quinta do Tedo ★ Marta Ràfols ★ Alessandro Ragni ★ Linda Rakos ★ Christina Rasmussen ★ Recife Japan ★ Philip Reedman ★ Magnus Reuterdahl ★ Tad Reynes ★ Les Reynolds ★ André Ribeirinho ★ Bernard & Treve Ring ★ Justin Roberts ★ Filipe Rodrigues ★ Art Rose ★ João Roseira ★ Pieter Rosenthal ★ Jim Roth ★ Denise Rousseau ★ Caroline Rowe ★ Nicole Rudisill ★ Stephen Ruffin ★ Pedro Sadio ★ Paul Sairio ★ Lynn Klotz Salt ★ Gonçalo de Mello Sampayo ★ Joana Santiago ★ Joel Santos ★ Ricardo Santos ★ Anda Schippers ★ Rachel Schneidmill ★ Luke Schomer ★ Herb & Yuliya Schreib ★ Ann Schroder ★ Joel Schuman ★ Anna Schumann ★ Lisa Schunk ★ Fabian Schutze ★ James Russell Schweickhardt ★ Kari Scott ★ Troy Seefeldt ★ Anne-Victoire Monrozier & Christian Seely ★ Elisabeth Seifert ★ JoAnn Serrato ★ Albert Sheen ★ Neonila Siles ★ Daniel Silva ★ Filipa M. Silva ★ Hugo Silva ★ Diogo Simoes ★ Aleš Simončič ★ George Sinnott ★ Katie Skow ★ Anthony Smith ★ Jimmy Smith ★ Sandra Smythe ★ Ana Isabel Soares ★ Victor Sorokin ★ João B. Sousa ★ Bruce Spevak ★ John Spurling ★ Arjan Stavast ★ Lee Stenton ★ Mont P Stern MD ★ Moritz Stumvoll ★ Gilles Suprin ★ Nancy & Thomas Sutton ★ Will Swenson ★ Dimitri Swietlik ★ Paul Symington ★ Symington Family Estates ★ Akos Szabo ★ Beppu Takenori ★ Taka Takeuchi ★ Gianluca di Taranto ★ David Tavakoli ★ João Tavares de Pina ★ Rupert Taylor ★ Sandra Taylor ★ João Tereso ★ Camillo Testi ★ Gary Thaden ★ The Wine Spot ★ Lars T. Therkildsen ★ Paola Tich ★ Mark Tilley ★ William Tisherman ★ Cathrine Todd ★ Sue Tolson ★ Ruben Augusto Trancoso ★ J. F. Tremblay ★ Michael Trowbridge ★ Chun Hsiang Tseng ★ Judy Tsiang ★ Katia Tsiolkas ★ James Turnbull ★ Ole Udsen ★ Udo van Unen ★ Van Belle Academy ★ Rachel Vandernick ★ Willem Velthoven ★ Alexey Veremeev ★ Martijn Verkerk ★ Bruno Levi Della Vida ★ Vinha.co.uk / Vinha.pt ★ Vins d'Olive Japan ★ José Vouillamoz ★ Bart de Vries ★ Stephen W ★ Filip de Waard ★ Evan D. Walker ★ Stan Walker ★ Scott Watkins ★ Timothy Waud ★ Ana Monforte Weijters ★ Elizabeth Y. Wells ★ Jeff Werthmann-Radnich ★ David Wesley ★ Simon Wheeler ★ Sacha Whelan ★ Daniela Wiebogen ★ Wijnhuis.Amsterdam ★ Colin Wills ★ Wine & Soul ★ Wine Republic ★ Adam Wirdahl ★ Michael Wising ★ Keita Wojciechowski ★ Stephen Wolff ★ Silven Wong ★ Dana W. Woods ★ Bethia Woolf ★ Chris & Sara Woolf ★ Inigo & Susan Woolf ★ Jon & Soumhya Venketesan Woolf ★ Phillip Wright ★ Robert Wright ★ YanFlorijn Wijn ★ Alder Yarrow ★ Ya-Ju Yu ★ YukonJen ★ Agnes Zeiner

Bibliography

Birmingham, David. *A Concise History of Portugal*. 3rd ed. Cambridge: Cambridge University Press, 2018.

Black, Jeremy. *A Brief History of Portugal*. London: Robinson, 2020.

Boylston, Anthea and Penelope Forest. *The Phelps Family and the Wine Trade in 19th Century Madeira: The Story from their Letters*. Self-published, 2017.

De Long, Steve. *Wine Maps of the World*. Las Vegas, NV: De Long Company, 2020.

Delaforce, John. *The Factory House at Oporto*. 2nd ed. London: Christine's Wine Publications, 1983.

Derrick, Michael. *The Portugal of Salazar*. New York: Campion Books, 1939.

Elles, M. J. *Letter in Reply to Mr Lytton's Report & Despatch on Port Wine*. Oporto, 1867.

Forrester, Joseph James, attrib. *A Word or two on Port Wine […] shewing how, and why, it is adulterated, and affording some means of detecting its adulterations*. London, 1844.

Forrester, Joseph James. *Portugal and its Capabilities*. London, 1860.

Gallagher, Tom. *Salazar: The Dictator Who Refused to Die*. London: Hurst, 2020.

Gibbons, John. *I Gathered No Moss*. London: Robert Hale, 1939.

Hatton, Barry. *The Portuguese: A Modern History*. Oxford: Signal Books, 2011.

Jeffreys, Henry. *Empire of Booze: British History through the Bottom of a Glass*. London: Unbound, 2016.

Liddell, Alex. *Madeira: The Mid-Atlantic Wine*. 2nd ed. London: Hurst, 2014.

Lynch, Kermit. *Adventures on the Wine Route: A Wine Buyer's Tour of France*. 25th anniversary ed. New York: Farrar, Straus & Giroux, 2019.

Maltman, Alex. *Vineyards, Rocks, and Soils: The Wine Lover's Guide to Geology*. Oxford: Oxford University Press, 2018.

Matos, Fátima Loureiro de. 'A paisagem Duriense a partir de uma obra de John Gibbons'. *Geografia*, Revista da Faculdade de Letras, Universidade do Porto, 3rd series, vol. I (2012), pp. 59–73.

Mayson, Richard. *Portugal's Wines & Wine Makers: Port Madeira & Regional Wines.* London: Ebury Press, 1992.

Mayson, Richard. *Port and the Douro.* 4th ed. Oxford: Infinite Ideas, 2018.

Mayson, Richard. *The Wines of Portugal.* Oxford: Infinite Ideas, 2020.

Page, Martin. *The First Global Village: How Portugal Changed the World.* 7th ed. Alfragide: Casa Das Letras, 2002.

Pereira, Gaspar Martins, et al. *Enciclopédia dos Vinhos de Portugal: Porto e Douro.* Lisbon: Chaves Ferreira, 1998.

Pessoa, Fernando. *Poems of Fernando Pessoa.* Edwin Honig and Susan Brown, transl. San Francisco, CA: City Lights Books, 1998.

Pessoa, Fernando. *The Book of Disquiet: The Complete Edition.* London: Serpent's Tail, 2018.

Robinson, Jancis, and Julia Harding. *The Oxford Companion to Wine.* 4th ed. Oxford: Oxford University Press, 2015.

Robinson, Jancis, Julia Harding and José Vouillamoz. *Wine Grapes: A Complete Guide to 1,368 Vine Varieties, including their Origins and Flavours.* London: Allen Lane, 2012.

Additional Resources

Wines of Portugal	winesofportugal.info
ViniPortugal	viniportugal.pt
IVDP – Instituto dos Vinho do Douro e do Porto	ivdp-ip.azurewebsites.net
Catavino	catavino.net
Foot Trodden	foot-trodden.com
Sarah Ahmed – The Wine Detective	thewinedetective.co.uk
Simplesmente Vinho	simplesmentevinho.com

INDEX
· · · · · · · ·

Afonso, Zeca 155

Aguardente 25, 73, 238

Ahmed, Sarah 52

Amaral, Bento 44, 76, 96, 231

Anthroposophy 56, 57

Barcos rabelos 73

Biodynamic farming 15, 48, 56, 57, 62–63, 67, 68, 69, 97, 121, 139, 142, 143, 173, 218, 220, 238, 240

Birmingham, David 22, 23, 28, 154

Bornstein, Marguerita 108

Botrytis cinerea 131, 133

Broadbent, Michael 103

Cabo da Roca 187

Campinas, Vicente 153

Carnation Revolution 30, 31, 155

Casa do Douro 71, 74

Catavino 13, 88

Chão de areia 198

Chão rijo 198

Chestnut flowers 69

Clarete 15

Clarke, Oz 136

Companhia Geral da Agricultura dos Vinhos do Alto Douro 23

Consumo 74, 95

Cooperativa Agrícola do Funchal (CAF) 207

Costa Felix, Rodrigo 34

Curtimenta 15, 108, 136, 223, 239, 240

D'Oliveira, Luís 212

Delaforce, John 48

Demeter 68, 143, 238

Douro Boys, The 81–83, 89

Esca 109

Escola Prática de Viticultura da Bairrada 131

Espumante 129, 131, 132, 147, 239

Essência do Vinho 19, 20, 235

Estado Novo 28–29, 30, 33, 34, 36, 43, 106, 111, 155, 164

Eucalyptus globulus 124–25

Eufémia, Catarina 153

Factory House 23

Fado 34–35

Falcão, Rui 117

Faustino, Rolando 131

Ferreira, Dona António 36, 82

Field blend 38–42, 43, 55, 92, 95, 112, 120, 199, 234, 239

Figueireiro, José Miguel 177–82, 183

Flamenco 34

Foot treading 43, 80, 220, 226

  Corte 43

  Liberdade 43

France 14, 19, 22, 37, 73, 77, 80, 111, 114, 122, 142, 202, 219, 232, 240

  Bordeaux 39, 77, 80, 83, 91, 106, 140, 175, 187, 191, 192, 207, 231

Fukuoka, Masanoba 109

Gallagher, Tom 28, 248

Germany 28, 33, 66, 82, 202

Gibbons, John 74

Gramoxone 129, 130

Grândola, Vila Morena 155

Grape varieties

  Alfrocheiro 224

  Alicante Bouschet 160

  Alvarelhão 55

  Alvarinho 52, 53, 54, 55

  Aragonez (Tinta Roriz) 160

  Arinto 56, 131, 140, 219

  Baga 30, 118, 130, 131, 132, 133, 136, 137, 139, 147, 150, 239

  Bastardo 92, 207

  Bical 131, 137, 140

  Bual (Boal) 202, 203

  Cabernet Franc 39, 219

  Cabernet Sauvignon 38, 39, 55, 107, 160

  Cainho 55

  Castelão 223

  Cerceal 131

  Chardonnay 38, 42, 136, 224

  Fernão Pires 182

  Gouveio 224

  Jaen 108, 118, 219

  Loureiro 49, 55, 61, 66

  Malbec 39

  Malvasia (Malmsey) 202

  Malvasia Candida 206

  Maria Gomes 131

  Moscatel 95

  Pedral 55

  Petite Verdot 39

  Pinot Noir 94, 111

  Ramisco 194, 195

  Sauvignon Blanc 91, 106, 219, 224

  Sercial 199, 202, 203

  Syrah 42, 107, 160, 219

  Terrantez 202, 206

  Tinta Barroca 80

  Tinta Cão 80

  Tinta Francisca 95

  Tinta Grossa 160

  Tinta Negra Mole 202, 203, 213, 214, 239

  Tinta Roriz 80, 113, 223

  Touriga Franca 80, 84

  Touriga Nacional 42, 80, 84, 95, 101, 113, 137, 219, 223, 224

  Trincadeira 182

Verdelho 199, 202, 203

Vinhão 49, 61, 62, 63, 66

Viognier 219

Vital 220, 221, 223

Green Revolution 129

Grémio dos Exportadores de Vinho do Porto (Exporter's Guild) 74

Guedes, Martim 33, 49

Harding, Julia MW 14

Independent Winegrowers Association of Portugal (IWA) 137

Instituto do Vinho do Bordado e do Artesanato da Madeira (IVBAM) 26, 205, 207, 208, 212, 213

Instituto do Vinho do Porto (IVP) 74

Instituto dos Vinhos do Douro e do Porto (IVDP) 10, 11, 44, 71, 74, 76, 92, 96, 226, 227, 231, 232, 240

International Wine Challenge, London 63, 133

Italy 14, 33

Japan 66

Jardim, Humberto 205

José de Carvalho e Melo, Sebastiao (see also Pombal) 22

Kramer, Matt 12

Lagar 43, 44, 47, 48, 67, 92, 94, 95, 120, 176, 190, 206

Leitão assado da Bairrada 132

Liddell, Alex 202

Lima, Marcelo 56

Lisbon

As centre of Fado 34

Earthquake in 1755 22

Migration to 217

Lynch, Kermit 37, 44, 66

Madeira 199

Madeira wine 26, 199, 202, 203, 205, 207, 208, 212

Definition of blends with age indication 203

Restrictions in trade of 26

Use of canteiro in 202

Use of estufagem in 202

Vinho da roda 202

Mayson, Richard 15, 38, 63, 103, 130, 150, 218

Medieval de Ourém 182, 183

Mestre, António 176

Metcalfe, Charles 63, 133

Moreira da Fonseca, Álvaro 74

Muhr, Dorli 82–83

Natural wine 15, 19, 37, 54, 66, 67, 69, 106, 108, 111, 112, 122, 137, 139, 142, 194, 213, 226, 240

Nolasco, Sonia 33

Nossiter, Jonathan 66

Oidium 26, 27, 206, 240

Orange wine 55, 108, 137, 219, 223, 226, 239, 240

Os Goliardos 19

Palhete 15, 66, 159, 182

Paraquat (see also Gramoxone) 129

Parker, Robert 14, 107, 192

Pato, Maria João 139

Patrão, Dinis 129, 144, 146, 147

Paulo, José Vicente 190

Pereira, Gaspar Martins 74

Pês 172, 178, 182, 183, 184

Pesgadores 172

Pessoa, Fernando 34, 249

Pét-nat 67, 95, 241

Petroleiro 159, 168, 182

Phylloxera 26, 27, 132, 136, 191, 193, 202, 215, 239, 241

Pinto, Gustavo 57

Polytechnic Institute of Bragança 69

Pombal, Marquês de 22, 23, 25, 28, 29, 52, 74, 130, 132, 199, 234

Poncha 212, 215

Port wine

18th-century trade 22

Adulteration with elderberry juice 23

Demarcation and regulation in 1756 23

History of 25

Use of foot treading in 43

Porto Santo 26

Producers

Adega Cooperativa de Sanfins do Douro 92

Adega Cooperativa de Vilarinho do Bairro 144

Adega Cooperativa Vidigueira 164, 167, 170

Adega de Monção 52

Adega do Vulcão 215, 238

Adega Honrado 173

Adega Regional de Colares 27, 190, 194, 198

Adega São Vicente 213

Adega Viúva Gomes 191, 194, 198, 238

Adega Zé Galante 168

Adegas Beira Mar – Paulo da Silva (Chitas) 198

Alves de Sousa 137

Anselmo Mendes 20, 44, 54, 61, 239

Aphros 15, 20, 62, 66, 96

Artur de Barros e Sousa 209

Aveleda 29, 33, 35, 36, 49, 52, 53

AXA Millésimes 37, 81

Azores Wine Company 215

Barbeito 26, 205, 206–07, 208

Blandy's 26, 36, 205

Bojador 184

Buçaco (Buçaco Palace) 58, 139

Bussaco – see Buçaco

Casa de Cello 137

Casa de Mouraz 118–25

Casal Figueira 15, 20, 218, 220

Casal Santa Maria 193, 198

Casca 187, 198

Caves São João 150

Chinado 224

Conceito 20, 91, 227

Croft 25

Daughters of Madness 224

Esporão 31–33, 35, 55, 144, 146, 147, 170, 217

Folias de Baco 95, 96, 227

Frey Blend 227

Fundação Oriente 192, 198

Henriques & Henriques 26, 205

Herdade de Coelheiros 146

Herdade de São Miguel (Casa Relvas) 170

Herdade do Rocim 170, 184

Humus 218, 219

J Faria & Filhos 205

José de Sousa 172–76

José Maria da Fonseca 30, 174, 194

Kopke 25

Lagar de Darei 20

Lima Smith 56

Luís Pato 20, 131, 132, 139

Madeira Vintners 205, 207, 208, 209, 212

Madeira Wine Company 36, 205

Marinho 219

Muxagat 19

Niepoort 36, 81–82, 91, 226

Olho no Pé 95

Pequenos Rebentos 55

Pereira d'Oliveira 205

Porto Cruz 26

Quevedo 84–89

Quinta da Boavista (Dão) 19, 105, 109

Quinta da Boavista (Douro) 56

Quinta da Costa do Pinhão 226–27

Quinta da Covada 20

Quinta da Palmirinha 15, 20, 68, 69

Quinta da Pellada 20, 112, 117–18

Quinta da Vacariça 139

Quinta das Bágeiras 20, 139

Quinta das Tecedeiras 56

Quinta de Baixo 139

Quinta de Covela 55, 137

Quinta de Passarela 118

Quinta de Saes 117

Quinta de Soalheiro 53–55

Quinta de Vale de Pios 20

Quinta do Ameal 55, 137

Quinta do Barão 199

Quinta do Crasto 39, 81, 82

Quinta do Infantado 19, 20

Quinta do Montalto 172, 182–83

Quinta do Monte Xisto 97

Quinta do Mouro 20

Quinta do Noval 9, 36, 37, 42, 81

Quinta do Poço do Lobo 150

Quinta do Vale D. Maria 12, 81

Quinta do Vale Meão 36, 77, 80, 82

Quinta do Vallado 11, 82

Quinta dos Roques 137

Ramilo 198

Ramos Pinto 55, 80

Rocha, António 139

Rufia 19, 108

Sandeman 26

Sogevinus 37

Sogrape 29, 30, 32, 33, 36, 106, 132, 217

Symington Family Estates 43

Taylor's (Taylor Fladgate partnership) 26, 37

Trans Douro Express 19, 97

Vadio 35, 144, 146–47

Vale da Capucha 218, 223–24

Villa Oeiras 199

Vinhos Aparte 224

Vinhos Cortém 218, 219

Vitor Claro 20

Warre 25

Quinta Casal do Paço 47, 56, 61, 63, 68

Região do Centro (Central Region) 130

Rocha, António (potter) 177

Rodrigues, Amália 34

Rouzaud, Jean-Claude 80

Salazar, António de Oliveira 25–30, 31, 111, 153–54, 155, 164, 190

Creation of the IVP by 74

Illness and death 30

Vineyards owned by 103

Saudade 33–34, 87

Serra da Estrela 101, 103, 111, 125

Serrão, Vera 125

Simplesmente Vinho 19–22, 44, 66, 109, 235

Smith, Tony 56

Soares, Mário 31

Spain 13, 14, 22, 28, 34, 48, 52, 88, 182, 183, 219, 220, 241

Galicia 48, 52, 55, 120

Steiner, Rudolf 48, 56, 238

Symington, Paul 30–31, 36, 75, 76

Talha 15, 66, 96, 158–84, 242

Batoque 159, 164, 242

Decline of winemaking in 164

Fermentation in 158

Ladrão 159

Lining with epoxy resin 172, 178, 183

Tasting the new wine direct from 159

Towns

Cuba 158, 168, 170, 173, 176

Mealhada 139

Régua 10, 11, 12, 71, 75, 97, 240

Sanfins do Douro 92, 96, 232

São João da Pesqueira 84, 86, 87, 89

Vidigueira 158, 164, 167, 168, 170, 173, 174, 176, 177

Vila Alva 155, 158, 160, 161, 165, 167, 168, 173

Vila de Frades 158, 165, 167, 168, 173, 174

Vila Nova de Gaia 25, 44, 73, 74, 77, 84, 89, 96, 238, 241

Vila Real 87, 89, 94, 106, 144, 232

United Kingdom 36, 57, 66, 81, 83, 88, 136

University of Trás-os-Montes and Alto Douro (UTAD) 106, 232

Vinha de enforcado 53

Vinho ao Vivo 19, 66

Vinho generoso 242

Vinho licoroso 242

Vinho seco 27, 212, 213, 215

Vini Portugal 137, 139

Viti Frades 168

Vouillamoz, José 101

Wine brands

Barca Velha 77, 80, 83

Casal Garcia 29, 49, 52, 53

Duas Quintas 80

Frei João 81, 150

João Pato AKA Duckman 139

Lancers 30, 36

Mateus Rosé 29, 30, 132

Phaunus 66

Planet Mouraz 122

Porta dos Cavaleiros 150

Redoma 81

Robusta 81

Wine regions

Alentejo 31, 38, 121, 146, 153–84

Antique talhas in 164

As pioneer in varietal wines 42

Modern-day talha making in 176

Political climate in 155

Poor working conditions in 154

Salazar's plan to plant wheat in 29

Talha DOC 169, 170, 183

Talha makers in 175

Azores (Islands) 15, 16, 199, 214, 215

Bairrada 20, 23, 101, 129–50, 218

Beira Interior 132

Dão 19, 20, 38, 101–25, 130, 150, 218, 233–34

As origin of Baga 131

Role of co-operative wineries in 27, 103

Salazar's vineyards in 28

Douro 10, 20, 71–97, 224–231

Baixo Corgo 73, 82

Benefício 71, 73, 74, 75, 76, 88, 97

Birth of the table wine industry 77

Cima Corgo 73, 75, 84, 91, 92, 227

Douro Superior 42, 73, 74, 75, 76, 89, 91, 97

Flooding of the river 73

Marcos da feitoria in 23

Old field blend vineyards in 39

Vineyard classification in 74

Encostas d'Aire 183

Lisboa 15, 20, 38, 183, 198, 217–24, 233

Bucelas 199, 218

Carcavelos 15, 23, 57, 58, 198–99, 218

Colares 15, 27, 187, 190–98, 218, 234, 241

Importance of African colonies as wine market for 218

Óbidos 218, 233

Setúbal 16, 30

Torres Vedras 224

Minho 23, 47, 48, 52, 53, 54, 55, 67

Ribatejo 23, 177, 182

Távora-Varosa 227

Trás-os-Montes 16

Vinho Verde 20, 47–69

Budget wines in 52

Growers in 53

High pergolas in vineyards of 53

Issues with viticulture 52

Monção and Melgaço 52, 53, 55

Winemakers

Amaral, Paulo 176

Araújo, Pedro 55

Baeta, Diogo 198

Baeta, José 195

Bandeira, Joaquim 31

Blandy, Chris 36

Blandy, John 36

Borges, Jorge Serôdio 39, 107

Caeiro, Teresa 170, 172

Carvalho, António 220–21

Castro, Álvaro 112, 117, 118

Castro, Maria 117

Cerdeira, Luís 54

Cerdeira, Maria 54

Claro, Vitor 20

Croft, Vasco 47, 56–68, 96

Cunha, Rui 56

Dionísio, Sara 118, 120, 121

Ferreira, Francisco 82

Figueiredo, Francisco 190–94, 198

Filipe, Rodrigo 218, 219

Franco, Domingos Soares 172–76

Freitas, Ricardo 206, 208

Frey, Pedro 227, 230, 231

Gonçalves, Lisandra 209

Lopes, Luis 112

Lopes, Márcio 55

Luper, Jerry 194

Machado, João Pedro 214

Madeira, António 105, 111–15, 118, 233–34

Marques, Pedro 223, 224

Marques, Rita 89, 91, 97

Mendes, Anselmo 20, 44, 54, 61, 239

Mendes, Paulo 207, 208, 209, 212

Morais, Miguel Monteiro 226–27

Nicolau de Almeida, Fernando 77, 80

Nicolau de Almeida, João 42, 77, 80, 94, 96

Nicolau de Almeida, Mateus 19, 20

Niepoort, Dirk 81–82, 107, 117, 139

Olazabal, Francisco 11, 82

Paiva, Fernando 68

Parreira, Daniel 160, 161

Pato, Filipa 44, 131, 140–47

Pato, Luís 20, 131–39, 150

Patrão, Luís 144–47

Pereira, André Gomes 172, 178, 184

Quevedo, Claudia 87

Quevedo, Oscar Junior 86–89

Ribeiro, António Lopes 118, 120–22

Ribeiro, João Ferreira Álvares 82

Roquette, João 32, 144

Roquette, José 31, 32

Roquette, Miguel 81, 82

Roseira, João 19, 35, 44, 109, 111, 235

Ruivo, 'Professor' Arlindo 29, 159, 165–69, 170, 172

Sampaio, Tiago 67, 74, 92–97, 232

Santos, Ricardo 158, 161, 169, 172, 184

Seabra, Luis 42, 43, 226–27

Soares, Marta 220, 233

Tavares da Silva, Sandra 13, 39

Tavares de Pina, João 19, 20, 105–11

Van Zeller, Cristiano 11, 81

Viseu, Miguel 67

Wouters, William 140, 143

Zero-zero winemaking 122, 219

About Ryan Opaz

Having graduated with a degree in sculpture and painting, Ryan's varied career has included time working as a chef, butcher, art teacher, speaker, event organizer and photographer. He eventually found his niche creating specialist wine and food tours. Ryan's photography is featured in two previous books, *Amber Revolution: How the World Learned to Love Orange Wine* and *Porto: Stories From Portugal's Historic Bolhão Market*. He is a knight of the Port Wine Brotherhood and a certified port wine educator.

Today, Ryan runs Catavino Tours, a company which creates customized luxury food and wine experiences throughout Portugal, and theLAB.Porto, a natural and organic wine and food shop based at Catavino's offices.

Ryan can often be found behind a hot grill surrounded by friends and enjoying a local artisanal beverage. He lives in Porto together with his wife Gabriella and son Mica.

Stay in touch with Ryan via **catavino.net**

About Simon J Woolf

Originally trained as a musician, Simon worked variously as a sound engineer, IT consultant and alternative currency designer before wine took over his life. His writing career began in 2011 with the founding of The Morning Claret — an online wine magazine which has become one of the world's most respected resources for natural, artisanal, organic and biodynamic wine.

His work is published in many print and online publications, including *Decanter, World of Fine Wine* and *Noble Rot*. Simon has twice won the Roederer International Wine Writing Award, most recently for his first book, *Amber Revolution: How the World Learned to Love Orange Wine*, published in 2018 and since translated into five languages.

Simon is also active as a wine judge, translator and editor. He is a keen cook and lover of music ranging from Stockhausen to ClownC0re. He lives in Amsterdam with his partner Elisabeth.

Stay in touch with Simon via **themorningclaret.com**

Portugal's Wine Landscapes MAPS
by: Zé Miguel Cardoso
hand-drawn with ballpoint pen